WINNIN'
TIMES

SCOTT OSTLER
&
STEVE SPRINGER

WINNIN'
TIMES

The Magical Journey
of the Los Angeles
Lakers

MACMILLAN PUBLISHING COMPANY
NEW YORK

Macmillan Publishing Company
866 Third Avenue, New York, N.Y. 10022
Collier Macmillan Canada, Inc.

Library of Congress Cataloging-in-Publication Data
Ostler, Scott.
Winnin' times.
1. Los Angeles Lakers (Basketball team)—History.
I. Springer, Steve. II. Title.
GV885.52.L67087 1986   796.32'364'0979494   86–16394
ISBN 0–02–594080–5

Macmillan books are available at special discounts for bulk purchases
for sales promotions, premiums, fund-raising, or educational use.
For details, contact:

Special Sales Director
Macmillan Publishing Company
866 Third Avenue
New York, N.Y. 10022

10 9 8 7 6 5 4 3 2 1

Designed by Jack Meserole

Printed in the United States of America

To ANNETTE,
who has made my life
a winning time.

To KATHY,
for insight, patience, and love.

CONTENTS

ACKNOWLEDGMENTS

A team's history is only as rich as the memories of its members. In writing *Winnin' Times* we were blessed with a lot of rich material supplied by a lot of wonderful people who were willing to bare their souls and share the laughter and tears of a quarter century. Our sincerest thanks go to: Kareem Abdul-Jabbar, Red Auerbach, Bob Baker, Elgin Baylor, Andrew Bernstein, Bill Bertka, Dave Blackwell, Jim Brewer, Jim Brochu, Jerry Buss, Scott Carmichael, Michelle Carpenter, M. L. Carr, Wilt Chamberlain, Steve Chase, Jim Chones, Mitch Chortkoff, Bart Christensen, Jack Kent Cooke, Michael Cooper, Wanda Cooper, Bob Cousy, Jack Curran, Bob Dwyre, Ray Felix, Jerry Fine, Don Ford, Harry Gann, Eric Girard, Ted Green, Allan Greenberg, Randy Harvey, Tom Hawkins, Spencer Haywood, Chick Hearn, Brad Holland, Hot Rod Hundley, Norm Hutchison, Jim Jennings, Earvin Johnson, K. C. Jones, Eddie Jordan, Jayne Kamin, Joe Kennedy, Don Kominsky, John Kundla, Mitch Kupchak, Mark Landsberger, Rudy LaRusso, Rich Levin, Mary Lou Liebich, Mike Littwin, Dr. Stephen Lombardo, *The Los Angeles Times,* the *Los Angeles Times* Electronics Department, the *Los Angeles Times* Library, Cedric Maxwell, Bob McAdoo, Mike McGee, Brian McIntyre, Barry Mendelsohn, Jim Mitchell, Larry Moulter, Johnny Most, Jim Murray, Sam Nassi, Don Nelson, Jeff Neuman, Norm Nixon, Miguel Nunez, *The Orange County Register,* Jim Perzik, Neal Pilson, Jim Pollard, Susan Ragan, Kurt Rambis, Wilbert Reitz, Jim Rhode, Wen Roberts, Chris Riley, Pat Riley, Alan Rothenberg, Bob Ryan, Frank Ryan, Satch Sanders, Fred Schaus, Frank Selvy, Bill Sharman, David Shaw, Bob Steiner, David Stern, Lucy Stille, Johannes Tesselaar, Joe Twit, Joe Vitti, Mark Wallach, Jerry West, Cassie Westhead, Paul Westhead, Jamaal Wilkes, Pat Williams, Max Winter, Janice Wise, Ervin Worthy, James Worthy.

Special thanks to Lon Rosen and Josh Rosenfeld.

WINNIN'
TIMES

PROLOGUE
Grinnin' Time

●

It was the first aisle seat on the left side of the DC-10, the bulkhead seat. On Los Angeles Laker flights, it always belonged to Kareem Abdul-Jabbar.

This day the seat was empty. Anybody could sit in it. But who could fill it?

The Lakers got the bad news Thursday morning as they arrived, one by one, at the United Airlines departure lounge at Los Angeles International Airport, bound for Philadelphia.

Jack Curran, the team's portly Irish trainer and traveling secretary, a man with a flair for delivering bad news with proper solemnity, handed each player his boarding pass and said, "Kareem's not making the trip."

"We were stunned, in shock," says Brad Holland, a rookie guard on that 1979–80 Lakers team. "Our main guy was not even going. It left a huge void. Everyone felt awkward, subdued."

Abdul-Jabbar, the Lakers' 7–2 center and captain, the league's MVP for the regular season, the greatest scoring machine since Wilt Chamberlain, was staying home. Their skyhooking superman had been grounded by a sprained ankle.

It was May 15, 1980, and the Lakers, who hadn't been in the NBA finals since 1972, were in the middle of a best-of-seven series against the Philadelphia 76ers for the league title. The night before, in Game 5 at the Forum, Kareem had wrenched his left ankle late in the second half. Curran and a team doctor assisted him to the dressing room, where the ankle was iced and taped. Kareem limped back onto the floor between quarters and told coach Paul Westhead he was ready to play.

His return was dramatic and effective. Kareem scored 14 points in the fourth quarter, and almost single-handedly—almost single-leggedly—led the Lakers to victory and a 3–2 series lead. But the ankle was ballooning badly, and, after a quick postgame shower, Kareem was hustled off to the hospital for X-rays.

His teammates stopped what they were doing to watch Abdul-Jabbar hop out of the locker room on crutches, ducking his head through the doorway. They knew they were in trouble. Kareem isn't the type of player to fake or exaggerate an injury. Some of the younger players, in fact, tended to think of Kareem as being impervious to pain or injury. Who could remember seeing him hurt? They knew he wouldn't be back.

Now, at the airport, it was official. Kareem wouldn't even

be flying to Philly. The doctors advised him to rest the ankle in hopes he could play in Game 7. A sound decision medically, but Kareem was the Lakers' rock, their leader, and even if he couldn't play, his teammates would have felt considerable comfort just having him around.

The Lakers were a supremely confident team. They knew no team in the world could run with them when they got their fast break rolling. But they also knew they had been lucky. They lost their head coach to a near-fatal bicycle accident. More recently they lost a power forward, Spencer Haywood, to cosmic forces (he was suspended during the finals for falling asleep during a practice and being generally disruptive). Norm Nixon, their superb jump-shooting guard, had a dislocated and badly swollen left ring finger. Through all that, the Lakers sailed along, never missing a fast-break beat, never losing their collective poise, momentum, sense of humor, and sense of destiny.

But now . . .

Waiting for the team's boarding call at the airport, Westhead huddled briefly with a few of the players whose roles would change drastically in Kareem's absence. He told the seldom-used Holland to expect significant playing time. Westhead informed forward Jim Chones he would guard Philadelphia center Darryl (Chocolate Thunder) Dawkins. And Westhead pulled aside Magic Johnson, the 6–9 rookie point guard, and let him know he would play center on offense, power forward on defense, and point guard on the fast break. In other words, he would play everywhere and do everything.

Chones seemed nervous after his chat with Westhead. When reporters asked him about his new assignment, Chones said, "Hey, I don't even want to talk about it."

Magic did.

"No problem, Paul," he told Westhead. "I played some center in high school. It's beautiful to be in a situation like this. It's gonna be enjoyable."

To the coach, Magic seemed like a boy in a candy store. He thought this was going to be fun.

Westhead expected as much from Magic, although the rookie interim coach couldn't help but wonder if his 20-year-old point guard fully realized the difference between playing center for

Everett High School in Lansing, Michigan, and standing in for Kareem Abdul-Jabbar in the NBA finals.

Westhead's plan of opening with Magic at center was equal parts strategy and theater. He knew Johnson was a strong rebounder and that his quickness and passing would cause matchup problems for Philly's big men. And Westhead, who had a flair for the dramatic and the unexpected, was hoping to inspire his team and unnerve the 76ers.

Of course the plan would fall apart if the Lakers were at all nervous or timid. They had to hit the floor at Philly with a swagger. Attitude would be everything.

As the Lakers filed into the first-class cabin of the DC-10, Magic went directly to the captain's throne, the seat always reserved for Abdul-Jabbar. Johnson stretched out, pulled a blanket up around his head, mimicking Kareem's preflight routine. Then he turned his head and winked and smiled at Westhead.

"Never fear, E. J. is here," Earvin Johnson announced to his teammates, who laughed their first laugh of the morning.

Either the kid was overreacting to the pressure or he was setting a new NBA record for cool. Westhead guessed the latter. Nervous was not Magic's style. This was the kid who had been telling the press all season, "I strive on pressure." And who had been explaining the Lakers' superb play in the postseason tournament by pointing out, "It's winnin' time."

A few minutes after takeoff reporters gathered around Magic's seat. He told them Kareem's absence would provide a fun challenge. He talked about how he would play each position on the court during the course of the game. Hey, he might even coach.

"Maybe you could write our stories too," one writer said.

"I *know* I could do that," Magic said. "I was sports editor of the Everett *Viking.*"

After the mini-press conference, Magic settled back, put on his stereo headphones, and spent the next five hours thinking about Game 6, about how he would have to score more, move around the court, play loose and free like in high school.

That night at the team's hotel near the airport, Westhead assembled the players in a suite to go over strategy and watch an inspirational film—the videotape of Game 5. When Westhead was through, the players took over. Nixon and Magic were angry. Every newsperson they had talked to in Philadelphia wanted to know what they thought about Game 7, back in L.A.

"They're writing us off, like we lost already," Nixon fumed. "They figure we got no chance without the Big Fella."

Most pro athletes thrive on persecution, real or imagined, and the Lakers were no exceptions. They whipped themselves into an us-against-the-world frenzy.

"I got to score more, look for my shot more," Magic said.

"I'm gonna close down the middle," vowed Chones, who despite his size wasn't known as an enforcer.

They talked about sucking it up on defense, and about running, and when they left the suite the players were on fire. Westhead wished he could load them directly onto a bus, phone the 76ers, and say, "Let's do it now."

Friday was a strange day in Philadelphia. There had been reports of Kareem sightings all over the city. A taxi driver phoned a radio station to report he had given the Lakers' center a ride into town from the airport. A woman swore she spotted Abdul-Jabbar at the Museum of Art. Some of the 76ers would say later that even up until tipoff they expected Kareem to make a last-minute grand entrance.

The Lakers arrived at the Spectrum 90 minutes before the game. It's a long walk from the players' entrance to the visitors' dressing room, a stroll along a narrow, curving hallway deep under the grandstands. The hallway walls are decorated with hundreds of framed photos of past 76er teams and stars, frozen moments of glory.

As the players walked along the hallway, there wasn't much talking. Off in the distance they could hear the sounds of carpenters at work. The nearer they got to the dressing room, the louder the sounds. When they rounded the last little bend they could see, just outside their locker room, workers building a platform of some kind. A less confident team might have figured it was a gallows.

The players went into the locker room, but Westhead paused and asked one of the workmen what all the hammering was about.

"We're building a platform for a postgame TV presentation

ceremony," he said. "I know it's kind of silly, but it's an NBA rule, you have to have one ready if either team has a chance of wrapping up the series."

The workman laughed. Westhead laughed. Obviously this was a rush job. Westhead could just picture a scene earlier in the day, two officials checking out last-minute details.

One guy says, "Uh, where's the victory platform?"

"The what?"

"The stage for the championship trophy presentation, for TV. The Lakers could win the series tonight. You gotta have a platform, just in case. It's league rules."

"Be serious. Kareem is back in L.A. The crazy Laker coach is playing his point guard at center."

"I know, but you better put something together fast, or we'll both be in trouble."

It suddenly dawned on Westhead that with all his intense pregame planning, until this very moment he hadn't paused to consider the possibility the Lakers *could* win this night. To Westhead, the pounding and sawing cut through all the X's and O's in his head and began to ring like a sweet song.

"This could happen," he said to himself.

As Westhead stepped into the locker room the pounding and sawing was drowned out by the full-volume pumping of Magic Johnson's stereo box and the shouting of the players. These guys were loose, much looser than normal, which is *real* loose.

I've just got to fire everybody up, Magic told himself. I've got to dance, just smack everybody, get everybody psyched up. I know we have to keep everybody loose. By dancin' and messin' around, they see that I'm loose and they can be loose too. We can't go in tight. I just have to keep telling them we're going to have fun. We're in a great position. They (the world) expect us to lose. It's gonna be cool. We're gonna run their tongues out.

Trainer Curran relayed a phone message from their captain. "Kareem says to go for it," Curran said.

More whoops. More hand slaps. "You heard the Cap!" "The Big Fella says go for it!"

The players talked some more about how they needed to

run the hell out of the ball, run like greyhounds. If they did, the 76ers couldn't keep up. That was the basic strategy: Run or die.

They felt good.

While the teams were warming up Westhead dispatched an assistant to the scorer's table to make sure Spectrum P.A. announcer Dave Zinkoff would introduce Earvin "Magic" Johnson as the starting center, not a starting guard. In psychological warfare, you don't want to misfire with the first volley.

After the P.A. introductions, the Lakers huddled around Westhead for last-second instructions, then the starters sauntered onto the court. Chones stepped into the midcourt circle to await the game-opening jump ball. He felt a hand on his back. It was Magic, gently pushing him out of the circle.

Chones was confused. He looked over to the bench at Westhead.

"You want me to jump center, right?" he yelled to Westhead.

The coach smiled—just a tiny smile—shook his head and said, "No, Jimmy. Earvin's jumping."

Chones's eyes widened.

The 76ers were also surprised to see Magic step into the midcourt jump circle, and even more surprised at his ear-to-ear grin. The kid was beaming.

"This was gonna be the greatest moment in my life," Magic explains. "I knew that. We were gonna have fun. See, the game was gonna be so fast, and they [the 76ers] didn't even know it. They didn't even know how that game was gonna be played. It was like the joke was gonna be on them. And that's what happened. If you watch that game ever again, you'll see—if they made it, if they missed it, that ball was up the side so fast! We'd move around so fast they did not have a chance to react. That's why I was happy, because I knew they were in trouble."

In the Spectrum, jazz supersax Grover Washington, Jr., the 76ers' good-luck charm, played the national anthem. Harvey Pollack, the 76ers' public relations man, retied the laces on his lucky pink shoes.

Back home in Bel-Air, Kareem Abdul-Jabbar, curled up on his bed in front of a TV, was beside himself.

"It was almost terminal for me," he says. "I was biting the

pillow, sweating, crawling under the covers, over the covers. It was very serious nervous time. Late in the game I went out in the backyard and yelled a little bit."

Nervous time? Mike-side in Philadelphia, Laker announcer Chick Hearn led off his broadcast by booming, "From the Spectrum in Philadelphia, this is Keith Erickson!"

The fans in the Spectrum waited. They waited for the visitors to crumble, waited for the laws of logic and reason to take effect, waited for the 76ers to take advantage of Kareem's absence. And waited . . .

—Magic lost the tip to Dawkins, but early in the first quarter Johnson drove Dawkins to the hoop and hit a layup over the 6-11 intimidator.

—In the Lakers' strategy, a fast start was essential. Don't let Philly take control. The Lakers scored the first seven points of the game.

—Holland, who had no right to be anything but scared and rusty, entered the game late in the second quarter with the Lakers down six. He moved the ball around efficiently, knocked in six quick points, and the Lakers were tied at the half, 60–60.

—The Lakers opened the third quarter with 14 unanswered points. Jamaal Wilkes scored 16 points in the quarter and a career high 37 in the game.

—Nixon, his jump shot rendered impotent by his mangled finger, stole a Dr. J pass near the end of the game and fed off for the clinching basket.

—Early in the fourth quarter Dawkins slammed Cooper to the floor on a layup attempt. Cooper hit his head and was out cold. "Where are you?" trainer Curran asked him. "I'm at home, right?" Cooper said. He staggered to the free-throw line and sank both shots.

—With five minutes left, the 76ers closed to within two points, but the Lakers rammed the throttle and ran off a 20–6 spurt. Run, run, run.

With 2:22 left in the game, Magic called time, the first time in his life he had ever called a timeout because of sheer exhaustion.

"Thanks, Buck," a gasping Chones told Magic. To the Lakers, Johnson wasn't Magic but the young, strong buck who would lead them to glory. Nixon had given him the title and it had gradually been shortened to simply Buck.

In the stands Jerry Buss, who had bought the team only ten months before, was in a trance.

A league official found him and told him, "You have to come out now to accept the trophy from the commissioner." About two minutes remained and the Lakers were comfortably ahead. The game was over, but not for Buss. It seemed to him like he was being interrupted in the middle. He had the kind of concentration you might expect if the Lakers had been ahead or behind by no more than a single point.

It was only then, as he marched off for his trophy, that reality began to dawn on him. He went into a stunned state of mind. He felt like he had a wall around him and sounds weren't coming in. He later couldn't even recall going back to get his trophy at the platform where a couple of workmen were congratulating each other on their foresight.

Final score: Lakers 123, 76ers 107.

Magic, the 20-year-old rookie two years out of high school, finished with 42 points, 15 rebounds, and 7 assists. He was 14-for-23 from the field and 14-for-14 from the free-throw line.

The Lakers, generally considered to be lacking in muscle, outrebounded the 76ers, 52–36.

It was not a typical championship locker-room celebration scene. Cooper poured some champagne on heads of friends and strangers, and there was some whooping and hugging, but for the most part the Lakers were strangely subdued.

Magic sat slumped at his locker with tears in his eyes. "I'm just stunned," he said. "I can't even talk."

Several of the 76er players pushed their way through the crowded room to pay their respects to the champs. Dr. J grabbed Holland's hand and said, "Congratulations, Brad."

Holland was speechless. "This isn't really me sitting here," he thought. "This isn't really happening. I'll come to my senses soon."

Rick Barry, who was handling the postgame interviews for CBS, said, "This is the quietest championship locker room I've ever been in."

"It was more a feeling of disbelief than anything," Magic

says. "It wasn't joyous. First there was the disbelief, and then Kareem wasn't there, so we didn't really celebrate. I was too tired myself. They had a party for us back at the hotel and I couldn't even attend. I was so tired I just laid on the bed. I could not move. I could not move."

In the hallway just outside the Lakers' locker room, Jerry Buss climbed onto the wooden platform. The TV lights blinded him. His gray hair was soaked with champagne. He had owned a basketball team for ten months, and now he was accepting a world championship trophy from NBA commissioner Larry O'Brien.

Buss hugged the trophy, wiped champagne out of his eyes, and said, "You don't know how long I've waited for this moment."

PART I

Beginnin' Time

•

The year is 1959.

In Santa Monica, Jerry Buss and Frank Mariani buy their first apartment building.

In Minneapolis, the Lakers decide to come West.

In Michigan, Earvin Johnson is born.

It is the genesis of a dynasty.

1.

From Ditches to Riches

WITH his right hand, the little boy pulled his coat tightly up against his neck to shield his body from the driving wind while tightly gripping a gunny sack with his other hand.

From his vantage point, the line of people in front of him stretched forever.

It was 1937. But Jerry Hatten Buss, age four, couldn't understand that the nation was still trying to pull itself out of the Depression, and that scarce money and scarce jobs had made food lines like this one common not only here in Evanston, Wyoming, but all across the country. All he knew was that his next meal was at the end of the line and that was reason enough to stand there in the bitter cold.

It was just Jerry and his mother—Jesse. It had been that way since around his first birthday when his father, Lydus Buss, had divorced Jesse.

Often there was no money to heat the house. So Buss, at age six or seven, would go around town collecting old telephone books, or maybe a Sears catalog, to bring home and burn in the fireplace. Sometimes he got lucky and found a real treasure in the streets—a discarded chunk of coal.

"I always had presents at Christmas," Buss says. "I don't know how that happened, but I always did. My mother was very good to me. You don't notice poverty if everybody's in the same situation. Looking back, standing in line with a gunny sack to get canned food doesn't sound like you were living the life of luxury. But at the time it doesn't necessarily hit you that way."

His mother was a beautiful, petite woman of 5–2 with dark brown hair, brown eyes, and fine features. She supported herself and her child by working as a waitress in Evanston, a community of about 3,000 people located in the southwestern tip of the state, right on the Utah border. The money Jesse made wasn't particularly good, but with government food handouts as a supplement, she and her son rode out the lean economic times.

When Lydus and Jesse divorced he moved to Salt Lake City and wound up joining the Navy. "Periodically, he'd get in our area," Buss says, "and he'd ask, 'Can I have Jerry for two days?' So I'd go down and see him. And I'd get letters from him once a month or something like that. I didn't know him well enough to like or dislike him. It was kind of a neutral relationship. I didn't have anything against him. He was always very pleasant to me."

After leaving the service Lydus Buss wound up at Cal Berkeley, where he earned a master's degree, became a CPA as well as a part-time teacher at Berkeley. An avid learner, he taught himself to read and write Chinese. He died of a stroke in 1952 at age 55.

When Jerry was nine he figured he had found paradise. Lured by the promise of better-paying jobs, his mother took him to Los Angeles, where she found work as an accountant in a greeting-card company. Compared to the bleak landscape and bitter weather of the only home he'd ever known, the palm trees and sunny skies of Southern California looked like the Garden of Eden to Jerry Buss.

After three years his mother married Cecil Orville Brown. When World War II ended, Brown, a former plumber, decided to take his new family back to his old home in Wyoming, where he had first met Jesse, and get back into plumbing. Buss didn't particularly want to go, but it's pretty hard to protest at the age of 12. Instead, he made a private vow: He would be back.

So off the family went to Kemmerer, a coal-mining community 50 miles from Evanston where J.C. Penney had opened his first store. Kemmerer was a six-block-long shopping and business center of nearly 2,000 in the late 1940s, surrounded by Diamondville and Frontier, mining camps containing around 1,000 people each. If you didn't work in the coal mines, you worked on the sheep and cattle ranches in the area, or perhaps for the Union Pacific Railroad, which ran right by Kemmerer, or in the gambling business.

Cecil Brown, or C. B. as he was commonly known, already had a son, Jimmy, who was a few months younger than Jerry. Brown and Jesse then had two children of their own—Susan and Mickey.

Brown was, according to Buss, "A very, very tough guy. A real throwback to the 1860s."

Big and muscular at six feet and 190 pounds, Brown enjoyed hunting and fishing. On one fishing trip deep into the wilderness, he suffered a broken leg. Brown set the leg himself and then literally crawled back to civilization over several pain-filled days. On another expedition he ran into a grizzly bear. He shot the animal, but not before the bear managed to attack him, shredding a good deal of the jacket he was wearing. Brown continued to wear what was left of that jacket around town. It made a pretty good conversation piece and served as a badge of his toughness.

Brown bought a plumbing store in what had formerly been a pool hall. It was an old and dilapidated wood frame house, a fixer-upper even by Kemmerer's standards. But it was available and it had boarding rooms upstairs where he could house his family.

Brown did better than average financially in a town where prosperity was a rare sight. When the railroads switched from coal to diesel fuel after the war, Kemmerer's major industry was hit hard. The underground mines were shut down, throwing those not lucky enough to work in the surface mines out of work. The other major activity in Kemmerer had been gambling. It was legal until around 1950 when it was outlawed, further drying up financial resources for the town.

No matter how well Brown did, however, Jerry was just counting the days until he could get out of the house.

"I had a lot of problems with my stepfather," Buss says. "He was a very tight-fisted guy who had all kinds of weird ideas. He wanted us to get up at 4:30 in the morning and go out and dig ditches in frozen ground so he could lay the plumbing. That was our contribution to the family. Then, after three or four hours of this, we were supposed to go to school. And after school we were supposed to go out for football. And after football I was supposed to go to work, which I did until nine o'clock at night."

Temperatures in Kemmerer, elevation 7,000 feet, have been known to fall to 40 below zero. Buss didn't work on those mornings, but he did work on 15-below mornings, shoveling snow along with the dirt in a town that usually experiences about nine months of winter.

As early as age 13, Buss got a job at the Kemmerer Hotel as a bellhop, working from 4 P.M. to 9 P.M., earning 20 cents an hour, plus tips. When there were no bags to carry, he would man the shoe-shine stand he maintained nearby. And when there were no shoes to shine, he was obligated to grab a broom and sweep out the hotel.

For all this, he made $2 a day.

Supplementing that income was the money from Jerry's company. Yes, at age 13 he was already an entrepreneur, having started a mail-order business. He would sell collector's stamps through the mail, buying them wholesale and then selling them for a profit. Not much of a profit. He might make a sale for 30 cents or, if he got lucky, maybe 80 cents. His profit for the month might be $2.

"The problem had been," Buss says, "that he wanted me to work for him for free and I wanted to work where I was getting paid. His idea of working was like 14 hours a day. He'd do that for four or five days and then go hunting for four or five days out in the woods. Then he'd come back and work like hell again. But I never got those trips out there to relax."

Relax? Buss couldn't afford to.

"I worked because without it," he says, "I hardly had any clothes or anything else. I wanted a car. I guess in your mind you keep thinking you'll save for a car and you keep saving, but it never happens.

"All the kids in town were hardworking, but most of them worked for their parents, helping to support the family. I was kind of a maverick to the extent I was outside the family framework. He [his stepfather] was making, in that town, somewhat more than the average income. It's just that I never received any of that."

●

Buss didn't know what he wanted to do with his life at age 15. But sleeping through the night seemed like a good start.

So after his junior year in high school Buss decided to quit high school, bid adieu to C. B. Brown and the wonderful world of ditchdigging, and go to work for the railroad, where he could make some real money as a gandy dancer. That's the guy who keeps the rails straight. Buss would get aboard one of the small, hand-driven railroad cars used by employees and flap his arms on the drive stick until he had made his way perhaps 10 miles out of town into the middle of the Wyoming desert. He and the other laborers, around eight or ten Caucasians and as many as 200 Indian workers from around the area, would jack up the ties and put rocks and dirt underneath to give them a firm base, or replace rusty creepers, the small metal objects that hold the tracks in place.

Buss would work at that job eight hours a day, and then take on four, five or six hours of overtime. It was a five-day-a-week job.

Except when it was more.

Because when the workman would tear up a mile of track, obviously no trains could come through until a new mile had been put in. And Mile-a-Day Mike McGuire, Buss's boss, was known as a man who would never keep a train waiting, no matter the strain on his boys. Buss worked in conditions where workers often pounded each other rather than the rails.

"After three months," Buss recalls, "I said, 'Wait, w-a-i-i-it a minute. This is not the right life. Go back and finish your education.' "

So he turned in his tools and again picked up his books.

If there was one thing Walt Garrett couldn't stand, it was to see a good mind go to waste.

He knew Jerry Buss had a good mind.

So it really bothered the Kemmerer High School science teacher to learn that Buss, back in school for his senior year, had moved out of his house and had worked out a deal at the Kemmerer Hotel to get his old job back with a room included. It wasn't an environment conducive to hitting the books, but, in Buss's mind, it was a lot better than going back home.

In the Wyoming environment of the '50s, many students

would drift in and out of school, attending only when their family's financial situation permitted it. Often they would have to quit for a stretch to work in the coal mines, or on a ranch, to get the family through another dismal period. It wasn't uncommon to find a 21-year-old or 22-year-old still trying to finish high school.

Garrett, however, did not want to see Buss follow that slow road to nowhere. One afternoon he approached Buss, then 16, in the pool hall that served as the local hangout.

"If you will stay in school, I'll give you a place to live," he told Buss.

"Where?" Buss asked.

"With me in my apartment."

It really wasn't much of an offer. Garrett lived alone in a tiny apartment, but to accommodate Buss, he got a cot and set it up in his kitchen. For Buss, though, it sure beat getting up at 4:30 to dig ditches for C. B.

"I still had no idea what I wanted to do with my life," Buss says. "He [Garrett] started telling me at the beginning of my senior year that I was a gifted student and, if I wanted to, I could really accomplish a lot of things in science. I knew it came very easily to me, but I didn't pay that much attention to it. It was just kind of easy, so I did my tests, I'd get an 'A' and I'd forget about it."

"You really have a gift," Garrett told him. "You could succeed at a university level."

"All I really wanted to do was get out of my house," Buss says, "have my own house, my car, and lead my own life. I never had any plans. Just get out of high school and go to California. That's all I could think of. I didn't know what I was going to do until this teacher started telling me that I really had a gift and I could cut it at a university if I wanted to. But I hated school, so him telling me I should go four more years when all I could look forward to was getting out sounded like nonsense."

One thing Buss liked about school was sports, but even that didn't seem to work out. He made the football team as a 6-0, 135-pound halfback and also ran the half mile and jumped hurdles on the track team. He was just average at both and he never got better because he always had to quit and go back to work when he ran short of money.

Still, he stayed in school. And he stayed with Garrett, who was determined to change his prize student's outlook. Garrett found that Buss liked card games. So he taught him cribbage. And he taught him pinochle. And he taught him chess. The two would play for hours in the tiny apartment. And while they played Garrett would drill Buss with chemistry questions.

Buss became a pretty good card player, a talent he would carry with him through life. But he also became, in spite of himself, a pretty good student as Garrett filled his head with thousands of pertinent facts. Buss became so proficient that, by the end of the semester, Garrett had the star pupil teaching his chemistry class.

Don Kominsky, the Kemmerer *Gazette* editor and publisher, remembers Buss as "an exceptional science student, a kid with a high IQ."

But what would Jerry Buss do with this unique talent of his?

"I was in a post office," Buss says, "and I saw you could get a job as a government chemist if you had one year of college. So I thought, well hell, one year can't be much. The salary was slightly better than I was making on the railroad. Already the economic value of education was starting to come home to me. I decided to go that one year."

Garrett helped Buss qualify for a science scholarship loan offered by an optics company and the student was off to the University of Wyoming, 300 miles away in Laramie.

Having chosen his own course in life, Buss found his relationship with his stepfather had deteriorated to a point where they were no longer speaking. C. B. didn't think his stepson was worth a damn. If he had been, he would have stuck his nose back in those ditches and worked for a living. Buss was still on good terms with his mother, but, at 17, he was making his own decisions. And this decision was final. He would go to college. But not for more than a year.

That was fine with Garrett. He figured they would take it one year at a time.

In Laramie, Buss got two jobs. One was cleaning a church in exchange for a room. In his other job he was a busboy in the school cafeteria, which entitled him to free meals, plus some cash. Thus he survived while pursuing his twin majors of chemistry and mathematics, working 35 hours a week while carrying a full load of 18 units.

It didn't seem to faze him in the classroom. "It was a snap for me," Buss says. "I got 'A's' in all the significant subjects, all the science and math. It was like falling off a log."

It wasn't easy financially. "At that time I didn't have the money to buy any books," he says. "The only time I could study was days and days before the test when nobody else was studying. That's when I could borrow the books.

"That's why that's all I do now is buy books. . . . I couldn't buy one, but since I worked hard at it, now I can buy a hundred. Same with sports. I really wanted to spend all my time and try to make the football team [in high school], but I always ended up quitting halfway through the season because I'd just run out of dough. So I kept telling myself, 'No problem. One of these days you'll have season tickets to all the great sports.'"

In those days Buss needed money for more practical things and he realized a second year of college would get him an even better-paying job. By attending summer school he could complete the curriculum in four or five months. So he stayed on and eventually decided to go for his degree.

In his senior year Buss got a job as a government chemist, working in the U. S. Bureau of Mines from midnight to dawn. He also had two other sources of income—a poker table and a pool table. For Buss, adept at both games, those activities were just as lucrative as his government job. He would come home from that job, shower, and head for school. After school he would head for the poker table or the pool table. Which didn't leave much time for sleep. So two days a week, usually Tuesday and Thursday, he would dispense with it altogether and just stay up around the clock to get in all his money-making ventures.

Word of Buss's academic accomplishments in college reached Kemmerer, where the number of local boys who went off and made good was not large.

In 1952, Buss decided to come home for Christmas. But only, in his mind, to see his friends. A lot of people in town were talking about this local kid who had gone off to Laramie and become an "A" student, but Buss didn't realize the degree of notoriety he had achieved until he stepped off his train onto the old platform of the train station at Kemmerer. It was good to be back among friends, among familiar sights. But Buss certainly wasn't prepared for the sight that greeted him at the other end of the platform.

As he stepped off his train, the bitter cold wind cutting into his chest like a sharp knife, Buss could make out a hazy figure, an apparition appearing through the steam of the idling locomotive. Buss had to look again to make sure it wasn't a mirage. Nope, it was C. B. Brown.

Buss knew it wasn't easy for C. B., a proud man, to greet the returning hero he had once labeled a bum. C. B. strode across the platform, stretched out his hand, and said, "Why don't you come home and spend the holidays with us?"

Buss did. He was too shocked to protest. Although the breach between the two was not totally healed, there was at least a grudging acceptance by Brown of his stepson.

A lot of young men aged 18 and 19 were getting drafted in 1952 to go off and fight in Korea. But Buss scored high enough on an exam to gain a student deferment.

In December of that year he married Joanne Mueller, a Wyoming coed. Buss graduated in the spring of 1953, before his twentieth birthday. A future as a government chemist no longer seemed like nirvana. Jerry Buss was beginning to think like a family man. He wanted kids. He wanted a more normal life. He didn't want to continue to depend on banking the eight ball into the side pocket or pulling an inside straight to put bread on the table.

He decided to go after a Ph.D. in physical chemistry. He wanted to go to Cal Tech, in Pasadena, California, but he couldn't get a full scholarship. Instead, he managed to land one at the University of Southern California. He grabbed it, figuring he would eventually transfer to Cal Tech. He arrived on the USC campus in 1953 and decided he didn't want to leave. He supplemented his income from his scholarship, which included $200 a month in spending money, with a teaching job and the money his wife earned from several jobs.

Still, it wasn't the best of times financially, and the couple had to work hard to stay within their food budget of $80 a month. They found chocolate milk was a penny a carton cheaper than white milk, so cold cereal in a bowl of chocolate milk became a staple of the Buss household. A meal might consist of one piece of lunch meat and a little bit of sandwich spread between two pieces of bread. Lunch might be one can of soup.

"We have it down to a science," the chemistry student would say.

One memorable day Jerry and Joanne discovered $5 lying in the street. They took their financial bonanza home and debated what they would do with this treasure.

The decision: "A dollar sixty-seven goes to you," Buss told his wife. "You can spend it anyway you see fit without taking the family into account. A dollar sixty-seven I get for the same purpose. And a dollar sixty-seven goes into the general kitty."

That money in the general fund drastically changed the lives of Jerry and Joanne. Until then they would occasionally add a real treat to their TV dinners—a wiener for the main dish. Until the $1.67 ran out, it was wieners all the time.

Jerry and Joanne had their first son, John, in 1956. There was another son, Jim, in '59; daughters Jeanie ('61) and Janie ('63) would follow. Expenses were rising.

Shortly before finishing his graduate work Buss took a job in Boston for a company called Operations Research, a firm that hired scientists to apply their expertise to business problems. He quit when the firm's promise of a transfer back to the West Coast fell through and he returned to L.A., where he got a job with the Douglas Aircraft Co. working on the development of rocket fuel and other classified material.

It was the era of Sputnik. The Russians had moved ahead in the space race and engineers and anyone with a science background could practically pick his position in America's budding aerospace industry. When Buss was hired in February of 1958 he was placed in a research group containing an even dozen. By June of 1959 that group, 160 strong, was divided into six smaller groups, with Buss promoted to a group leader. That didn't make what he saw as the regimentation of his job any easier. He looked at himself and his colleagues and saw "a herd of educated cattle."

His first love, however, remained teaching, but he decided he just couldn't make any money at it.

It was at Douglas that he met Frank Mariani, a fellow scientist. They had a lot in common. Mariani, too, had struggled as a child, in a poor neighborhood in Boston. And they both loved poker. To the sound of shuffling cards, a lifelong partnership was born. Over endless hands they talked and dreamed about becoming financially independent.

In July of 1958 they decided to take their first, small financial steps toward that distant goal. They would form a company to buy real estate. To do so, they would need $1,000 each. So they began to save exactly $83.33 from each paycheck, a paycheck that totaled a little over $500 a month for Mariani and a little over $700 a month for Buss.

A third partner joined the savings club: Ted Ward, Mariani's roommate. The plan was to save for a year in order to buy a duplex in the Los Angeles area, which the trio figured would cost about $25,000, with a down payment of about $3,000. If there was a vacancy, Mariani or Ward would move in to save money. And the three would do their own repairs.

The group started to grow. Two of Mariani's brothers in Boston, Bobby and Angelo, saved up $1,000 each to get in. A sixth partner, Sam Wilson, chipped in his thousand.

Six thousand was enough, they thought, for a four- or five-unit building. Instead, in 1959, their broker landed them a 14-unit building in West Los Angeles for $105,000.

"Real big stuff then," Buss says. "We were scared."

The group, calling themselves Cal-Ven Inc., put $6,000 down and took out a first, second, third, fourth, and fifth mortgage on the place.

By keeping every unit occupied—which they could guarantee since the plan called for group members to personally occupy any empty apartment—and by doing all the repair work themselves, the investment team could just about break even. But it wasn't easy; Buss and Mariani may have had a genius for science and real estate, but heavy labor was a different matter.

One night, after a full day at work, Buss and Mariani were painting one of their apartments when they found a hole in one of the pasteboard walls.

"You know, I have never been able to figure one of these things out," said Buss, staring at the hole. "How the hell do you plaster over this stuff? With this space here between the wall and the frame, you put the plaster in and it falls through. What holds the plaster up?" Mariani shrugged. He had no idea either. Jacks-of-all-trades they weren't.

Something had to be done. It was getting late, both men had put in a full day at Douglas and were facing another full day tomorrow. They were tired, they had paint on their hands, their arms, and their old work clothes. And they had an apartment that couldn't be finished until that damn hole was filled.

They stared at that hole as if sheer willpower could make it disappear. And then suddenly, Buss, ever the master of practicality, had an idea. Not an idea common among plasterers, but an idea nonetheless.

He smiled, pulled his dirty T-shirt over his head, wadded it into a ball, and jammed it into the hole. He and Mariani then plastered over the shirt and, *voilà,* one hole filled.

Every day brought new problems, new crises, new skills to learn, like laying carpet and moving refrigerators. Unfortunately, they weren't much more skilled at moving appliances than they had been at plastering. On one occasion they were hauling a refrigerator up a flight of stairs that made a sharp turn to the left. Maneuvering the refrigerator on a dolly, they made too sharp a left, leaving Buss trapped between the appliance and the wall. They laughed at their own ineptness. Finally, after 15 minutes of twisting, turning, and grunting, the pair figured out a way to squeeze Buss out without sending the refrigerator tumbling back to the ground floor.

The original plan had called for the six investors to divide into two-man repair teams, each team working every third weekend. But it became impossible to get it all done on weekends, so the teams had to start working weeknights after their regular jobs. That began to get real old real fast.

The other partners made an offer to Buss and Mariani: If

they would work every weekend, they would receive a management fee from the others. The pair agreed. "We kind of enjoyed it," Buss says. "I don't know, owning your own place—we had colored lights and palm trees—you felt like you were really accomplishing something."

Besides, it was easier than working for Mile-a-Day Mike.

There were 12 partners in Cal-Ven by now, saving $125 a month each. One year later Mariani-Buss and company had a second building, a 16-unit structure in Cheviot Hills, purchased in July of 1960 with a down payment of $18,000.

Buss and Mariani each planted a palm tree in front of that second building, twin symbols of a dream that their holdings would grow as surely and as strongly as those trees.

"We had big aspirations," Buss recalls. "We had this whole thing all figured out. We figured we would buy one building every year. Then, after 10 or 12 years, the first one would be somewhat paid off. With inflation, the rents would be up, but your payments would be fixed. With the income from that— the seconds and the thirds would be paid off—I think we figured we could pull out maybe five, six hundred a month. Six hundred a month plus teaching would be about the same as I was making from industry by that time. To pull out some money from real estate would allow me to teach."

But the more money Buss pulled out, the harder it became to get back to teaching.

For their third unit Buss and Mariani saved $200 a month. Again, their goal was one year of saving, but a good buy came on the market in Santa Monica sooner than that. So they took in additional partners and made a purchase, ahead of their timetable, for $150,000.

Buss and Mariani were still doing all the repairs. But it was taking them seven days a week now. "We were running out of juice, working nights, days, everything," Buss says.

The solution wasn't far away. His stepbrother, Jimmy, had just come out to L.A. from Wyoming. With adequate money coming in from the real estate holdings, Buss made Jimmy the full-time maintenance man.

By now Buss himself had a new job. He left Douglas in February of 1960 and moved on to TRW, where he worked on long-range research with a physics group dealing in subjects like particle propulsion. Eight months later Mariani followed him over. But the real estate empire remained priority No. 1.

In 1962, Buss and Mariani began a second company—Dyna Real (for dynamic realty) Inc. They continued to buy real estate and added a second employee in maintenance. Jesse, Buss's mother, divorced from C. B. Brown, had also moved to L.A., and she became the bookkeeper for her son's growing business.

But Buss couldn't quite shake that long-nagging urge to teach. And in July of 1962 he quit TRW and applied for a teaching job at SC. The best they had available was a lecturing position. Buss took it and ran the real estate company full-time while Mariani stayed at TRW.

That lasted one semester. By then the money from real estate was pouring in as if someone had left a cash valve open. Buss's annual income from his holdings had grown to $80,000 by 1963, more than a university president's salary, perhaps as much as the president of TRW was taking home.

"I've totally lost interest in teaching," Buss told Mariani. "I want to see how far we can take this real estate thing."

Mariani quit TRW and also devoted all his efforts to real estate; the days of plugging up walls with T-shirts was just a funny memory.

Buss has a lot of funny memories of Frank Mariani over the years.

While Mariani has proved himself to be an astute businessman in his own right, capable of successfully carrying off a million-dollar deal without a hitch, carrying a cup of coffee, getting out of his car in one piece, and various other daily routines sometimes seem beyond his capabilities. This guy, according to Buss, is the Inspector Clouseau of the business world.

While Mariani and Buss were still working at Douglas, Mariani was constantly spilling his coffee on Buss's desk. Buss was always checking out classified documents and then bringing them back with coffee stains all over them.

Finally he had enough. He saw Mariani heading his way one afternoon, the ever-present deadly cup of coffee in one hand.

"Hold it! Stand back," said Buss, holding up the palm of his hand.

He grabbed an important set of documents spread across the top of his desk, tucked them into one neat stack, opened the bottom drawer of the desk, placed the documents in there, and shut it.

Only then did a smile cross Buss's face.

"Okay," he told Mariani, motioning him to come over.

As the two started talking Mariani set his coffee cup down on Buss's desk. A question arose over something they were working on.

"Just a minute," Buss said, "I have it right here. Let me get it for you."

He reached down and opened the bottom drawer to get the documents.

Mariani leaned over to look and hit the coffee cup, sending its contents spilling over the top of the desk, down into the drawer, and all over those classified documents.

Another time Buss and Mariani went to dinner at the highly exclusive Jonathan Club in downtown Los Angeles. As they were getting out of their car Mariani caught his jacket on the door, badly ripping one sleeve of the garment near the shoulder.

"You can't go into the Jonathan Club like that," said Buss, shaking his head at his partner's latest misadventure.

"Don't worry," Mariani assured him, "I'll just hold my shoulder, pretend I've got some injury."

"Okay," said Buss, sure that an embarrassing moment was ahead.

Mariani was carrying it off until the waiter brought the dinner rolls to the table. Forgetting his problem, Mariani reached over for a roll, dropping the arm of his jacket into his plate before a wide-eyed waiter.

Getting out of his car at a Southern California racetrack one day, Mariani managed to catch his pants on the door, ripping them badly.

Once again there was Buss telling him, "You can't go in there like that."

Once again Mariani disagreed. "Sure I can," he said. "I'll just hold them up."

And he did until the middle of a race in which the horse he had bet on was fighting for the lead. Caught up in the excitement, Mariani leapt up and forgot to hold on to his pants, causing them to drop to the floor.

Nearby, a couple of women watched the scene in disgust. "I told you," one said to the other, "that a lot of people who come to the track can't afford it."

The Mariani stories are a favorite of Buss. He tells about his partner accidentally dropping drinks over a railing at a race-track, raining booze on the people below; of Mariani leaning against an office partition, causing it and its surrounding supports to topple like a row of dominoes; and of the time Mariani leaned against an office water cooler, tipped it over, caught the upside-down water bottle, and watched helplessly as the water cascaded over him and across the floor.

The man may have left his mark on the Southern California real estate market, but to Jerry Buss that mark will always be a coffee stain.

When Mariani-Buss started to grow, the added pressure failed to diminish the laughs and good times. One reason is that the two partners made their company a family affair, and when they ran out of family, they employed friends or friends of friends. Outsiders were rarely hired. Jesse moved into a full-time position as an accountant and receptionist. Mariani's brothers worked for the company. So did an aunt and uncle of Buss's along with his mother. There were long hours, but a lot of camaraderie—pizza after work, weekly poker sessions, and sports. Always games to attend, Lakers, Rams, USC. Or the horse races.

Even at the track Buss seemed to have some kind of magic, long before he had ever heard of Earvin Johnson.

A case in point: It was during the late '60s. Mariani-Buss had been anxious to purchase a piece of property they felt was very important to their financial holdings. It was at the corner of Second and Arizona in Santa Monica. But the woman who owned it refused to sell.

One day Buss got a call. "If you can come up with cash outside of escrow by Monday," he was told, "you can have this piece of property."

All they needed was $20,000.

They were off to the races.

Mariani and his father, Buss and his mother, and several other family members went to Santa Anita racetrack, bought a stack of about 20 tickets at $2 each, and made identical bets after Buss, who fancied himself a pretty good handicapper, assessed the field. He was good enough that day; they hit the daily double and racked in $632 per ticket, giving them over $12,000. They soon raised the rest and had their property.

"Everybody just felt like God loves us," Buss says. "Everything we did just went the right way."

Another case in point: Shortly after Mariani-Buss bought one Los Angeles apartment building, oil was discovered underground. The company's royalty rights just about paid off the mortgage.

Still, it wasn't all good times. In 1967 a recession hit, gobbling up many real estate companies. But because Mariani-Buss had gone the family route, it survived. Family and friends were willing to work extra hours and defer some pay until the rough waters had smoothed. Thus they rode it out together.

By age 34, Jerry Buss was a millionaire.

But he was no longer enchanted with his position. He felt like merely the middleman between his renters and the bank. Collecting rents, which continued to soar, became a real hassle at times as people often fell behind in their payments.

He and Mariani began to diversify. Resorts were the first alternative. They bought the Ocotillo Lodge in Palm Springs, a hotel in Phoenix, and another in Mammoth, a California ski resort. They had a trio of hotels on the Sunset Strip. They owned the International Towers Building in Long Beach—eight stories of hotel rooms, eight stories of office space, and eight of apartments.

Then came another recession in the early 70s. While oil prices were skyrocketing, real estate was crash-landing upon the Southern California landscape. This was worse than '67 and it required more extreme measures than merely asking family and friends to pitch in. So Buss and Mariani went back to those they knew best—aerospace engineers.

His track record with the horses may have been good, but it was nothing compared to his track record with investors, many of whom were engineers he knew from his days at Douglas and

TRW. He coddled them, he courted them, and he always made them money. He knew they were the lifeblood of his organization so he kept them informed and he kept them in the black, and when he needed them in '72 and '73, they were there.

"You as engineers, you as aerospace people understand numbers. You understand things that fit into formulas," Buss would tell a group of potential investors. "You can make real estate work the same way. Something you design has to have these kinds of things to make it work. Your investment has to have these kinds of things. You get so much appreciation. You get so much return on investment and you get so much tax advantage."

Buss was a master at getting up before a microphone, which he referred to as his "sword," and driving home a point.

"You know," he once told Bart Christensen, an aide, "ninety-nine percent of the people that know me don't know what my real talent is. They respect me for my education. They respect me for my ability to think on my feet. They respect me for my ability with numbers. But my real forte in life, what I am better at than anyone I've ever met, is being a salesman. The secret of all this is being able to sell. I'm a great salesman."

Christensen, who worked for California Governor Ronald Reagan in the state's Commerce Department, worked on several presidential campaigns and later ran for Congress and lost, didn't argue with Buss's self-analysis.

"I realized he was right on the money," Christensen says. "I would go to these [investment] meetings and he was absolutely the best person I've ever seen behind a microphone. He probably would have made a great politician if that had been his bent. He's talked about politics a lot, very knowledgeable about it. He's said that someday he might want to find somebody that he would back and try to help, somebody who believed the way he did. He had no interest himself, no ego to be involved."

Buss was not only a great salesman, he offered a great product, nearly guaranteed to make money. It may be hard to reconcile his flashy cars, his flashy ladies, and the flashy wad he might toss on a football game with a straight-arrow approach to business, but that's the way it has always been for Buss.

"There's a 180-degree difference between Jerry Buss, the

social person, and Jerry Buss, the business person," according to his longtime P.R. man, Bob Steiner. "To me, they are about as diametrically opposed as you can be. The businessman is an ultraconservative, operates on an absolute cost-effective method and manner. Nobody here has an unlimited expense account. Yet he's perceived by the public as being this flamboyant guy. And socially he lives that kind of a life. He works hard to enable himself to do these other things of which he says, 'If people don't like me for them, I'm sorry, but I've earned the right to do this.' He's a mathematician, and mathematicians aren't gamblers."

Buss does gamble on sporting events quite a bit, often employing unique theories. He would, for example, have an assistant who bet pro football games weekly, bring in his picks. The assistant had no inside information on the games and bet the way most casual fans do. Buss would look at the picks, then bet the opposite, figuring a little knowledge was dangerous. Unlike his assistant, Buss usually wound up winning.

When he moved on his theory that the '70s recession would be another short-term plunge, Buss didn't see it as a gamble. He and Mariani bought up buildings that had been foreclosed by banks or savings and loan institutions. Going that route, they were able to acquire millions of dollars worth of property with little or no down payment. The financial institutions were more than happy to find someone to take the buildings off their hands and manage them.

When the economy turned back around there they were, Buss and Mariani, sitting on four-, five-, six-story gold mines. They'd staked their claims at just the right time. By Buss's fortieth birthday, in 1973, he and Mariani were each worth several million. But that was just spending money in comparison to the gusher that was to follow. An incredible real estate boom hit Southern California in the mid and late '70s. People were literally buying and selling homes overnight for huge profits. Buss and Mariani had bought up eight pieces of property along Wilshire Boulevard, property that increased nearly tenfold in value in three years. One piece of Mariani-Buss land along Wilshire had been worth about $20 per square foot. It was felt it might have gone up to $50. Buss asked $100 a square foot for the property.

And got it. From '76 to '78 a share in Mariani-Buss soared in value from around $10,000 to $85,000. Buss himself owned around 200 shares, whose worth leapt from $2 million to $17 million.

By now those two palm trees he and Mariani had planted when their dreams were budding had grown to full size, but they were dwarfed in comparison to a real estate empire that, by its peak in 1979, stretched across California, Arizona, and Nevada. They owned, through about 45 different limited partnerships, 1,000 houses, 200 pieces of land. They employed 400 people, including hotel employees. Their holdings were worth an estimated $350 million—on paper, that is, because that included a lot of unpaid mortgages. If they had liquidated at that stage, they probably could have realized about $80 million. Since the various other partners owned about 60 percent of that, Buss and Mariani together could have pocketed about $35 million. Frank Mariani, who had grown up in a tiny apartment, four to a room, and Jerry Buss, the kid who had stood in that food line so long ago in Evanston, had moved near the front of the line among Southern California real estate magnates.

Buss had begun with simple desires—to get out of the old house above the plumbing shop, perhaps someday to get to California, and eventually to teach. But money had always been a problem, from the days when his next meal lay at the bottom of a gunny sack at the end of a line to the days when finding $5 was a cause for celebration. What he wanted was enough income to make his dreams of teaching possible. What he got was beyond the wildest of dreams.

But still it wasn't enough.

Entering middle age, Jerry Buss was bored.

2.

The Team: Crashing in Iowa, Reborn in L.A.

IN the early hours of January 18, 1960, somewhere above America, the Lakers weren't California-dreamin' about L.A. millionaires in their far distant future. They were Minneapolis-prayin' for their immediate future. Nobody in the world knew where they were, including their pilot.

The roar of their airplane flying very low overhead awakened Joe Twit from a sound sleep.

It sounded like a big plane, and big planes didn't buzz Carroll, Iowa. Not at 1:30 in the morning, and especially not in the middle of a hellacious snowstorm. Something was wrong, and when something went wrong in Carroll, Joe Twit was needed. He and his wife lived upstairs at the Twit Funeral Home, and Joe drove the town's ambulance, which doubled as a coroner's wagon.

He was already starting to dress when the phone rang. It was the sheriff's office.

"Joe, we've got an airplane down in a cornfield out on the Steffe's farm," the dispatcher told Twit.

Elmer Steffes's farm was less than a half mile away.

"I'll be there in five minutes," Twit said, and hung up the phone.

The previous day had been a lousy one for the Minneapolis Lakers. They had lost a game that afternoon to their division rivals, the St. Louis Hawks, 135–119. By 5:30, when the team arrived at Lambert Field in St. Louis to board the team plane back to Minneapolis, a heavy winter storm was blowing. Worse, the players were informed that their plane had a generator problem and that the airport was temporarily shut down for landings or takeoffs because of the sleet and snow.

37

The players shuffled into the airport dining room to wait and to fuel up for the two-hour flight home. The team's private DC-3 was equipped with a hot plate, suitable for heating cans of soup or spaghetti, which helped stretch the players' $7 per diem, but under the circumstances most of the players opted for a greasy coffee-shop burger. They ate, played cards, and watched the snowstorm rage. Just after eight o'clock word came that the plane was ready and the airport was open. The players bundled up for the sprint from the terminal to the plane.

"Hey, Boomer, better check your Ouija board," guard "Hot Rod" Hundley said to Jim Krebs, the team's young center. Krebs had been given the Ouija board for Christmas, and less than a week ago it had warned him that the team plane would crash.

This news unsettled some of the players. They read the newspaper headlines. Less than two weeks before an airliner had crashed in North Carolina, killing 34, and the previous October a commercial airliner had crashed in Charlottesville, killing all 26 passengers. An AP newspaper story referred to "a series of baffling recent plane crashes in widely separated parts of the world."

A couple of months earlier Hundley had been discussing the topic of winter air travel and crash landings with the one of the team's copilots in a New York bar, and the copilot assured Hundley that if you had to crash-land, the DC-3 was as good a plane as any to do it in.

"We could set that baby down in a cornfield," he had boasted to Hot Rod.

It was 8:30 when Vernon Ullman, a retired Marine pilot and the captain of the Lakers' plane, received clearance from the tower, taxied down the runway, and lifted off into a white sheet of a sky. He had to take the plane out low, under the air traffic stacked up in the sky over St. Louis by the storm. The flight was bumpy from the start, which was no surprise to the players. The DC-3 is a sturdy and reliable aircraft, having served nobly during World War II, but it is an airplane short on comfort.

The cabin was unpressurized, drafty, and small, seating three across, two on one side of the aisle and one on the other. This being a propeller plane, it flew *through* the weather, at about 15,000 feet, not over it. Commercial jet travel had come into being two years earlier, but teams in the National Basketball Association almost never flew jets on their winter-long wandering through the East and Midwest. Bucking storms was an everyday fact of NBA life.

In the front of the cabin, the only part of the Lakers' plane ever noticeably warmed by the heating system, the team's card players quickly set up shop. Hundley, Elgin (Motormouth) Baylor, Dick Garmaker, Frank (Pops) Selvy, Bob (Slick) Leonard, Boomer Krebs, and Larry (Desert Head) Faust wedged their custom-made card table into the narrow aisle. No Laker flight ever took off without the card table in place and the game already in progress, usually poker, dealer call, $2 limit. The card players all smoked (rookie Tom Hawkins was the only nonsmoking player aboard), kibitzed, and chattered unceasingly.

The card games helped relieve the tedium of travel, helped the players through the exhausting grind of NBA travel. Before this 75-game regular season had even started, the Lakers had played a barnstorming series of 10 exhibition games in 13 nights, all against the Celtics, up and down the New England coast. During the season the Lakers often played back-to-back games, sometimes arriving in town just in time to drive to the arena and suit up. On one trip into Chicago weather grounded their plane and the Lakers were forced to take a train, changing into their uniforms in the baggage car as they pulled into Chicago. If the road was tough on the Lakers, home wasn't much more glamorous, since they were drawing an average of only 3,400 in the old Minneapolis Armory.

Less than 10 minutes into the flight the cabin lights flickered, dimmed, and finally died. The card players scrambled for flashlights to keep the game alive, but this flight was unusually bumpy, and the heater had gone out when the lights died. It took a lot to discourage a card game, but this one was called on account of coldness, darkness, and bumpiness.

The players weren't yet aware that the plane's two generators had blown shortly after takeoff, and the crew was now flying with no radio, no heat, no defroster, and no cockpit lights. Within 15 minutes of takeoff the storm had closed off visual contact with the ground. With no radio, and with heavy traffic in the sky above the airport, Ullman couldn't risk returning to St. Louis.

He pointed the plane toward Minneapolis, using the compass, but soon it began to gyrate wildly. The boys in the cockpit didn't know where they were or where they were going, but there was no turning back.

The passengers—nine players, coach Jim Pollard, six other adults, and four children—were calm and quiet. There was nothing to do but sit back and ride out another storm. That was something the Lakers were good at, in the air and on the ground.

This was a team floundering, going nowhere, literally and figuratively. Some games, barely a thousand fans showed up at the Armory. Team owner Bob Short, a dynamic young Minneapolis lawyer and trucking magnate, was running short of cash. Short was one of about 20 Twin Cities businessmen who bought the Lakers in 1957 for $150,000 in order to keep the club in Minneapolis. They put an additional $50,000 in as operating capital, and that was gone in two weeks.

The committee of owners would hold weekly "prayer meetings" to brainstorm on how to keep the Lakers afloat. At one prayer meeting they calculated that the team needed $14,000 to meet immediate expenses. Short wrote out a check for the entire amount. The other owners were so appreciative they voted to issue him all the outstanding common stock at five cents a share.

It was a symbolic gesture, but it would result in Short owning about a third of the franchise. By acclamation he had become the group's leader and unofficial Laker "owner." The token gift certainly didn't look like a windfall, considering that, at the rate it was losing money, the franchise would be $300,000 in the red before the start of the next season.

When the team would hit a losing streak Short would visit the locker room and plead, "Listen, guys, I like basketball as much as the next guy, but not to the tune of $50,000 a week."

Short was selling players to meet his payroll. He peddled one very good guard to the New York Knicks for $25,000. The season before, in desperation, Short had drafted, recruited, and signed Elgin Baylor after Baylor's junior season at Seattle University. Baylor came to Minneapolis hailed as a superman, an acrobatic and creative player the likes of whom had never before been seen anywhere. Baylor adjusted to the NBA game immediately, lived up to every word of his advance billing, led an otherwise ordinary team into the NBA finals his rookie season, and was primarily responsible for whatever meager box-office success the Lakers were having.

"If Elgin had turned me down, I'd have gone out of business," Short said. "The club would have gone bankrupt."

After Baylor's first season Short signed Elgin to a five-year contract at $50,000 per year.

"Are you happy with your contract, Elgin?" a reporter asked at the press conference.

"No," Baylor said. "Short's got a smile on his face. There must be something wrong with the deal."

In truth, Short did consider Baylor a bargain, but even Elgin couldn't save the franchise in this town. Short was talking about moving the club, and there were rumors he was even considering the West Coast, San Francisco or Los Angeles. Those rumors didn't mean much to the Lakers. Playing basketball in a city that had sunshine and movie stars and palm trees was an almost surreal prospect, too distant and foreign even to contemplate. The Dodgers and Rams were packing 'em in at the Coliseum, proving that pro sports could thrive in the virgin West, but the Dodgers and Rams were in the big leagues. The NBA, Elgin Baylor or no Elgin Baylor, was still bush league. The Lakers couldn't relate.

In the cockpit Ullman pulled back on the stick and tried to climb over the storm, get high enough to see the stars and fly by celestial navigation. The cabin temperature dropped and the passengers huddled in blankets. With no pressurization, the air in the cabin became thinner. As the plane climbed many of the passengers became short of breath.

Baylor, who hated and feared flying under the best of circumstances, would have given up a year's salary for a parachute on this particular flight. He pulled his blanket tighter and fought back the waves of nausea. Normally, Elgin was a nonstop talker, a combination of a walking trivia encyclopedia, kibitzer, putdown comedian, play-by-play commentator on card games or on life in general, and a Mark Twain-class storyteller. He could keep a roommate awake half the night telling a tale of a dead uncle who came back to visit.

On the court Baylor was even more spectacular, a sleek yet powerful 6–5 forward with a noble bearing and a repertoire of acrobatic shots that continually amazed even his teammates. Elgin didn't perfect old moves, he invented new ones, seemingly every night. Just this afternoon he had scored 43 points in the loss to the Hawks. Fans around the league were turning out in big numbers to marvel at Baylor and at the league's other new superstar, rookie Wilt Chamberlain of the Philadelphia Warriors.

Because of Baylor, and because fans still remembered the George Mikan-led Laker teams that dominated the NBA in the early '50s, the Lakers were the NBA's glamour team. Hot Rod Hundley, a fourth-year veteran from West Virginia, provided a perfect artistic complement to Baylor's majestic grace. Hundley worked an arena crowd with the flair of a circus juggler and the bravado of a midway barker. To Hot Rod, basketball wasn't a war, it was a performance, a show, a wonderful outlet for his creative impulses. It was Hot Rod's fortune, good or bad, to come to the pro game in an era where any intentional razzle-dazzle was considered a capital offense, where a behind-the-back pass was unconscionable showboating. If anything, the prevailing tight-ass attitude toward fancy play only inspired Hot Rod to greater hot-dog heights. If the Lakers had a comfortable lead, or were being badly beaten, he would throw incredible wrap-around passes, dribble behind his back and between his legs, shoot hook-shot free throws. The fans loved it, the opposing players hated it.

St. Louis coach Harry (the Horse) Gallatin once warned Hundley not to pull any of that hot-dog, circus stuff on *his* team. Hot Rod snapped back, "Don't get too far behind tonight, Horse, or it'll be showtime in St. Louis."

Off the court Hot Rod was a nonstop party. When the team checked into New York he would phone Tommy Hawkins and proclaim in dramatic tones, "Hawk, it is six o'clock. The streets of the naked city beckon, telling of the glamorous wonders that await us."

One evening in St. Louis, an off night before a big game, Hundley was standing on the sidewalk in front of the team hotel awaiting a cab to take him in search of adventure. Bob Short approached and smiled.

"Listen, Hot Rod," Short said, "you need your rest. I don't want you to wear yourself out chasing all over town. If you'll go back to your room, I'll send up a beautiful girl. I'll pay for everything."

Hot Rod threw his arm around the owner's shoulder.

"Bob, you know I don't work that way. The thrill is in the chase, baby."

Short was understanding, to a point. That point was finally exceeded, however, by Hundley and his most frequent off-court running mate, Slick Leonard. After too many missed curfews, Short summoned the two players to his office. He called Hundley on the carpet first, while Leonard waited outside. Short informed Hundley that he and Leonard were being fined $1,000 each. Hot Rod's salary was $10,000; Leonard's was $9,000.

Hundley sauntered out of Short's office. Leonard, worried sick, whispered, "What happened, Hot Rod? How bad is it?"

"He fined us a big one, baby," Hot Rod said.

"A hundred bucks!" Leonard moaned.

Short used the fine as a kind of probation collateral. If the two behaved the rest of the season, the fines would be rescinded. Hot Rod wondered if $1,000 wasn't a small price to pay for the right to party. A guy had to do something to rise above the boredom and low-rent atmosphere of the NBA. This was, after all, a league fighting to stay alive, always teetering on the brink of financial collapse, operating on a tattered shoestring. The NBA featured frequent franchise shifts, low salaries, tight schedules, cheap hotels, cold arenas, racism, thugism, and bumpy flights through winter storms. According to one National Football League insider, the NFL team owners referred to the NBA as "Eight Jews doing business out of a phone booth."

Not all the owners were Jewish, but the phone-booth analogy wasn't far from wrong. The league was only 15 years old, and the eight teams were owned by men of modest wealth compared to the owners in other sports and to the tycoons who would come along in the NBA of the '70s and '80s.

"They weren't rich guys," Wilt Chamberlain would say years later. "They were barnstorming owners who fell in love with the game of basketball but didn't have enough money to make it a class operation. They were struggling. My first year, in order for Eddie Gottlieb [the Philadelphia Warriors owner] to get back the money he paid me [about $100,000], he scheduled about 25 exhibition games [teams today play about six]. And they were in remote areas—Missouri, Arkansas, North Dakota, Nevada. I'm talking about *small* towns."

On this particular Laker flight the passengers were beginning to worry. The scheduled two-hour flight was already three hours long, the lights and heater were out, and still there was no word from the cockpit. Tommy Hawkins, the rookie forward from Notre Dame, was sitting in the back row taking stock of the situation. The roaring storm was all but drowning out the noise of the twin prop engines. Visibility was nearly zero. Hawkins noted the ice accumulating on the wings and on the cabin-window glass. At his feet a layer of ice was beginning to form on the aisle floor. And now one of the engines seemed to be sputtering and coughing.

"So this is professional basketball," Hawkins thought.

Up in the card players' section, Boomer Krebs was making pious vows about what he would do if this plane ever landed safely. Lord, he would clean up his act. Be nice to everyone. Throw out his Ouji board.

"And I swear I'll never cheat at cards again," Boomer said earnestly.

Hawkins thought about how, in many ways, including travel, playing basketball in the NBA was a step down from college ball, especially from the style of life he was accustomed to at Notre Dame. The NBA provided its players no medical or dental plan, no retirement or pension fund. Most contracts were for one year and not guaranteed even for that length of time. The league's eight arenas, as rookie Wilt Chamberlain had noted, were all "old, cold, big, empty, and dark."

Heating the arenas was a constant problem. "Your hands are cold, and the ball is cold," Chamberlain would later reminisce. "The ball feels like a brick. In the Detroit Arena I remember playing in front of about 3,000 people, and every time someone opened a door the wind would blow through like a hurricane. Paul Arizin had asthma, and I remember him rubbing his hands together, blowing on his hands, and you could see the vapor."

To keep travel expenses down, the Lakers would fly into a city the day of a game instead of the previous day. The team would rent two rooms instead of the normal five or six, and the rooms would serve as lounges for pregame relaxation. After the game, no matter how late, they would fly home.

Apart from the bargain-basement traveling and playing conditions, the game itself had a look that present-day NBA fans would barely recognize. The NBA game of 1960 was much simpler, tougher, and whiter.

The sport of basketball was still in the early stages of integration at the beginning of the 1960s. The NCAA college tournament wasn't integrated until 1948, and the NBA was lily-white until 1950, when Celtic owner Walter Brown, at the league draft meeting in a Chicago hotel room, announced, "Boston takes Charles Cooper of Duquesne."

There was silence in the room, according to a later *New York Times* account.

Another owner broke the silence, saying, "Walter, don't you know he's a colored boy?"

"I don't give a damn if he's striped, plaid, or polka dot!" Brown roared. "Boston takes Charles Cooper of Duquesne."

Whether this historic draft pick was made out of an enlightened sense of equality or was simply a desperation move is not clear. The league was in big trouble at the time, six teams having gone under that spring, and several others were in trouble. The Celtics were $460,000 in debt.

Whatever the reason, by 1960, two years after the St. Louis Hawks won an NBA championship with an all-white roster, blacks had begun to make an impact on the league. In Boston, Bill Russell had already helped hatch a dynasty. Russell, Chamberlain, and Baylor were the first black superstars, the first to be true drawing cards, and the first to have enough power to stand up against some of the racism commonly encountered by blacks.

In Baylor's rookie season the Lakers scheduled an exhibition game against the Cincinnati Royals in Charlestown, West Virginia, Hot Rod Hundley's hometown. When the Lakers checked into their hotel they were informed that Baylor and the team's other black, Eddie Fleming, could not stay in the hotel. Baylor, a proud man, said he would not play in the game, and Fleming said he wouldn't either.

Baylor's teammates, bowing to pressure to fulfill the contract, didn't join Baylor in boycotting the game, but they did join him in walking out of the hotel. The team bussed across the tracks to the black section of town and spent the night at Edna's Rest Home.

The NBA had an unofficial racial quota: three blacks per 10-man roster. Most of the teams were still at a 9:1 or 8:2 ratio, and black bench warmers were rare. If a black player wasn't good enough to make the starting lineup, he was cut.

"I could understand the quotas, even if I didn't like 'em," Chamberlain would say. "You were in white America. The fans were all white, and the owners weren't bigots, they were businessmen trying to survive."

Blacks were struggling for acceptance, especially in St. Louis. Every time Chamberlain's team played there he was bombarded with borderline racial verbal abuse from three men who had front-row seats.

"One day in St. Louis I hit every fucking shot you can imagine," Wilt would say. "I had about 50 points by the end of the third quarter. Those three guys got up, said, 'Enough of this shit,' and walked out, never to be seen again. Ben Kerner [the Hawks' owner] told me later they turned in their season tickets."

In time black players would play a strong role in changing the structure and style of the sport, but in 1960 the NBA was still short on finesse and long on brutality. Years later, with graceful leapers on every team, the game would be played above the rim. In 1960 much of the action was below the belt. Thugs and enforcers ruled.

Rudy LaRusso, a Dartmouth graduate, was the Lakers' muscle, a 6–9 power forward before the term was invented. LaRusso had no qualms about fighting, but he wasn't the toughest player in the NBA. The Celtics had Jungle Jim Luscotoff, considered by many the prototype enforcer. The Warriors had Handy Andy Johnson, whose job it was to protect Wilt. "Don't mess with my meal ticket," Johnson would snarl at opponents. Cincinnati had big Wayne Embry.

In one exhibition game Warrior forward Woody Sauldsbury was matched up against LaRusso, then a rookie. LaRusso hit a jump shot in Sauldsbury's face. Then another, and another. At the other end of the court Woody took a pass, looked at LaRusso, placed the ball carefully on the floor, and punched LaRusso in the face, knocking him off his feet.

"The man was guarding me too close," Sauldsbury explained.

By now the Lakers had been airborne three and a half hours. Copilot Howard Gifford opened the cockpit door, stepped into the passenger cabin, and gave a quick status report: We have no lights, no generator, no radio, and we're lost, he told them. We have no idea where we are, not even which state we're over, and we're running out of fuel. We came down to about 500 feet to get below the storm, and we can see some lights below. It looks like a town. The captain's been shining a flashlight down there, hoping to get someone to turn on airport lights, if there is an airport, but no luck. He spotted what looks like a cornfield. We can see the dark corn against the snow background. The captain thinks that's our best shot.

"Shit, let's go for it," Hundley said.

Baylor got up from his seat and lay down in the aisle, wrapping himself tighter in his blanket.

"Just put it down anywhere," he moaned. "I don't care."

The copilot stepped back into the cockpit, but the door didn't latch behind him. As the plane pitched in the storm the door swung open and closed, affording the players a view of the cockpit drama. They could see the frosted-over windshield and Ullman with his head out the side window. With one copilot reading the altimeter by flashlight, Ullman took the plane down to 200 feet and was buzzing the town, formulating a landing plan. The three crewmen debated whether to land the plane with or without landing gear. They decided to lower the gear.

On one pass over town the players could see a large, white water tower with black lettering, and they saw they were about to attempt to land in Carroll, Iowa. On a flight of about 500 miles, they had strayed some 150 miles off course.

"We're gonna make it," Pops Selvy kept saying. "We're gonna make it."

Below, Carroll was waking up to the sound of a low-flying DC-3. The fire department was alerted, then the sheriff and Joe Twit at the funeral home. Ullman made several more roaring passes over the town and the cornfield, but whenever the plane got below 200 feet, the storm would obscure visual contact with the ground and Ullman would pull up and circle around again.

Finally there was slight clearing, enough visibility to attempt a landing. Ullman rolled down the flaps, throttled down, and took his airplane toward the cornfield, heading north by northwest toward a slight incline in the standing corn. The players watched through the swinging door as one of the copilots read the air-speed gauge aloud: ". . . eighty knots . . . seventy . . . sixty . . . fifty . . . *take it up! Take it up!*"

There was a high-tension power line directly in the intended landing path.

So they circled again and approached the landing area a second time. This time the plane cleared the high-tension wire, Ullman cut the engines, and the Minneapolis Lakers floated down toward Elmer Steffes' field of standing corn. The DC-3 plopped into the corn and bounced softly three or four times. Any snowdrifts or mounds could have been disastrous, but the standing corn served to keep the snow flat. After plowing a neat furrow 100 yards long through the corn crop, the plane came to a gentle and noiseless stop.

Inside the cabin there was complete silence, not even the sound of breathing, for several seconds. "Are we dead?" Baylor wondered. Then, as if on cue, the players erupted in whoops and shouts of joy and relief. The door was opened and they all scrambled out, into two feet of powdery snow. When Ullman climbed out the players threw him into the corn and pelted him with snowballs.

They could see the road, about two hundred yards across the field, and a line of fire trucks, police cars, civilian cars, and Joe Twit's ambulance. As the players slogged through the snow to the welcoming party, someone standing by the ambulance called out a greeting: "We thought we were going to have some business tonight, boys!"

The motorcade took the players and other passengers directly to the Burke Motor Inn. By now, back in Minneapolis, the wives and families would be in a panic. All they knew was that the plane had taken off from St. Louis in terrible conditions and hadn't been seen or heard from since and was long overdue, so the first order of business for the players was to phone home. They all lined up at the motel's three pay telephones.

Desert Head Foust, who in the course of his married life had employed many excuses for coming home late, phoned his wife, Toni.

"I won't be home tonight," he told her. "We just crash-landed in a cornfield in Iowa."

"Call me back when you sober up," she said.

Back inside the motel, the players celebrated, sang, talked, and drank beer, a bottle of liquor supplied by Twit, and hot coffee. Someone broke out a deck of cards. During the first hand Elgin Baylor caught Boomer Krebs cheating.

The year 1960 was a big one for new beginnings. John F. Kennedy, nominated at the brand-new Los Angeles Sports Arena, was elected the thirty-fifth President. The United States space program sent a chimpanzee into space, and Russia one-upped us by putting a man into orbit.

And Bob Short, his Lakers clinging to life as a franchise, decided to move from Minneapolis to Los Angeles after the 1959–60 season. It was a bold move, a Lewis-and-Clark-like expedition for a cozy little eastern league that considered St. Louis to be the wilderness. The Lakers had no way of knowing what to expect in L.A., whether they would be embraced or rejected, accepted or swallowed up in the vast, sprawling sea of freeways and suburbs.

If Los Angeles had basketball fans in 1960, most of them hadn't yet come out of the closet. The UCLA Bruins, with a coach named John Wooden, were struggling to stay above .500 and were drawing an average of just over 6,000, counting double-headers. The Bruins played in the new Sports Arena, which they shared with the USC Trojans, who were drawing about 6,400.

Bob Short didn't know if Los Angeles was ready for pro basketball—or for any basketball—but he had to take his team somewhere. He had borrowed $87,500 to buy enough shares to own one third of the team. The following year he would buy out the others completely. Now he had a sizable investment in a very speculative venture.

"A gamble?" Short would say when asked years later about the move. "Hell, we were broke in Minneapolis. We did have some confidence in L.A., but it wasn't the basketball capital of the world then. Kids out there hardly knew what a basketball was in those days."

To get a feel for the potential hoops market on the Coast before committing to a move at season's end, Short booked the Lakers to play regular-season games on January 30 in San Francisco and February 1 in L.A. against the Philadelphia Warriors in the new Sports Arena.

So 11 days after the Lakers' unscheduled cornfield landing in Carroll, the players boarded their old DC-3 in Minneapolis for the long flight west. There was considerable grumbling. The players' wives—and some of the players—protested strongly the idea of *ever* flying in the DC-3 again, let alone all the way to California. There are no cornfields in the Rocky Mountains. But Short convinced the players of the necessity of the trip and of the shortage of funds that prohibited sending his team west by jet.

A crowd of 10,202 fans turned out in the Sports Arena to watch the city's first regular-season NBA game. They also saw a bonus prelim game between Los Alamitos Navy and the Vagabonds, billed as "an all-Negro basketball team."

The Warriors beat the Lakers, 103–96, and the fans seemed to enjoy the show. Elgin Baylor scored 36 points, and, according to *The L.A. Times,* "the audience cheered the Lakers' Hot Rod Hundley when he pulled his behind-the-back dribbling routines."

Short was along on the trip, and he told the L.A. media, "We don't want to leave Minneapolis. It's more than just a dollar-and-cents thing, it's a civic venture. However, if we can't see a way to operate without constantly subsidizing our investment, we'd ask permission to move our franchise."

Short booked the Lakers into L.A. for two more games later that month against the Hawks. The games drew a combined 8,300. But Short knew he had to move his team. If the Lakers stayed in Minneapolis, they would soon be financially squeezed even more by competition from the baseball Twins and the football Vikings, two new pro teams that were settling in Minneapolis in 1961. Short made his decision: Los Angeles or bust.

He very nearly got the latter. The league refused to let the Lakers move.

At the 1959 league meeting at New York's Roosevelt Hotel, at eleven o'clock in the morning, Short submitted the proposed move to L.A. to a vote of the eight owners. The tally was 7 to 1 against the move.

The problem was cost. Flying the teams all the way to the West Coast would put a strain on the other owners' already overstrained finances. If the Lakers folded, so be it, they figured. Another team would pop up somewhere in the East or Midwest.

The owners broke for lunch. Short and his attorney, Frank Ryan, were dejected. They buttonholed St. Louis Hawks owner Ben Kerner.

"Ben, we've *got* to move," Short insisted. "We're going to die in Minneapolis."

"Then that's the way it's gonna be," said Kerner with a shrug.

Short and Ryan looked at one another helplessly. This was the final blow. By the end of the day the Minneapolis Lakers would be history and Short and Ryan would be out of basketball.

As they walked past a newsstand in the Roosevelt's lobby, Short spotted a newspaper headline: "Saperstein Announces ABL."

Abe Saperstein, a shrewd business and basketball man who originated the Harlem Globetrotters, was announcing the formation of the American Basketball League to challenge the NBA. NBA owners knew if Saperstein put teams on the West Coast, he would get a nice foothold on a huge section of the country.

The other owners also saw the headline. They reconvened after lunch and voted once more on Short's request to move the Lakers West.

Says Ryan, "By two o'clock the vote was 8–0 and we were on our way to Los Angeles."

Then the NBA held its college draft, and Short made a move that would have an impact on his franchise for at least the next three decades. He drafted Jerry West, a shy, skinny forward from West Virginia who had been hoping to be drafted by the New York Knicks. The kid was too short and too frail to play forward in the NBA, and he had never played guard. But the scouting report said the kid could shoot. If he panned out, he might take some of the pressure off Baylor to carry the offense. Now Short needed a new coach. He hired Fred Schaus, Jerry West's coach at West Virginia.

"Had I known the real financial condition of the franchise," Schaus would say years later, "I'm not sure I would have taken the job. It was nearly bankrupt."

To run the business end of the club, Short—who would remain in Minneapolis and commute to many of the games—hired Lou Mohs, a newspaper executive from Kansas City, and gave him a budget.

"If there's any money left over, send it back," Short told Mohs. "If you need *more* money, forget where you came from."

Short considered changing his team's nickname, but decided to stick with Lakers.

"I can't call them the Oceaneers," Short reasoned. "Besides, we have a lot of trophies."

In order to get league approval to move his team to the Coast, Short had to agree to pay the difference in travel expenses between Minneapolis and Los Angeles for every team. "You can gamble on pro basketball in L.A.," the league was saying to Short, "but not with *our* money."

Short didn't plan to sneak up on L.A. Mohs would arrive early and act as an advance P.R. man, wining and dining the local media. The players were urged to move to L.A. in the summer of '60, well before training camp, and circulate in the various communities, making public appearances, giving clinics, scrimmaging, doing radio and TV interviews and promos. The players did everything but go door-to-door.

The cultural significance of the move from Minneapolis to L.A. was not lost on Hot Rod Hundley. As soon as he heard the news he started packing. It was early summer, but within the week he had his 1959 Oldsmobile Super 88 convertible— one of the few convertibles in Minnesota—loaded up and pointed toward the setting sun. Rudy LaRusso was anxious to get West, too, and he and Hot Rod decided to race to L.A.

They drove straight through to Las Vegas and stopped to tour the town, checking out the shows, the casinos, the lights. Minneapolis was already a distant memory. By 5 A.M. they were at the Stardust, watching the action at a blackjack table.

"Let's bet a hundred bucks each," Hundley suggested.

"Okay, here's my hundred," said LaRusso, who didn't play cards but trusted his buddy.

Hundley took a seat and slapped the $200 on the table.

"Hey, don't bet it all at once, Hot Rod," said the stunned LaRusso, reaching to snatch his money off the table.

Hundley brushed him aside and winked at the dealer, who flipped Hot Rod an ace and a king. Blackjack.

They took their chips and their drinks outside to celebrate beside the hotel pool. LaRusso, wearing a suit and tie, laid seven silver dollars on the ledge of the pool, took off his shoes, and dived into the pool.

"I'll bet you those seven silver dollars you won't come in," said LaRusso, treading water.

Hot Rod pulled off his shoes, adjusted his tie, and jumped.

By now the sun was rising. The two newly baptised L.A. Lakers walked to the parking lot in their drip-dry suits, which were dripping and drying, got into the cars, and raced across the desert to the promised land.

L.A. was everything the Lakers had hoped it would be, except in terms of fan support. In spite of the ambitious promotional efforts of Mohs and the players, the team got off to a slow start at the turnstiles. They opened at home October 24 against the Knicks and drew only 4,008 fans, nearly half of whom were season-ticket holders. They lost, 111–101.

The following night, against the Knicks again, the Lakers scored their first Los Angeles win, 120–118. Only 3,375 turned out to see Baylor collect 36 points and 17 rebounds.

For the season the Lakers would average only 5,045 for their 30 regular-season home games, despite playing in the NBA's only modern arena, despite Elgin Baylor's 34.8 scoring average (second in the league to Chamberlain's 38.4), despite the mid-season emergence of Jerry West, and despite finishing second in the Western Division, albeit with a 36–43 record.

The Lakers and pro basketball were still novelties in town, a fact reinforced by their home-court problems during the play-offs. The Sports Arena was already booked for other events, so the Lakers played a game at Cal State Los Angeles against the Hawks and another on the stage at the Shrine Auditorium against the Detroit Pistons before a full house of 3,705.

Appropriately, the theatrical Hundley was the star of the Shrine game, a series-clinching 137–120 win. Hot Rod, who had been eased out of the starting lineup when Schaus took the wraps off West, scored 14 points and had 15 assists. The Shrine stage was barely big enough to hold the portable court, and Piston center Walter Dukes, scrambling for a loose ball, tumbled into the orchestra pit. West remembers the game. Looking up for a rebound, he was elbowed in the mouth; he stuck out his right hand and caught two of his front teeth.

The Lakers stretched the Hawks to seven games before losing the Western Division finals, the fifth game of which deserves a historical footnote for being the first Laker broadcast by a local announcer named Chick Hearn. Chickie Baby, as Hot Rod called him, would do more than any other Laker figure to establish the team's popularity and define its personality through the years.

Hearn's enthusiasm and sense of humor were perfectly in sync with the Laker team he joined that winter. This was a loose group, fast and flashy on the court, fast and fun off the court.

Baylor and West were clearly the stars, and the offense was built around them almost to the exclusion of the other players, but there were no ego problems. Baylor, unaffected by his pro fame, was a nonstop source of outrageous stories, games, and nicknames. West was still the wide-eyed rookie, Zeke from Cabin Creek, as Baylor nicknamed him, or Tweet Bird.

Schaus broke NBA custom, indeed defied an ancient tradition of American sport, by integrating his team. On road trips it had been customary for blacks to room with blacks and whites with whites. To prevent cliques from forming, Schaus regularly shifted rooming assignments on the road and did so without regard to race.

The Lakers hung together. They enjoyed a social unity that would be foreign in pro sports today. It wasn't unusual for a group of seven or eight players to go to dinner together or to a movie. And for some of the players the season was a six-month card game, interrupted only by occasional basketball games, meals, and cab rides. Slick Leonard was the chief instigator.

Baylor was the most consistent winner, and a consummate good sport, even when he lost. Hundley, though, was more volatile, likely to react to a disappointing hand by picking up the deck and hurling it out the hotel-room window. On plane flights Baylor and Chick Hearn would lock up in titanic gin battles or have newspaper crossword-puzzle speed races for $5, both having cheated by working out the puzzle ahead of time.

They were a group of men not overburdened by pretense or sophistication. In each town they would pile into two or three rental cars and race from the airport to the hotel. In Cincinnati they poured soap bubbles into a public fountain. And outside a gift shop in the Detroit airport LaRusso engaged in a furious wrestling match with a huge stuffed tiger. The combatants rolled around the floor until the shop owner called security guards, who separated the tiger and the Dartmouth graduate. The next time the Lakers traveled to Detroit the tiger demanded—and got—a rematch.

The Lakers were knocked out by Los Angeles. "This is *my town*, baby," Hot Rod would tell whoever happened to be riding with him in his convertible as he cruised the Sunset strip or swung up LaBrea Avenue to Ernie's House of Serfas, where he would hang out with various Dodgers, Angels, and Rams. Dean Chance and Jim Fregosi were two of Hundley's regular running mates.

As for working conditions, the Sports Arena was a space-age wonder compared to the rest of the league's ancient buildings. With their glamorous home, and with their flashy running game, with Elgin and Jerry and Hot Rod and Chickie Baby, the Lakers caught the attention of the Hollywood crowd. Doris Day sat courtside almost every game, yelling at players and screaming at the referees. James Garner, Pat Boone, Gardner McKay, and other entertainers were regulars. The Lakers were establishing a following, a style, and a tradition. And they were winning.

After losing to St. Louis in the Western Division finals the first season in L.A., the Lakers won the West the next two seasons, losing to the Celtics in the finals both seasons. That's another tradition they were establishing.

The Lakers' problem was they never had a center to match

up with Bill Russell, and they might never have gotten one if not for a bombastic, transplanted Canadian named Jack Kent Cooke, who bought the team in 1965. Cooke, who then owned a minor-league baseball team in Canada and one quarter of the Washington Redskins, was a retired publishing and radio tycoon. In '65 he was living in Pebble Beach, playing golf, and gardening. And bored stiff. He wanted to buy another sports franchise. "I was rather well off and could indulge myself," he says.

Cooke had earned his fortune in Canada, first selling sets of cheapie encyclopedias door-to-door, then selling soap store-to-store, then stumbling into the radio and publishing business, where he went from $25-a-week exec to multimultimillionaire in a few years.

Cooke is a man of boundless enthusiasm and energy. "He is one of the most forceful men I have ever known," wrote Lord Beaverbrook, the late British press chief. "He is quick, pungent, full of ideas. He has qualities that sometimes provoke dislike: invincible confidence in himself, a fluent, rushing anxiety to tell you about his work and his projects. Yet Cooke is likable. He is sincere and straightforward and he has humor."

Cooke is a former musician, bandleader, and competitive yacht skipper, an expert bridge player, a social lion, and a voracious reader. But by 1965 his abiding passion was sports ownership. He had tried to land an American League expansion franchise but lost out to Gene Autry. Cooke was rich and restless, so he flew to L.A., dropped by the law offices of O'Melveny and Myers, and posed the question "What team can I buy?"

"How about the Lakers?" asked Dean Johnson, a senior partner in the firm.

Cooke said he wasn't familiar with the team. He had never seen a pro basketball game, live or on TV.

"Let's see if we can't buy these Lakers," Cooke said.

The problem was, the Lakers weren't for sale.

"I didn't want to sell," Short said years later. "We were talking about a merger with the Dodgers, and of building a facility adjacent to Dodger Stadium." It was to have been a straight merger, Frank Ryan says, with Short and Ryan owning 20 percent of the two-team, two-facility package. Negotiations were near completion, but were delayed a couple of months when Dodger

owner Walter O'Malley ran into a snag negotiating a TV contract.
While Short was waiting to finalize the Dodger-Laker merger,
Cooke stepped in. "I said, 'The team is not for sale,'" Short
recalls. "But my banker told me, '*Everything* is for sale.' When
I heard Cooke's offer I called my banker back and told him he
was right. When Cooke took me into the stratosphere, I had
to sell. O'Malley said, 'Hell, you *gotta* sell. That's a tremendous
amount of money for ten pairs of tennis shoes, as long as you
get it in cash.'"

Cooke doesn't remember Short being reluctant to sell.

"To the last day that he breathed a breath, Bob Short was
a wheeler-dealer," Cooke says. "He'd buy and sell *anything,* that
was Bob. He told me, 'I want five million.' I said, 'Just let me
see some kind of profit-and-loss statement and I'll let you know.'
Well the next thing I got was one sheet of paper, the damnedest
P-and-L you ever saw, the kind of a thing a housewife might
make up if she had no idea what she was doing but her husband
said, 'Look, I want to know where that money is,' and so she
makes up something she hopes will pass. So there was no sense
depending on the P-and-L. Short demanded five million dollars
and I agreed."

The amount was stunning, considering that the famed Boston
Celtics had just sold for $3 million. Yet Short wanted more.
After the deal was set he thought about how he had already
sold $350,000 worth of season tickets. He felt entitled to half
that money and informed Cooke that the asking price was now
$5,175,000.

"By now," Cooke says, "I wanted the team so damn badly,
had he asked for $575,000 extra, I would have paid him. There
was Bob, holding me up. That's all he did, he held me up for
the extra 175, figuring, 'What the hell, this guy's got all the
money in the world, I might as well get it out of him.' That's
the way Bob operated."

Another way Bob operated, at least in this deal, was on a
strictly-cash basis. At first he was willing to accept a cashier's
check from Cooke, until Ryan, heeding the advice of O'Malley,
convinced Short to insist on cash.

"We made 'em come up with 'good funds,'" Ryan says, "cash
on the table."

The money changed hands in a New York bank vault. Cooke's

people laid $5,175,000 on the table. The stack of money looked as big as a bale of hay. It took 12 bank vice presidents to sign the deal off. The money was transported from one bank to the other under the street in a four-wheel wagon.

Ryan and Short strolled out into the fresh air and stood on a street corner. Once again a newspaper headline caught their attention: "NFL Contests Cooke's Right to Buy Lakers." Cooke owned 25 percent of the Washington Redskins. The NFL prohibited its owners from having teams in other sports.

"We weren't worried," Ryan says. "We had the money. We went to the Peppermint Lounge to celebrate, the two of us and [then NBA commissioner] Maurice Podoloff. Short picked up the check."

Meanwhile, Cooke had himself a pro basketball team, and he was determined to make his investment pay off, financially and artistically. He took command of the Laker ship immediately, working 12 hours every day at the Laker offices, overseeing every detail of the organization with a zeal that some found refreshing and others found suffocating. It's doubtful that any NBA owner ever thought bigger or smaller. No plan was too grand for Cooke to consider, no tiny cog in the machine was trivial enough to ignore.

He detested mediocrity and despised anything less than 100 percent attention and commitment. He fired off scores of memos. The team switchboard operators *will* answer the phone before the third ring, and will do so *cheerfully.* The secretaries and other office staff members *will* be at their desks, *with* their coffee, at nine o'clock sharp. The preferred pronunciation for the word *grimace,* Cooke memoed to Chick Hearn, is with the accent on the *second* syllable. When Cooke built his own arena in 1969 his first memo to employees was "Never call it an arena. This is the Fabulous Forum, or a sports theater. It is NEVER an arena." One of Cooke's aides circulated a memo chastising staffers for wasting too much paper on sending memos.

"Was I tough to work for?" asks Cooke. "I think not, in this respect: No one ever had any misunderstanding about what I wanted done. In that respect I was easy to work for. The toughest guy in the world to work for is the fella who waffles, who vacillates, you never know quite what he wants done, who then raises hell because you failed to do what he failed to communicate to you. There was never any question about my ability to communicate with people."

When he bought a hockey team Cooke invented nicknames for many of the players—Gary (the Bull) Croteau, Eddie (the Jet) Joyal—and ordered the nicknames to be used on all broadcasts and in all press releases. For the Lakers, Cooke selected new purple and gold uniforms to replace the traditional blue and white. But he hated the word *purple,* and ordered his announcers to refer to the color as Forum blue. Says Hearn, "I constantly had to remind the TV viewers not to adjust the color on their sets."

Until Cooke, NBA teams always wore white uniforms at home. Cooke wanted his team in gold at home.

"I spoke to [NBA commissioner] Walter Kennedy about it," Cooke recalled. "He said, 'Oh, I don't think you can *do* that.' I said, 'Tell me why not, Walter.' He said, 'Frankly, I haven't got any reason a'tall. Go ahead and do it.'"

Cooke spent lavish, unheard-of sums on teams, players, and later on his own stadium, but he kept a watchful eye on the small change. He did not overpay his staff, and he was conscious of every expenditure.

In a recent interview Cooke couldn't remember the specific amount of money involved in a transaction 20 years previous. "I think it was two and a half [million dollars]," Cooke said. "It was either 2.3, 2.4, or 2.5, something like that. Now, for goodness sake, don't get the impression that I treat lightly the difference between 2.2, 2.3, 2.4, 2.5. I do not. As a matter of fact, I raised hell downstairs [in a hotel gift shop]. They charged me 60 cents for a package of those Tic-Tacs, when you can buy them anywhere for 39."

Under Cooke, head coach Schaus and general manager Lou Mohs continued their vigilant watch on outgoing cash. Mohs would turn down the heat in the press lounge, hoping to encourage the freeloading drinkers not to stay so long. Schaus told his players that free passes were available only for close family.

"How about my sister?" one player asked.

"Not close enough," Schaus said.

In financial negotiations Cooke was not a man to be trifled

with. Shortly after he bought the Lakers he sent word to Chick Hearn to come in for a meeting. Hearn brought along his agent, Harry Abrams.

"I understand you do satisfactory work," Cooke said to Hearn. "Would you like to continue broadcasting the Laker games?"

"Yes I would, Mr. Cooke," Hearn said.

"What do you propose as a salary?" Cooke asked.

Abrams suggested a figure, a very high figure.

"You're sure that's the figure?" Cooke asked.

"Yes," Abrams said.

"Sir, would you leave my office?" Cooke said to Abrams. "Get OUT! NOW! Mr. Hearn, you stay. YOU—OUT!"

Says Hearn, "Right then he could've signed me for $20."

The morning after a home game against Cincinnati, facing an early flight for a game against the Pistons in Detroit, Hearn was summoned to Cooke's office in Beverly Hills. Cooke cued up his tape recorder and played a portion of the previous night's broadcast, making marks on a yellow legal pad. Finally Cooke stopped the tape and said, "Now, you have said nice things about Cincinnati 15 times! You said something decent about the Lakers *three* times! I've got to put people in those seats!"

"Wait a minute, Mr. Cooke," Hearn said, "what was the score?"

"I don't know."

"The score was 142 to 110. How the hell am I going to say something good about a team getting beat 142 to 110?"

"I didn't think about that," Cooke said. "Anyway, you give our team due credit, will you?"

"I won't be a cheerleader."

"But you'll give them due credit, won't you?"

"If they earn it," Hearn said.

"All right," Cooke said, "be on your way to Detroit."

Early in Cooke's Laker reign, when it became apparent to him that the Coliseum Commission was not treating him fairly, Cooke pulled off one of the most grandiose acts of one-upmanship in sports history. He built his own arena.

The friction developed when Cooke was trying to land a

National Hockey League expansion franchise for Los Angeles. The Coliseum Commission, however, had already granted exclusive Sports Arena hockey rights to the minor-league L.A. Blades, whose owner was also seeking the NHL franchise.

Cooke wanted that new franchise badly, and he painted himself into a corner by promising the NHL board of governors he would build a glorious new 16,000-seat arena, the first privately built indoor stadium to be constructed in 30 years.

"We want to be fair with Mr. Cooke," said Supervisor Ernest Debs, chairman of the Coliseum's finance committee. "He can accept the contract we gave Mr. Short, which runs for two more years, and then negotiate a new contract. Otherwise, on January 15 he has no contract at the Sports Arena. He's got to fish or cut bait."

Cooke recalls the meeting where his bluff became a crusade.

"I figured I was being euchred out of the entire setup," he says. "They were treating me contemptuously. It was just *awful.* I thought, 'Holy gee, what's going on down here?' I'd only been out here three or four years and I didn't know about the machinations of these guys, Machiavellian kind of birds.

"So I said, 'You know, you're making this whole thing so difficult, I'm liable to build my own arena.' And this fella looked at me and said, 'Ha. Ha. Ha.'

"Now if he'd only laughed, I would have laughed with him, you see? But he actually said, 'Ha. Ha. Ha.' I said, 'In that case, I *am* going to build my own arena.' I turned to [Cooke lawyer] Clyde Tritt and said, 'Close your briefcases. I've had enough of this balderdash.' And away we went."

The Forum was built with what Cooke calls "lavish money and attention. . . . I said, 'If we're going to build it, we're going to do it as perfectly, as perfectly as man can do it. We *poured* money into that place.' "

The building itself cost $12.5 million, compared to the $5 million spent to build Philadelphia's Spectrum earlier the same year.

The design concept was all Cooke's. He went into the offices of architect Charles Luckman and was shown various sports arena designs. Cooke didn't like any of them.

"What would you like, then?" Luckman asked.

"Something about 2,000 years ago and about 6,000 miles to the east of here," Cooke replied.

Dick Niblack, a Luckman associate, said, "I know *exactly* what Mr. Cooke is talking about."

Niblack grabbed a sketch pad and drew a Roman column. "That's what I want," Cooke said.

A press release said the Forum "will be in essence a modern version of the greater Colosseum of ancient Rome."

The finished product was a perfect circle, supported by 80 white concrete columns, with an oval interior. It was attended by a legion of toga-clad ushers and kept spotlessly clean and meticulously repaired.

Along with the details of his teams and his organization, Cooke was vitally concerned with the big picture. Big as in seven feet tall. It was glaringly apparent the Lakers needed a legitimate center if they were to contend for an NBA championship. When they lost yet another final series to the Celtics in 1967–68, Cooke traded Darrall Imhoff, Archie Clark, and Jerry Chambers to the Philadelphia 76ers for 33-year-old, 7–2 Wilt Chamberlain. Four seasons later, in the team's twelfth season in Los Angeles, Cooke and the Lakers had their first NBA championship.

Three years later, with Chamberlain and West gone and the team having failed to make the playoffs for the first time ever in Los Angeles, Cooke acted again. Portland was offering Bill Walton, who had just enjoyed a very promising rookie season, and Milwaukee was offering Kareem Abdul-Jabbar. Cooke consulted his advisers. Which center should he get for the Lakers?

Hearn, one of the five advisers, arrived at the voting meeting a half hour late.

"We can get either Walton or Abdul-Jabbar," Cooke explained.

For Kareem, Cooke told Hearn, the Lakers would have to give up David Meyers, Junior Bridgeman, Brian Winters, and Elmore Smith. Same package for Walton, except the Lakers could keep Winters, who was then a very good guard.

Hearn considered the packages and the ages. Abdul-Jabbar is five and a half years older than Walton.

"I vote to take Walton," Hearn said.

"What do you *mean,* you vote to take Walton!" Cooke raged. "The rest of us have *agreed* on Kareem."

"Then why did you ask me?" Hearn said.

"Because you have the right to vote," Cooke sniffed.

So the Lakers traded for Kareem. In succeeding years Cooke signed rookie Norm Nixon and free agent Jamaal Wilkes. Still, even these three genuine NBA stars didn't make the Lakers a genuine NBA contender.

The overall picture was not bright. Laker attendance was down, the NBA was in financial and artistic trouble, and Kareem was rumored to be near the end of his career. The team and the league were beset by the most deadly disease in pro sports— boredom.

"Bloody boring," Cooke said just before selling the team. "That's what we've been the last two years—bloody boring."

Times had changed quite a bit since that happy day more than a decade earlier when the Forum had first opened its doors.

Cooke was conducting a last-minute inspection tour with aide Alan Rothenberg. Cooke stopped at a lobby vending machine, which was owned and operated by an outside company. He dropped a quarter in the slot and pushed a button. Cooke's soft drink dropped into place, and about $10 in small change clattered into the coin return.

Cooke was delighted. Grinning, he put the change into his pocket, turned to Rothenberg and said, "Story of my life!"

But the story—at least the Laker story—was growing stale for Cooke by 1979.

After 13 years Cooke's last act as Laker owner was to preside over the team's selections in the NBA draft. The Lakers had the No. 1 pick. Cooke didn't need a list or a scouting report. He had been watching this fellow from Michigan State, a charming young man. His name was Earvin Johnson.

3.

Magic

EARVIN JOHNSON knew he had leadership qualities, a flair for showing others the way, but this was ridiculous.

It was 5:30 in the morning—May 28, 1983—and Magic was hurrying along a hallway in Philadelphia's Bellevue Stratford Hotel. The hotel (as it turned out, just a hallway drape) was on fire. Alarms were clanging, people were shouting and screaming, and the hallway was filled with smoke. Several people, none of whom he had ever seen before, were following Magic, who wasn't sure just where he was going.

One woman in the pack cried out over and over, "We're going to die! We're going to die!"

"Pleeease, lady, *please* calm down," Magic pleaded.

As he searched for an exit Magic considered the very real possibility that they *were* going to die. He was choking on the smoke, becoming light-headed, and nobody around him seemed to have any idea how to get out. All they knew was they were following Earvin Johnson. He was called Magic, wasn't he? Surely he'd find a way out.

The night before the Lakers had lost to the Philadelphia 76ers to fall behind 2–0 in the NBA Championship Series. The Lakers were scheduled to fly home later this morning . . . if they managed to get out of the hotel alive.

Magic and his raggedy band of followers were on the eighth floor of the Bellevue, a 79-year-old structure. On other floors his teammates were also busy playing hero. On the sixteenth, Michael Cooper was banging on hallway doors, sounding the alarm. Kurt Rambis was making sure team doctor Robert Kerlan, who is partially disabled, had help.

But on the eighth floor Magic was the man. He found a stairway and led his group down two flights, until the smoke got too heavy. Then he led the people out onto the exterior fire escape. They climbed down the metal stairway to the third floor, where the stairway ended. The only way down now was a ladder suspended from the third-floor landing. In order to lower the ladder to the street, somebody had to stand on the end of it to weigh it down.

Magic hesitated. Then he heard someone behind him say in a calm, confident voice, "Go ahead, Earvin. You can do it."

Magic turned. It was Kareem Abdul-Jabbar.

Johnson gingerly stepped onto the bottom rung of the ladder and rode it slowly to the sidewalk. He climbed down, followed by his instant entourage.

He would find out later that the fire had caused little damage. Just a lot of smoke. As they stood on the sidewalk, though, Magic and his followers felt they had escaped the jaws of death.

A fire truck pulled up to the hotel, lights flashing and siren blaring. The first fireman off the truck recognized Magic and asked for his autograph. He signed. Magic always signs. Besides, it never occurred to him that this sidewalk scene was particularly strange or unusual. In the life of Earvin Johnson, the strange and unusual is the usual.

Besides, as he had said often during his rookie season with the Lakers, "I strive on pressure."

When Johnson was a high school star in Lansing, Michigan, a local sportswriter summed up in one word the kid's zenlike mastery of the game, his enormous fan appeal, his ease in the spotlight, his style.

The sportswriter nicknamed him "Magic." As in the Sammy Cahn–Jule Styne song, "It's magic . . . How else can I explain that rainbow when there is no rain? It's magic."

How else can we explain:

—Magic appearing in seven end-of-season championship series in the last 10 seasons. Result: one state high school title, one NCAA title, three NBA titles.

—Magic the rookie playing three positions and causing the 76ers to disappear in the NBA finals.

—Magic the veteran *not* making the crucial plays and causing the Lakers to disappear in 1981 and 1984.

—The five-bedroom, one-disco, one-indoor-basketball-court

bachelor pad in Bel-Air . . . and the 600-guest, black-tie birthday parties.

—The stories, some almost Babe Ruthian, about Magic and kids.

Like the time Magic is driving his new Mercedes to an appointment in Lansing when he spots a young man, a total stranger, in a high school football uniform huffing along the sidewalk, seemingly in distress. Magic pulls over, asks if anything's wrong. The kid says his car broke down, he's going to be late for practice and will be in big trouble with the coach. Magic hops out, gives the young man the car for the morning, and walks to his appointment.

Or the time a 15-year-old Pittsburgh boy, dying of leukemia, has his wish granted by the Make a Wish Foundation. The boy is flown to L.A. to meet his hero, Magic Johnson. They are introduced at a morning Laker practice session. Wish fulfilled. Magic invites the boy to shoot around with him, they play some HORSE, laugh it up. Magic invites the boy to come to the game that night and work the sidelines as a Laker ballboy.

The kid is beside himself, of course, his wish more than fulfilled. But when the game is over he's sad at the thought of going back to Pittsburgh. In the locker room he thanks Magic and says goodby.

"What's this goodby stuff?" Magic demands. "You're not leaving tomorrow."

"My parents and I are flying out in the morning," the boy explains. "We already have our plane tickets."

"Forget it," says Magic. "Make some new reservations. I'm taking the three of you to dinner tomorrow night."

Magic meets the boy and his parents at a Benihana restaurant, treats them to dinner, then drives them back to their hotel. Months later, when Magic hears that the boy has died, he sends a huge floral arrangement to the family.

These stories do not come from a public relations firm or an agent.

"When he does this kind of thing, which he does all the time, he always keeps it secret," says a friend of Magic's.

Going into the NBA draft of '79, it's likely that nobody in the Laker organization fully realized what kind of teenager they would be getting with their No. 1 pick. Even in their optimism there's no way they could have foreseen the impact Magic Johnson would come to have on the city, the team, and the league. But then-owner Jack Kent Cooke seemed to have a pretty good idea.

It was Cooke who stole Magic for the Lakers, or at least stole the draft choice used to bring him to L.A. And it was Cooke who took one look at the young man's smile and called off the spirited debate among his advisers over which player to draft.

For the Lakers the choice came down to Magic or University of Arkansas guard Sidney Moncrief. It was not all that clear-cut. The team already had a fine point guard in Norm Nixon, who had spent his first two seasons learning to be a floor leader, and learning well. Nixon was considered one of the league's bright young stars. What the Lakers needed was not another ballhandler, Magic's specialty, but a prototype off guard, someone who could play without the ball, complement Nixon, defend against the league's large, high-scoring guards, such as George Gervin, Paul Westphal, and David Thompson. Moncrief, a 6–4 skyleaper, seemed the ideal man in every respect. He would go on to be a wonderful NBA player, a great guard, and team leader.

Magic was rated only average on leaping ability, speed, and outside shooting, and his defense was suspect since he had played mostly zone in college. The report on Moncrief at the time: no shortcomings. Except that his smile and his personality didn't radiate quite as brightly as Magic's. Whose did?

Cooke had seen the smile on television, when Magic was leading Michigan State to the NCAA championship. He loved the kid's style. Cooke had been in show business, and he knew a showstopper when he saw one.

The previous season the Lakers, a team well stocked with marquee-value stars, had won 47 regular-season games and yet sold out the Forum only once in 41 home games, averaging 11,700 fans in the 17,505-capacity building. Cooke had to choose between a solid, star-quality, college graduate and a flashy teenager with the potential box-office appeal of an Eddie Murphy.

Easy choice.

"There was never any question in *my* mind," Cooke says.

"There was some thought among my counselors that Sidney Moncrief might have been the better choice. Never any question in *my* mind. I said to my counselors, 'I don't give a damn *what* you say, it's going to be Magic Johnson.' "

If Cooke is smug about bringing Magic to L.A., he has a right to be. It was Cooke and his attorney, Alan Rothenberg, who pulled off the sports theft of the decade in obtaining the draft pick used to select Johnson from Michigan State.

Less well known is the fact that Cooke, after obtaining that precious draft choice from the lowly New Orleans Jazz, wanted desperately to give the pick right back to the Jazz in exchange for a player who was on the verge of fizzling out like a spent skyrocket.

The scenario went as follows:

After the 1975–76 season Laker point guard Gail Goodrich played out his option, became a free agent, and signed with the Jazz. By league rules of that time, the Jazz was required to compensate the Lakers with players, cash, or draft picks in an amount to be mutually agreed upon by the two teams. If they couldn't agree, NBA Commissioner Larry O'Brien would step in as arbitrator.

Rothenberg met with Jazz general manager Barry Mendelsohn to negotiate the compensation package. Mendelsohn, incidentally, had worked for Cooke and the Lakers six years earlier and had formed a friendship with Goodrich, which probably contributed to Mendelsohn's eagerness to sign the aging guard. Mendelsohn now says that Jazz coach Bill Van Breda Koff, assistant coach Elgin Baylor, and player personnel adviser Bill Bertka all agreed that obtaining Goodrich would be a wise move.

But at what price? Rothenberg informed Mendelsohn the Lakers wanted the Jazz's No. 1 draft picks in 1977 *and* 1979 and a second rounder in '80.

Ridiculous, Mendelsohn said. And it was. Goodrich was 33 years old at the time, a veritable geezer considering that few NBA players perform effectively beyond age 30, especially if their forte is quickness. Indeed, Goodrich would play the equivalent of only two more seasons with the Jazz before retiring.

But Rothenberg wouldn't budge, and the deadline was closing in. Soon the commissioner would be called in, and Mendelsohn was convinced O'Brien would lean heavily against the Jazz. There was a feeling that the league wanted to discourage teams from signing free agents because too much of that type of player movement fostered overall roster instability and pushed up the league's salary level. Just before the deadline Mendelsohn threw up his hands and agreed to the Lakers' demands.

Cooke was delighted with the bold heist his team lawyer had pulled off, but he wasn't finished dealing. Cooke wanted Sidney Wicks badly. Wicks was a former UCLA product, a five-year NBA veteran power forward who could score and rebound. Cooke saw Wicks, 6–9 and 225 pounds, as the answer to the Lakers' desperate prayers for a great power forward. Plus, Wicks, a charismatic former hometown hero, would be great box office.

The Jazz had just worked out a conditional trade to acquire Wicks from the Portland Trail Blazers. Cooke instructed Rothenberg to take the compensation package the Lakers had just snatched from the Jazz and offer it back to them in exchange for Wicks. If the Jazz said yes, the Lakers, in effect, would have lost an aging point guard and gained a hot power forward seven years younger than Goodrich. They had no way of knowing, of course, that they would also be kissing goodby to Magic Johnson, who was just completing his junior year in high school.

But the Jazz said no. New Orleans owner Sam Battistone had promised the Portland management he would never send Wicks to a rival team in Portland's division. Rothenberg persisted, reminding the Jazz that the agreement with Portland was a handshake deal, not legally binding. Battistone said no, he had given his word. The Portland–New Orleans deal involving Wicks fell through and Wicks was sold to Boston, where his performance level began to skid.

The Jazz then did the Lakers another enormous favor by finishing with the league's worst record for the 1978–79 season, earning for the Lakers the conference's No. 1 pick. Still, however, they had to flip a coin with the worst team in the Eastern Conference, the Chicago Bulls, to determine which would get the overall No. 1 pick.

The coin was flipped by O'Brien, who was hooked up to the Bulls' and Lakers' front offices via conference call.

"Chicago, do you want to make the call?" O'Brien asked.

"We'd love to," said Bulls general manager Rod Thorn.

"Is that okay with you, Los Angeles?" O'Brien asked.

"Fine," said Chick Hearn, speaking for the Lakers.

"We call heads," Thorn said.

A pause, then O'Brien said, "Tails it is."

Hearn and Bill Sharman whooped and hugged.

"That terminates the exercise," O'Brien said.

And that commenced the *real* exercise, a fast break such as the game had never seen.

The Lakers couldn't officially sign Magic until after the actual draft, but Cooke flew Johnson to L.A., along with his father and two advisers, for salary discussions. They met in Cooke's Forum office and he ordered lunch sent in from the Forum Club. Cooke insisted on ordering for Magic.

"You'll love these," Cooke said when lunch arrived. "They're the finest sand dabs you've ever tasted."

Magic agreed, since they were the only sand dabs he had ever tasted. He tried a few bites.

"How is it?" Cooke asked.

"It's all right."

"All *right!*" Cooke shouted. "Only all *right?*"

"Yeah," Magic said, "but I'd rather have a hamburger. Please."

After lunch Magic and Cooke reached a tentative contract agreement and the Johnson contingent flew home to Michigan. Asked his impressions of his first visit to L.A., Johnson said, "It was nice. The only thing I don't like is the gas [shortage] situation."

Responded Cooke, "I would think with his peripheral vision, he could find gas stations no one else could see."

Cooke introduced his new star to the L.A. media at a lavish Forum press conference. Magic was magic, facing the lights and mikes and sea of faces, fielding questions with grace and humor. He instantly charmed the audience. Then he met informally with a smaller group of reporters, the Laker beat writers from a few L.A. papers. They warned the kid he would be dealing with a hard-to-please crowd in L.A., where the yawns sometimes were louder than the cheers.

As Rich Levin wrote in the next day's *Herald-Examiner*, "Magic's mission in Los Angeles will be to wave his wand and resurrect a team that has turned the Forum into a basketball mausoleum."

The challenge seemed to intrigue the young man.

"If there are some crazy basketball fans," Johnson told the beat writers, "tell 'em to come on out. The Lakers already be winnin' without me. Now we're gonna be exciting."

The reporters and photographers left to spread the word about this teen sensation (Magic was 19, a college sophomore), and the Forum lights were dimmed. Earvin walked across the court and sat down in the stands, alone. He stared down at the highly polished hardwood floor and, in his imagination, he could see a game. He was in the middle of the action, naturally, wearing a Lakers gold uniform, No. 32, dashing full-tilt up and down the court, dealing off to Kareem and then to Jamaal Wilkes. He could hear the crowd, feel the excitement.

He sat back and stared at the 1972 NBA championship banner hanging on the wall, signifying the Lakers' only title since coming to L.A. He surveyed the 17,000 seats and looked all the way up to the ceiling high above. What a *building*, Magic thought. This isn't an arena, it's a *palace*.

Then Magic walked back across the floor and into the tunnel leading under the stands, through a hallway and into the Lakers' locker room. That room was also dark and empty, and he filled it up with more imaginary action. Magic sat in the dark for an hour, in a near trance, staring at the dressing stalls with their nameplates—Abdul-Jabbar, Wilkes, Nixon . . . and the new one: Johnson. He was frightened and excited, and so happy he felt like singing or laughing. But he just sat.

He thought about the hundreds of make-believe NBA games he had played, just him and his basketball, alone on the playgrounds of Lansing. He was always the star player of both teams, as well as the play-by-play announcer.

"Dave Bing for the jumper," he would call out across the empty playground, acting out the action. ". . . Yes! . . . Two seconds left on the game clock, down low it's Wilt! He's backin' up! There's that *fingerrr* roll! . . . The 76ers win it!"

Those were the rehearsals. Now it was showtime.

The Los Angeles fans got their first in-person look at Magic three weeks later when he flew into town to play a game with the Lakers' rookie team in a local summer pro league.

The summer games draw 200 to 300 spectators at most, but for this game the Cal State L.A. gym was jammed well beyond capacity with about 3,600 fans, many standing in the aisles and around the court. Outside, temperatures were in the high 90s. Inside the gym the heat was stifling. When the last ticket was sold and the doors slammed shut, there were still about 1,000 people outside trying to get in, including latecomers Bill Sharman and Jack McKinney, the Lakers' general manager and new head coach. Traffic was snarled on the two nearby freeways, and cars were parked on campus lawns and sidewalks. Sharman and McKinney, amazed at the fan turnout, finally talked their way into the sweltering gym.

Portland coach Jack Ramsay, Philadelphia coach Billy Cunningham, and San Diego coach Gene Shue just happened to be in the neighborhood and stopped by to watch. So did actors Rob Reiner and Al (Grandpa Munster) Lewis. And Jerry Buss, who had just taken delivery on an expensive new team, arena, and rookie.

Paul Westhead, McKinney's assistant and head coach of this rookie squad, kept Magic out of the starting lineup in deference to the team's regular starters, and to the dismay of the fans. But Westhead sent Johnson into the game early in the first quarter. Magic, college basketball's coolest player and slickest ballhandler the season before, was so nervous he silently prayed nobody would pass him the ball.

The first time he did touch it, the ball was immediately stolen by Pistons rookie Roy Hamilton, a guard from UCLA. Magic stole it right back and the play ended in a jump ball. Within minutes Magic was loose, into his game rhythm. On one drive he wrapped the ball around his back and laid it in left-handed. The fans entered nirvana.

Magic played 28 minutes, scored 24 points, and flashed enough spectacular moves to satisfy the delirious crowd. The Lakers won, and Magic, on his way off the court, was detained for a brief TV interview and was mobbed by fans. He seemed stunned.

"It was beautiful," he said in the locker room, still dazed

by the warm welcome to his new hometown. "These fans are really basketball fans, not like I'd heard. They really cheered. I'm really kind of excited everyone came out."

Sharman made a feeble attempt at being the voice of reason. "I hope people don't expect a lot from Magic too quick," he said.

Sharman might as well have tried to cool off the 3,600 screaming sweating fans by fanning them with a scorecard. Magic had arrived. The heat was on.

By the start of training camp, Johnson had played in numerous summer-league and exhibition games around the country, against many top NBA players, and had more than held his own. He felt calmer, more confident than in the rookie-game L.A. debut. On the first day of camp he shook hands with Westhead, and told *him*, "Welcome to the team."

Camp was at Palm Springs, and Magic played it hot, and cool. He wanted to make an impression, to break out his best game, but he also wanted to blend in, to be accepted. Competition among the guards was particularly fierce, so Magic worked hard and kept his mouth and his emotions under wraps.

He was playing well, but he wasn't quite the Magic Johnson that Jack McKinney remembered seeing in college games. After one evening practice session in the junior college gym that serves as the Lakers' training headquarters, McKinney called Magic aside. They sat down in the wooden bleachers.

"Look, I know you're a rookie," McKinney told him. "I know you feel overwhelmed at times. But you have a lot of talent. This team has been so bland. It's had no personality. If you can bring the enthusiasm you generated at Michigan State to this team, I think it would really help us. The other players will accept it. *If* you back it up."

Magic wasn't about to shy away from this challenge. He knew the team needed his spirit as much as it needed his technical skills, but until now he had been more concerned with honoring the traditional rookie role of being seen and not heard, of being humble, and it hadn't felt right.

"I'd like to do that," Magic said. "And I'll back it up."

Magic began taking the wraps off his personality. His teammates accepted the change. They got into the shouting, the high fives after every good play, the whooping and laughing even during layup drills, the almost childlike exuberance and emotionalism. Still, Magic's style was new to the NBA, it certainly wasn't the Lakers' accustomed style, and at times it took his teammates by surprise.

On opening night the Lakers were in San Diego to play the Clippers, one of the league's weakest teams. But the Clippers played over their heads and it took a majestic 18-foot skyhook by Kareem at the buzzer to beat them.

The Laker center started to jog casually off but got only as far as midcourt, where he was intercepted by Magic. The rookie gave Abdul-Jabbar the most sincere sports embrace since Yogi Berra's leaping bear hug on Don Larsen after Larsen's perfect game in the 1956 World Series. Magic was ecstatic. Kareem was dumbfounded. Hitting 18-foot skyhooks at the buzzer was his *job*.

"They [his teammates] all thought I was crazy," Magic says. "So did Kareem. He told me, 'Hey, we got 81 more.' Everybody was shocked. But I was used to showing my emotions."

But how long could this show of emotion last in the physically and spiritually draining grind of an NBA season?

"I think half of Magic's appeal is his enthusiasm," said 76ers' general manager Pat Williams before that season started, "but you have to remember that happiness and glow and joy often turn to dust in our league."

There was no crumbling that season. The fun was infectious. The newer Lakers—Michael Cooper, Jim Chones, and Spencer Haywood—got caught up in the good-time feeling. The veterans—Kareem, Wilkes, and Nixon—could have put a lid on the giddiness, could have restored the team to its former level of sanity and boredom, but they didn't. They allowed the Magic show to go on, because along with the grinning came the winning. Magic was talking big and backing it up.

Early in the season Wilkes scored on one particularly breathtaking fast-break layup off a Magic pass and was fouled. Johnson raced to Wilkes, hugged him, and whirled him under the basket in a dance of delight. Wilkes, easily the least flashy Laker, was obviously startled. He laughed and hugged back.

"They seem to be happy out on the court," said Jerry Sloan, coach of the Chicago Bulls, after getting his first look at the new-look Lakers. "They seem to be excited about the game. They're loose, free and easy, and enjoying the game."

A measure of Magic's impact was how much he was missed. The Lakers' third game of the season was against the SuperSonics in the Seattle Kingdome. Early in the second half Magic made a cut and fell to the court, grimacing in pain. He was carried to the locker room, where a Seattle orthopedic surgeon examined him and gave a preliminary diagnosis—torn ligaments. Magic would be out for months, maybe the whole season.

He seemed to be almost in shock as attendants wheeled him out of the locker room into the waiting ambulance. His rookie season had seemingly ended with a snap.

The next morning Magic was flown ahead to L.A. by private jet. His teammates, waiting at the Seattle–Tacoma airport for their own flight home, were quiet and glum. Chick Hearn was almost in tears. He paced up and down in the airport waiting area, shaking his head.

"This is terrible, *terrible,*" Hearn said. "Even if he comes back, he might not ever be the same player he was."

Late that afternoon Laker doctors released their own findings. No ligament damage. Only a sprain. Magic would miss three games. Among the Lakers, from Buss down to the ballboys, the news was considered nothing short of a miracle.

It would be that kind of miraculous rookie season for Earvin Johnson, although there would be a full quota of rookie-type blunders. Like the time Johnson's agent and attorney both convinced the *The White Shadow* TV show people to sign Magic and build an entire episode around him. His role, Magic playing Magic, would be filmed over two days. On the designated first day of shooting, the cast and crew were on location, ready to go, and a limousine was dispatched to pick up Magic at the airport, where the Lakers were landing after having played in Portland the night before.

But Magic was tired. His body and mind were being stretched thin. The schedule of games, compared to college, was brutal. And he already had endorsement agreements with Buick, 7-Up, Converse, Spaulding, Bonnie Sportswear, Quality Dairy (in Lansing), and a company that was marketing Magic Johnson Cookies. Magic shook his head and waved off the limo driver.

"I'm played out," Magic said to the astounded driver. "I'm worked out. Maybe I can do it another time."

Even in the prima donna world of Hollywood, this was a shocking no-show. The *White Shadow* producers were amazed, and mad. They quickly sent out a call for Elgin Baylor, and the show was hastily rewritten and filmed with the new guest star. Estimated cost in delays and reworking the script: $20,000.

Magic shrugged it off. Hey, it wasn't as if he had missed something important, like a basketball game.

On the team's only visit that season to Detroit, near Magic's home, the local media turned out in force to welcome back their hero. Reporters and TV and radio crews packed a large conference room in the Lakers' hotel for the scheduled press conference. But Magic never showed. There had been a mix-up. He hadn't been informed of the press conference. Or he had forgotten. He was off visiting old friends, and about 200 newspeople paced and fumed and grumbled.

Two hours later a team official located Earvin at his parents' home and a helicopter was dispatched to fly him to the hotel for the press conference.

The next morning the Lakers boarded a bus in front of the hotel for a short ride to a nearby gym for a pregame shootaround. One minute before the bus was scheduled to leave, Magic was the only player missing. Nobody had seen him since the previous evening's press conference. Suddenly there was a loud noise overhead and a helicopter landed in the parking lot, just yards from the bus.

"It *couldn't* be," one of the players said.

It was. Magic, wearing purple sweatpants and a fur overcoat, climbed out of the chopper. He had enjoyed the ride the day before, so he had chartered the helicopter to facilitate visiting his family and friends.

It never occurred to Magic that the helicopter landing might appear to some to be an ostentatious show of power and wealth, and it didn't bother his teammates. They laughed at the spectacle and razzed the rookie as he boarded the bus. Still, dissension was brewing. Talk was starting among some of the other players that Magic was handling the ball too much, freezing his team-mates out of the action. Also, his intensity on defense was suspect.

Well into the season, during a game against the Nets in New Jersey, on two fast breaks in a row Magic took the ball all the way to the hoop, both times ignoring Jim Chones, who had hustled to fill an outside lane. The Lakers called a timeout and assistant coach Pat Riley pulled Johnson aside.

"You missed Chones twice," Riley said. "You have to look for those guys. They're busting their ass to fill the lane. You have to look for them."

Magic was visibly upset. He stiffened his arms and said, "I can't do *nothin'* right."

But Magic listened, and toward the end of the season Norm Nixon told *The New York Times,* "Magic had to learn to keep everybody in the game. He was losing 'em. He had to make an effort and he did. I like playing with him much more now. We complement one another."

There was also a league-wide Magic Johnson backlash. The NBA had been crying for hot new talent, for an injection of excitement, and suddenly they had Magic *and* Larry Bird. But maybe Johnson was getting *too much* press coverage. When the midseason All-Star game voting was tabulated, Magic was a starting guard for the Western Conference team by vote of the fans.

"It's a travesty," Celtic coach Bill Fitch said. "Magic is a good enough kid, but some of those people must have thought they were voting for Dennis Johnson when they voted for Earvin Johnson."

The New York Times polled the league's players and Magic wasn't even among the top *six* Western Conference guards.

"If that's how they pick 'em, what can I say?" Magic responded.

He didn't say anything more, but he did a lot. He improved his game. Magic not only did a better job of ball distribution, but he also began to play a lot at power forward when Westhead would go to his greyhound unit. Magic became the team's most rugged rebounder, averaging 10 over the last month of the regular season.

For his rookie year he averaged 17.6 points, 7.7 rebounds,

7.3 assists, and shot 52 percent from the floor, a 6 percent improvement over his collegiate mark. In the 16 playoff games he averaged 18.3 points, 10.5 rebounds, 9.4 assists, and kept his shooting at 52 percent.

"We all thought he was a movie-star player," said Westhead, "but we found out he wears a hard hat. It's like finding a great orthopedic surgeon who can also operate a bulldozer."

As the Lakers and the league discovered that season, it wasn't so much Magic Johnson's numbers but his personality and spirit that influenced the chemistry of a team and an arena.

"It was the mood and atmosphere he brought with him," Michael Cooper says. "When he came into the gym it was like, 'Oh, okay, it's time to come to life.' Everyone comes alive and the place starts hummin' and buzzin'. He brings something with him. And any basketball player can relate to that. You always want to play the game at a playground level. I don't care how fundamental you are, you know that the best feeling you ever get is when you're playing with the fellas. As you go up from the playground to college and then to the professional ranks, players have a tendency to say, 'It's my job. I gotta do this. I'll give it this much effort.' It's not exciting. It does get boring.

"But here comes this guy, Magic Johnson, him and Larry Bird, and they make the game *exciting*. I was enjoying myself that first year. I'm jumping up and down, night after night. We're up 20 points and I'm jumping and yelling like I'm still in college, and our whole team was like that. And we *sustained* it, for 82 games, and the playoffs."

Brad Holland, a rookie from UCLA, was in awe of the other new kid, Magic.

"I didn't know anyone could affect a team like that with his enthusiasm, personality, style of play," Holland says. "He truly loves to play the game. He's very special. He has a knack for the game no else has. It's amazing how he sees the court. No one resented him. Everyone was surprised and excited and grateful that he made such a quick impact. It was a whole new world for the Lakers.

"Kareem had a reputation of looking like he didn't care. I think he got caught up in the enthusiasm like everyone else.

Kareem started thinking, 'We can *win.*' I think he got excited. Magic played the crowd, the team, he was an orchestrator. That's Magic; that's him. It all came naturally. He was a kid in a candy store, grabbing for everything he could get."

Typical play: Against the Jazz in Salt Lake City, on the front end of a fast break, Magic drives to the hoop, scores, is hammered by a Jazz player, gets the foul call, and, without breaking stride, makes a sharp U-turn and sprints past the Laker bench, slapping hands with four alert teammates.

Midway through the season Magic spotted O. J. Simpson in the Laker locker room after a game and called out, "How ya doin', Juice? What's happenin'?"

"You're what's happenin'," Simpson said.

With a rookie setting the tone, the Lakers that season were a tight group, friends off the court as well as on. The NBA life-style had changed a great deal in 25 years, but the '79–80 Lakers were somewhat of a throwback. They hung out together. Often several of them would go to a movie or dinner rather than go their separate ways. They always had their music blaring in the locker room, and they even played cards on plane trips, just like Hot Rod and Elgin and the boys in the old days.

The Lakers had their own informal soul glee club. On long bus rides at night, between airports and hotels, several of the players would congregate in the back of the bus and sing *a cappella.* Magic and Cooper and Chones and Haywood and Jim Brewer and one or two other Lakers would transform themselves into Kool and the Gang or the Four Tops.

This was a group of close friends playing a game they loved.

"A lot of what we did was effortless," says Jim Brewer. "Even practices were fun. We were winners, and we were all good friends."

"That's when it was really fun," Magic says. "We just had some good-natured guys. We could kid each other. It's different now, no question. Everybody is really an individual. You have to have more space for yourself. So many more guys [on the '85–86 team] are married, so many more families, so things have to change. And we've got more young guys now. Then it was me and Brad the rookies, and everyone else was a vet."

Nowhere does Magic have more fun than on the basketball

court. Nowhere else does he feel as much pure joy and freedom of expression. It is possible that Magic moves the basketball around the court, finding open teammates, better than anyone who ever played the game.

Don Ford was going into his fourth season as a Laker forward when Magic was a rookie.

"All of a sudden I'm getting passes like I'd never seen before," says Ford.

When Kurt Rambis became a Laker he wasn't accustomed to Magic-style passing either.

"I had a few of his passes bounce off my hands, shoulders, head," Rambis says. "Some passes, even though I was watching Magic and I knew the pass was coming, I didn't catch them because I honestly didn't believe there was any way he could get the ball to me. He would throw the ball through a crowd of eight people, just like *that.* It shocked the hell out of me. I learned that even though you *know* he can't get the ball to you, you stick your hands out anyway because the ball's coming."

And this from Michael Cooper, who has played alongside Magic for seven seasons: "There are times I'll be running on the break and I'll say. 'Naw, Magic's not gonna pass me the ball,' and sure enough, he'll pass it, and I'll say, 'Well, they're gonna intercept it.' I'll put my hands out just in case, and the ball will hit me right in the hands for a layup."

While many experts assert that Larry Bird is the greatest player in the game today, maybe the greatest ever, Magic has his supporters too.

"The man is the maestro out there, he is the conductor," says Wilt Chamberlain. "I don't want to compare players, I'm sick and tired of comparisons, but nobody can come up to Magic.

"Plus, he's fun to watch. Earl Monroe was fun to watch, too, but as a team player he wasn't shit. Same way about Dr. J. He was spectacular, but he didn't rebound or play defense. Other guys on their teams did the hard work. A guy who does it both, gets the job done and puts on a show, is Magic.

"Oscar [Robertson] was great, but his defense stunk up the place and he would belittle and scold his teammates. Baylor didn't play much defense, either. Neither could do as much for his team as Magic. I like Bird, and [Kevin] McHale, but Magic is closer to a consummate basketball player. He runs the team, rebounds, creates the flow of the game, does so many things I can't believe it. I don't know if there's ever been a better player than Magic."

Magic is 27 now, still a young man, but he knows he has been paying a price for his greatness. All the fast breaks and the falls tick onto his odometer.

"I'll only play about three or four more years, that's it," he said late in the '85–86 season. "I give all I can give on the court, and it's showin' up now. I wanna be able to play with my kids someday, run with 'em and do things, without hobbling.

"I think I'm different than most guys, and I really believe that. I'm gonna go 125 percent every night, play as hard as I can for 10, 11 years, then that's it. That's better than trying to hang on and be another kind of player, where you come in for five or 10 minutes and relieve. That's not me. I can't see anybody just taking me and using me up, goin' by me. Oh, no. I pride myself on being at top form. It's better to go out that way. Then you can be remembered, and you can remember yourself."

Johnson will quit when he can no longer make plays like the one he made his rookie season at Phoenix during the Western Conference semifinals. Series tied 1–1, Lakers lead by three points, two minutes remaining. Magic has his dribble slapped away by a Suns player. Walter Davis picks up the loose ball and loops it long downcourt to Paul Westphal, alone and seemingly headed for an uncontested breakaway dunk. Just as Westphal reaches the ball, Johnson, seemingly coming out of nowhere, sprints in from the side, steals the ball, dribbles back upcourt, and throws an impossible, over-the-head, no-look pass inside to Kareem for the game- and series-breaking basket.

The next day a reporter is walking through the airport with Johnson.

"That play on Westphal, how did you do that?" asks the reporter, still amazed.

Johnson puts his arm around the writer's shoulder and explains:

"It's magic, baby."

4.

Boardwalk and Park Place
for Marvin Gardens
and the Lakers

HE always followed the bouncing ball.

The fact that Jerry Buss was forced to abandon his athletic career, mediocre though it may have been, in order to earn room and board during the rough years in Kemmerer only increased his desire to get involved again when he could afford to. So he became your old-fashioned sports nut once he reached the gravy years in Los Angeles.

Tickets? Buss had them all—season seats for everything from the Rams to USC football, with an occasional Trojan road trip thrown in. In 1972, when the Lakers won their first NBA championship in L.A., Buss was right there, cheering with the rest of the Forum fans from his $7-per-game seats.

It was that year that he first thought about being more than just a fan. He was eating lunch with his Beverly Hills attorney, Jerry Fine.

"See that article in the paper about something called World Team Tennis?" Fine asked.

As a matter of fact, Buss had. According to the story, the founders of this new concept wanted a club in L.A. There was speculation about possible owners, with names like Bob Hope being tossed around. Price tag for obtaining a franchise: $50,000. No big deal by then for Jerry Buss.

"Let's get involved," Fine said. "We'll each put in $25,000 and we'll operate it carefully so we don't lose any money."

"Okay, but I don't really have the time," Buss replied, "so you are going to have to run it."

That was fine with Fine. Buss took such a low-key stance

in the operation of the team, named the Strings, that when *The Los Angeles Times* did a feature story on the squad after its first year of operation, the entire focus was on Fine. The first mention of the other major owner came in the next-to-last paragraph, where he was identified as Jerry Buss.

The way things were going, however, such anonymity was welcome. Buss and Fine were in on a venture that just couldn't seem to catch on; the public just wasn't interested in watching tennis stars in a team situation. Buss and Fine lined up Johnny Carson, one of their limited partners, to serve as master of ceremonies for their team's inaugural night. But while the doors of the Los Angeles Sports Arena were opening on a spring evening in 1974 for the first appearance of Jerry Buss's first sports team, the Symbionese Liberation Army, kidnappers of Patty Hearst, was involved in a shoot-out with police just down the street. The shoot-out drew a bigger crowd than the Strings. After one year of "careful" operation the team, with an investment of $600,000, lost nearly $200,000.

"That's it," Fine told Buss. "Good-by. Good luck. The franchise is dead."

"No," insisted Buss after some deliberation, "I like it. This is going to be my education in sports. I want to be into the next tier—major-league sports. Whether team tennis makes it or not is not as important as it is to learn effectively at a small amount of money how to really run a team, how to do it from the ground up, from a business standpoint. I want to try it another year, but I'll run it."

So Buss took over his first sports operation. With him at the helm, the Strings, in their second year, lost a million dollars.

No matter. Jerry Buss was no longer bored. He had found a new challenge. He loved being a sports owner, being a fan who could actually call the shots, the guy in the seats who could yell about what a team ought to be doing and then go out and do it.

He quickly applied the let's-make-a-deal techniques he had developed in real estate to his newly chosen field. Buss wanted Jimmy Connors for his Strings, but the superstar resisted all offers. Then one day Connors was showing off a new Porsche to a friend and fellow player, Ilie Nastase, when up drove Buss in a Maserati. The Strings owner jumped out of his car, keys in hand, dangled them in front of Connors, and said, a devious smile on his face, "You want it? Sign with me and you've got it." This was one bargain Jerry couldn't strike. Connors held firm, but Buss didn't come away totally empty-handed: He wound up signing Nastase, who became one of the Strings' biggest draws.

But while Buss loved the wheeling and dealing, he would only wheel on a road bordered by his own ethical boundaries.

Buss and one of his attorneys, Jim Perzik, were trying to finalize a deal for one of the Strings' superstars in 1977. There were tax angles, there were investment angles, and the more Buss talked, the more the other side was trying to outsmart him. In the end they outsmarted themselves. Obviously overwhelmed by a myriad of side issues, the player's negotiators proposed a new plan. When he heard it Buss looked at Perzik and rolled his eyes. Both men nodded and excused themselves.

"Hey, they are totally lost," said Perzik in the privacy of an anteroom. "They do not understand what we've offered. If we agree to this deal, they are going to take $100,000 less than they could have had."

"Nope," Buss said, "we've already agreed on what we want. We thought the original plan was fair. Go back in, nicely put them back on track, and go ahead and close the deal out."

And with that Buss left.

One of his first orders of business for the Strings was to get out of the Sports Arena, which had become a white elephant with the departure of the Lakers. Buss decided to follow the Lakers to the Forum.

Since the WTT season ran in the summer when the Forum had plenty of open dates, Jack Kent Cooke was happy to offer Buss a break on the rent. "I'm going to pay just a little more than I was at the Sports Arena," said Buss when a deal was signed for the 1976 season, "and the Forum is ten times nicer."

One evening in '76 he invited Bart Christensen to drive down with him to Palm Springs. Buss was well-stocked for the 90-minute journey. He had one of his secretaries arm him with a six-pack of Coca-Cola, a fifth of rum, and silver bucket full of ice. He and Christensen hopped into Buss's Maserati, and Christensen, with the bucket between his legs, mixed the drinks while Buss drove.

Buss was a man in a hurry that night. Hitting speeds of 80 miles an hour, he peered out at the road ahead and told Christensen just where it would lead.

"I am going to own one of the major teams in Los Angeles, if not two, in the next two to four years," said Buss between sips. "Tell your people not to lose sight of the bigger picture. Tennis is only our stepping-stone."

Bart nodded and kept mixing while keeping one nervous eye on the speedometer, the other on the road.

Buss's need to speed was cured months later on a solo trip to Las Vegas. Hitting the open stretch of desert between the California state line and the desert city, Buss decided to really push his faithful Maserati. That he did, hitting 80 . . . 90 . . . 100 . . . 110 . . . 120 . . . 130 miles an hour. That's when the fear finally hit him, like a cold slap in the face. He "slowed down" to 75, then glided to a complete stop on a shoulder of the road amid the cactus and a few curious rabbits. He sunk his head into the steering wheel as the full awareness of what he had been doing sunk in. His knees were shaking uncontrollably, and he vowed he would never again exceed the speed limit. It was a vow he kept.

His vow to own a major sports franchise would take a little longer to fulfill. For the time being Buss was happy with the WTT, but few of his fellow owners were, as financial problems mounted for the league. It needed fresh money, and Buss, anxious to keep his new enterprise alive, knew just where to get it. The San Diego Friars were purchased by Frank Mariani. Another Buss business associate, Larry Noble, bought the Indiana Loves. And still another of his business partners, Dennis Hall, took over the Anaheim Oranges.

Buss wouldn't give up. He had hungered for a piece of the sports pie for a long time and all he'd gotten so far was a taste. If the solution was to feed his rivals, that's what he would do. Need a player? Buss used his influence to try and sign players for competitors. Need money? Buss bought a life insurance policy for one team and offered to lend $200,000 to the New York franchise when its losses reached $1 million.

It wasn't enough. The Strings won the WTT championship in 1978, but it was a hollow triumph. Buss cried tears of joy at the victory celebration, but there were other tears around the league as rival owners looked at their profit statements. Or rather lack-of-profit statements. Red ink? World Team Tennis had become one big red machine, a machine heading for a total breakdown. Tennis was becoming bigger than ever, but rather than helping the WTT, that fact was killing it. The number of tennis events were doubling and tripling. A Japanese tournament director might call Chris Evert and offer her $100,000 to spend a weekend in his event. Players were weighing that against a $150,000 or $200,000 WTT contract, a contract that tied them up for three months, and they were becoming increasingly restless.

At one league meeting Buss was trying to push some legislation through. He had six votes, more than enough to pass it. But two of those opposing him were the Boston and New York teams. Buss didn't want to offend them for fear they'd pull out of the league, so he tabled the legislation. The two eventually pulled out anyway.

By the end of '78 continuing losses by the WTT had resulted in its demise. Buss could point to his own profit-and-loss ledger with pride. The Strings' season-ticket sales had moved steadily upward, from 700 the first year to 1,500 the next, then 3,000, 4,500, and, finally, 6,000 with a gross of $1 million the last year. But when you subtract the money he had given in loans and support for other teams, Buss dropped nearly $5 million in the WTT. Still, he would have stuck it out if he could have convinced enough others to do the same. Unraveling the Strings was a very emotional thing for Buss, who wasn't used to seeing his enterprises end this way.

"When the WTT was approaching major-league stature, it was okay," Buss told a *Times* interviewer when he announced he was getting out of the tennis racket. "But I didn't want to suffer a credibility loss. I could have saved the league, set up two new franchises, gone to work to build back to where we were. But I'd spent five years building this into a major sport already. It was too much heartache, too much worry, too much emotion for something less than top drawer."

And then, the resolve evident in his face, he declared, "I don't know what sport I'm going into. I have an offer out on a couple of baseball teams, at least one, possibly two, football teams, and I'm interested in basketball. I have enough money to own a major-league team and I intend to do so. I'm literally going to go to Hawaii for a while, get some sun, and regroup my thoughts. Then I'm going to come back, buy a major-league team, and win a damn world's championship with it."

It was in 1977 that Buss first heard the rumors that Cooke's empire might be for sale. Cooke was going through a divorce that had triggered a desire to sell his sports holdings and leave Southern California. And Buss, looking at his own rapidly growing holdings, began to think the unthinkable for the first time. He might actually be able to afford both the Forum and Cooke's teams—the Lakers and the Kings hockey club.

The pair met in 1977. "I'd like to buy the Forum if it's for sale," Buss told Cooke. Cooke was noncommittal, but he certainly didn't discourage the talks.

This was Buss's most serious shot at the big leagues. He had already sent out fruitless feelers about buying the Philadelphia Eagles and the New Orleans Saints of the National Football League, the California Angels, Chicago White Sox, and Oakland A's baseball teams, and a couple of clubs in the old American Basketball Association.

With the divorce looming ahead, Cooke got out of town, moving to Las Vegas. But every few weeks Buss would get a call. Cooke's forceful voice would boom from the other end of the line. "Why don't you come up and talk to me this afternoon?" he would say.

An hour later Buss would be on a plane.

The talks, usually about three or four hours in length, never got down to specifics concerning the sale of the Forum. "You see," Cooke would tell Buss, "there are certain people I wouldn't sell anything to because they are what I call buccaneers. All they are interested in is bucks. They don't care about winning or losing."

What Jerry Buss, fan, got in those sessions was the opportunity to listen to the owner of the Lakers, one of his favorite teams, discuss all the moves he was making, or at least contemplating. It was as close as Buss had ever been to the seat of power of a major team in a major sport. And it was enough to keep him on those afternoon flights to Vegas whenever the call came.

When it finally happened, it was quick.

It was a Tuesday in May 1979. Buss, always a night person, was sleeping late when the long-distance call came. He was told Cooke was on the line. Buss tried to brush the sleep from his eyes, but those eyes popped to twice their normal size when he heard Cooke's question.

"Are you ready?" Cooke asked.

"Was he ready?" Buss thought. This was the moment he had awaited for so long that it didn't seem real now that it had arrived. And by this point the Lakers and Kings were also in the deal.

Cooke's call was prompted by the end of a long and arduous divorce from Barbara, his wife of 42 years. The settlement took two and one half years to resolve, involved 41 lawyers, 12,000 pages of documents, and resulted in $41 million going to Cooke's former wife, a record amount for the state of California, where divorces are as common as avocados. After signing the final papers, Cooke was ready to start a new life back in Virginia.

"Jack is a more emotional man than people realize," a friend said. "I've gone to restaurants with him, places he'd been to with his wife, and I'd spot a tear in his eye. The divorce was a bitter experience. I think he wants to wash his hands of the entire California scene. California, to put it simply, reminds him of his wife."

The reasons for the sale didn't matter to Buss. All he knew was, he had an opportunity to purchase two teams and the most impressive sports arena in Southern California. Whatever the cost, he would do so. But he never dreamed what that cost would be.

Buss and Cooke had a series of meetings at Las Vegas's Desert Inn. Cooke had 20 years on Buss, but they were a pretty even match, these two self-made men, the *nouveau riche* cowboy with the dirty jeans, Western shirts and boots against the immaculately dressed Canadian, the soft-spoken self-assurance of Buss against the blustery, self-confident Cooke. Two financial heavyweights, they would enter their meeting once a week, briefcase-laden attorneys and tax advisers serving as seconds, to spar and look for some advantage, each man used to winning, neither ready to give a monetary inch. They met across a large table, but it might as well have been a ring. It was like a championship fight, the early rounds used to feel each other out, spot some weakness. Between rounds each would head for his corner—Cooke back to his hotel, Buss back to Los Angeles—to discuss strategy.

Cooke had built the Forum for $12.5 million. So if he should sell it for $33.5 million, which he had pretty much established as the price, it was going to cost him $6 million to $8 million in taxes.

Buss had a better idea. "How about a trade?" he said at one session. "We have some high rises in L.A. That way you can avoid the taxes."

That was something Buss and Mariani had become good at over the years. They were always trading properties and opening new partnerships to take advantage of the tax laws. The idea was just what Cooke had in mind. But after Buss had put together a package over several weeks, Cooke hit him with a new plan.

"Jerry, I'll tell you what I want to complete this deal," said Cooke, his voice echoing off every corner of their Desert Inn meeting room. "Let's make it a three-way trade. I've always liked the Chrysler Building in New York. Get it for me, you can trade it for your apartments, and then I'll trade you for the Forum."

These financial giants were playing real-life Monopoly without a board. Buss broke into a large grin. This was fun. If you could have put a stethoscope to his forehead, you would have heard the wheels turning. Buss had always loved to play Monopoly, loved it so much that he had memorized every square on the board and, indeed, often played without a board. He would play imaginary games, making the moves for all his imaginary players. Fine, he thought when Cooke had made his demand, I want Marvin Gardens and it's going to cost me Boardwalk.

There was talk of expanding the trade concept to include the Lakers. Buss would buy another team and he and Cooke would swap. The Baltimore Orioles baseball club was for sale. The possibility of purchasing it was explored, but an acceptable deal couldn't be worked out.

Just in case the 77-story, $40 million Chrysler Building was unattainable, an alternate property was needed. Buss's side looked at the Watergate complex in Washington, then for sale.

It wasn't needed. Cooke's side had already contacted the Chrysler people and had worked out most of the details of the deal. But the Chrysler owners didn't want Buss's high-rise buildings; they wanted cash. So what Buss had to supply was not only the buildings, but buyers for those buildings.

It was Buss, the deal-maker, at his best. He tossed five of his Southern California high rises into the pot along with a buyer for each and dealt his hand.

The deal, simplified, would go as follows:

—Buss would get the Forum, the Lakers, the Kings, and Cooke's sprawling Raljon Ranch in the Sierras.

—Cooke would get the Chrysler Building and some property in Virginia, Massachusetts, and Maryland.

—The Chrysler people would get the high rises. They would immediately sell them to Buss's buyers and collect their cash.

Buss would buy the Forum for $33.5 million, the Lakers for $16 million, the Kings for $8 million, and the California ranch, all 13,000 acres of it, for another $10 million. He was throwing most of his real estate fortune into the deal and would emerge with sole ownership of the Lakers and Kings. Mariani would share in the ownership of the Forum.

The transaction was so huge, it was split into three segments. The final escrow was to close at 12:30 P.M. on May 18, 1979.

Fait accompli? Not quite yet.

On the night of May 17, Buss got a phone call. "One of the buyers has dropped out," he was told.

"How short are we?" Buss asked.

"Two point seven million."

Even for Jerry Buss that was a lot of money to come up with in 15 hours. A conference was held involving Buss, Mariani, and their lawyers and advisers.

The name Sam Nassi was brought up. Nassi, a Los Angeles businessman and a friend of Mariani, would later buy the Indiana

Pacers; he had owned the Indiana Loves of the WTT. It was decided to borrow the money from him—if he could be found. He was in Las Vegas, but a series of phone calls failed to produce him.

Finally Mariani reached Nassi at a midnight dinner show.

"I've got a ticket on a 7 A.M. flight to L.A. waiting for you at the airport," Mariani told him. "We need you to get back here immediately."

Nassi made the flight and rounded up the money upon his arrival home. An additional loan was supplied by Donald T. Sterling, another Mariani business associate and the man who would one day buy the San Diego Clippers and move them to Los Angeles to rival the Lakers. But on this day Sterling was happy to add a loan of approximately $1 million to seal the deal for the Buss forces.

At noon, Cooke, in Las Vegas, got his first hint of the problem in a call from one of his attorneys. "Buss is $2.7 million short," he was told. "What do you think?"

"Well," Cooke said, "we told the man he had until 12:30. We'll wait."

In a San Fernando Valley escrow office, Jim Perzik, a Buss attorney, casually pulled back his jacket sleeve and looked at his watch. It was 12:01. He looked at a phone on a nearby desk. Nothing.

At 12:05 it rang.

It was Mariani. He was with Nassi at a bank in the Beverly Hills area and they had, in hand, a cashier's check for $2.7 million. It was too late to make the 30-minute journey out to the Valley. Perzik asked Jim Jennings, an attorney for Cooke, if the money could, instead, be brought to an escrow office in Beverly Hills, just a few minutes from the bank. Fine, he was told.

Perzik hung up and went back to waiting. And waiting. And waiting.

At 12:17 the phone rang again. It was Angelo, one of Mariani's brothers.

"Where's Frank?" Perzik asked anxiously.

"I don't know," Angelo said.

"What do you mean you don't know?" Perzik asked. "Weren't you with him?"

"Yeh," Angelo said, "but we took two cars. He should already be there. He left before me. Maybe he got lost."

Angelo hung up and Perzik went back to looking at his watch and wondering if this whole thing was going to come crashing down.

At 12:20 the phone rang again. It was Mariani.

"We're here," he said. "Uh, just a minute." With that he put the phone down and walked away.

"But, I . . ." Perzik never finished his sentence. Mariani was gone. Perzik sighed. The clock kept running. It was 12:22 . . . 23 . . . 24.

At 12:25 Mariani got back on.

"Get the escrow officer," said an exasperated Perzik, "and hand her the check."

Again Mariani put down the phone.

"Okay," he said, returning at 12:27.

"All right, put her on to confirm that she has the check and I'll put Cooke's attorney on," Perzik said.

Jennings took the phone, listened for an instant, then nodded his approval at Perzik. Buss's attorney looked at his watch. It was 12:28.

So by 12:30 P.M. on May 18 the deal was complete. It involved nine pieces of property, 12 separate escrows in three states, and the efforts of more than 50 lawyers and advisers. With the sweep of various pens in various cities, Jerry Buss had turned his real estate empire into a sports empire.

Buss knew it was a silly thought. He knew what he wanted did not exist. And yet he couldn't shake a natural feeling. Don't I even get a key? I mean I spent nearly $70 million for the building and its teams. Don't I even get a key to the damn place?

He smiled. It was a brief smile. The fall of 1979 would soon be at hand and there were a lot of holes to plaster in this new acquisition, holes that wouldn't be satisfied with a T-shirt. He had spent a lot of money and he had to conceive new ways of generating revenue in the building.

He was also a little frightened.

He was quickly learning that power was more fun to imagine

than it was to possess. It was like another fantasy he had long harbored, that of being a general in the Napoleonic Wars, ordering up this army, cutting off that route, surrounding these troops.

Now that he was living out one of his fantasies, he found it scared the hell out of him. He had sunk almost his entire fortune into a business he knew relatively little about and every move was going to be crucial.

Buss dressed in his old Wyoming jeans—incredible wealth hadn't changed his style, so why should a few basketball and hockey players—and went off to work.

The Forum offices snake through the building, a labyrinth, winding in a circular fashion through a walled-off section high above the floor. At the back, two wooden doors off the main hallway lead into a long, narrow reception area. Two wooden doors on the left of that area lead into the inner sanctum from which Cooke used to issue his stinging memos. This would be Buss's office, where the financial wizard would push the buttons that would operate his Oz.

On that morning after The Great Swap, Buss marched into his new office to find paper and boxes everywhere. Rose Marie Garmong, Cooke's private secretary, apologized profusely for the mess. Buss waved her off. She'd find he was nowhere near as demanding as his predecessor.

The hours slipped away as Buss perused volumes of records and figures. When he looked up he was alone. Rose Marie and the other secretaries were long gone.

He looked at his watch. It was 8:30.

He stood up and walked down the circular hallway. The Forum was dark this summer evening and the only bodies still stirring somewhere in the bowels of this structure belonged to a couple of security guards. Buss made his way through the press lounge out into the entryway that leads to the court. On the walls on both sides were action shots of Laker and King players. *His* players.

It took him just a few steps to reach the entrance to the actual arena, where he paused. A couple of lonely lights cut a thin swath down to the dark, empty floor, 14 rows below. Another light beamed up at the Laker championship banner from the 1971–72 season, spread across one wall near the ceiling, 40 rows above. Buss retreated into the press lounge, took a folding chair, and marched down to the floor, where he set it up.

The silence was deafening, broken only by the low hum of a generator. Buss sat down and lit up a cigarette. He looked to one side and saw, in his mind's eye, a Laker streaking for a layup. He flipped to the next frame on his mental projector and saw a King streaking down the ice, puck in control. He imagined 17,000 fans screaming at every move.

The cigarette was warm and satisfying, but he still felt a chill run up and down his body. He took a drag, exhaled, and watched the smoke follow the shafts of light blazing a trail to the ceiling.

Then he said softly, "You've come a long way, baby."

PART II

PART II
Hirin' Time, Firin' Time

●

The characters are in the wings.

The curtain is set to rise.

Showtime is about to begin.

And before the last act is played out there'll be laughs and tears, careers launched and lives shattered, games won and friendships lost. Few if any playwrights have ever packed more twists of fate into a single drama.

Jerry Buss dreams of being a sports owner.

Jack McKinney, Paul Westhead, and Pat Riley dream of being head coaches.

Magic, Kareem, and Norm Nixon dream of glory.

But none can possibly dream how their lives will intertwine on the national stage.

5.

The Rise and Fall of Jack McKinney

THE DAY after purchasing his teams Buss met with two longtime guardians of the Laker crest—Jerry West and Bill Sharman. Buss could be sure of one thing: He wasn't hurting for experience.

Sharman had been a star for the USC Trojan basketball team, a guard on four of the Boston Celtics' championship teams (1957, '59, '60, and '61), is a member of the Basketball Hall of Fame, was one of ten named to the NBA's Silver Anniversary squad, is the only coach to have won championships in three separate pro leagues: with the Cleveland Pipers of the American Basketball League in 1961–62, the Utah Stars of the American Basketball Association in '70–71, and, of course, the Lakers in '71–72. On the day he met Buss, Sharman was getting ready for his fourth year as the Lakers' general manager. West had his own plaque in the Hall of Fame, his own spot on the Silver Anniversary team, his own niche as one of the greatest guards in league history. He had spent the previous three years as Laker head coach.

Facing two such brilliantly credentialed figures, the natural inclination for Buss, who admittedly didn't know an X from an O, might have been to keep his mouth shut and his eyes on the financial end of the business, letting these guys keep doing whatever it was they had been doing.

But that wasn't Buss's way. After all, who would have thought an aerospace worker with no background in real estate could plunge into the Southern California market and emerge a multimillionaire? So he kept his insecurities to himself and dived right into the decision-making process. He wanted everyone to know this was his team. The last thing he wanted was to be perceived as a figurehead supplying the bankroll.

It wasn't that Buss didn't have faith in West and Sharman. Just the opposite. He knew West wanted out of coaching and the first thing Buss wanted to do was to try and change his mind.

West is nothing less than the heart and soul of the Lakers. Along with Elgin Baylor, he pioneered and popularized the NBA and the team in L.A. Then he coached the Lakers for three seasons before moving into the front office.

"I feel like I'm a piece of the furniture here," West says. "I can't imagine what my life would be like without my involvement with this team. I have a tremendous allegiance to the Lakers."

As a player, West was high-strung, a skinny, 6–4 bundle of nerves and energy. Elgin Baylor nicknamed him "Zeke from Cabin Creek," and the name was a perfect fit, especially in his first couple of seasons in L.A. West spoke with the high-pitched country twang of his native West Virginia. Off the court he was painfully shy, the classic country kid in the big city.

"I was so bashful, it's hard to believe," West says. "If anyone asked me if I played basketball, I'd get red in the face, I'd lower my head and say, 'Yes.' There's no question I was a country bumpkin. A lot of people think I still am."

West was very much the extrovert on the court. His game was fast and fluid, and he hit so many game-winning shots, he became known as Mr. Clutch. Hearn used to say West never had to look at the scoreboard with time running out because "he had a clock in his head."

West didn't just get by with his brilliant offensive skills, either. He was a marvelous defensive player, and he could run and pass. He is generally considered one of the two greatest guards [Magic may soon join this group] in the game's history, along with Oscar Robertson.

Bob Ryan of the Boston *Globe* is one expert who gives West the nod.

"Oscar was a cold player, a robot, an automaton," Ryan says. "Oscar was a crybaby, he yelled at his teammates. West was incredibly human, he had a heart. You had to love West."

Says Tommy Hawkins, who played with both men, "With

Oscar, if you made a mistake, he was all over you, screaming at you, berating you. Jerry would pat you on the back, say 'That's okay.' He was a pleasure to play with."

But West was tough on himself. He was driven.

"He had the standards of Zeus," says former *Los Angeles Times* sportswriter Ted Green. Green recalls a scene in the locker room after one Laker playoff win over the Knicks. West had played circles around Walt Frazier and turned in a performance that was scintillating even for West.

Green, on his way out of the locker room, said to West, "Jesus, Jerry, you were really something tonight."

West shook his head. "Remember the two-on-one early in the second quarter? I had a guy open and I threw it behind him."

"To tell you the truth, I don't remember that play," Green said.

"God, it pissed me off," West said.

West retired at age 36, when he felt his skills slipping somewhat. Comfortably wealthy through investments, he played golf every day. But after two years of leisure West was itching to get back to basketball. Cooke hired him to coach the Lakers.

West's perfectionist nature served him well as a player, but turned him into a basket case when he was coaching. Every loss plunged him into depression and anger. He couldn't understand why lesser mortals couldn't bring the ball downcourt with seconds remaining and pump in a game winner from 25 feet out, why others didn't gravitate to the ball with the game on the line, why others couldn't perform at the incredible level he consistently did. It wasn't hard being a Jerry West. At least it hadn't been hard for him. He had no patience for those who failed. He didn't have the temperament to be a loser.

He criticized himself and his players. The frustration often surfaced in the form of negativity. He once referred to Kareem Abdul-Jabbar as a dog, and was chagrined when the quote showed up in the newspapers. After star forward Lou Hudson played a bad game West grumbled to a reporter, "If Hudson were a horse, we'd have to take him out and shoot him."

After three seasons West was ready to be taken out and shot. Coaching was killing him.

And sportswriters were killing him, particularly Green and Rich Levin of the *Herald-Examiner*. West felt those two were unduly harsh in their criticism of Abdul-Jabbar, causing a rift between the coach and the star.

Still, under West, the team revived. The Lakers had missed qualifying for the playoffs in '75 and '76, snapping a 14-year streak. West led the Lakers to the playoffs in each of his three seasons, and in '76–77 the team had the league's best regular-season record, 53–29. But the Lakers were a player or two short of being a genuine NBA title contender.

"We had glaring weaknesses on the team," West says, "and yet we prospered in the three years. I think we turned the franchise around in my three years, put it on a path where we could continue to win.

"I can say I'm glad I had an opportunity to do what I did, but two of those years were the most miserable years I have ever spent on this earth. No player is as lonely as a coach. You don't know about this until you become a coach. I learned some bitter lessons."

The lessons were bitter enough that no entreaties by Buss could make West unretire. Not that Buss didn't try.

"I'd like you to continue to coach this team, Jerry," Buss said.

I just can't do that, West told him.

"I'm asking you to do this for me," Buss said. "I'm pleading with you. Please, please help me out! I'm new. I don't know what I'm doing."

West knew it would be a bad move to unretire as coach. Deep down, Buss knew it too. West no longer had any stomach for waking up on a weekend in some strange hotel and preparing for a game he wasn't even going to play in. He begged off.

Sharman was, in many ways, an ideal candidate for the job. The consummate gentleman, Sharman is also the consummate competitor. With Boston he had been an eight-time All-Star guard who played in the classic Celtic tough-guy style. West's first encounter with Sharman came early in his rookie season. In an exhibition game, guarded by Sharman, West hit two or three jump shots in a row. The next time West touched the ball, Sharman hit him in the face and knocked him to the floor.

Here's Sharman's intensity: In 1981, when he was 54 years old, he was invited to participate in an old-timers exhibition shoot-out at halftime of the NBA All-Star Game in Cleveland. For the other old-timers it was more or less a lark. Sharman practiced daily, for weeks. The day before the game he rented a car and drove an hour through a Cleveland blizzard to the arena for his own private shoot-around. But he couldn't find a basketball, so Sharman walked around the court in the dark, simulating the shots.

Just before the shoot-out reporters were invited to predict the winner and his score. The most accurate prediction would win a TV. Two L.A. writers asked Sharman for an honest analysis of his chances. He shook his head and said glumly, "There's no way I can beat Oscar [Robertson]. He tours the country, putting on shooting clinics and exhibitions. He'll *kill* me."

Sharman blew Robertson off the court and won easily.

Sharman shot 88.4 percent from the free-throw line in his career (third best in league history) and 91 percent in the playoffs (second best ever). It's a skill he takes a lot of pride in. In preseason camp in the fall of 1980 he and Magic staged a free-throw shooting contest. Magic nonchalantly stepped to the line and hit 27 of 30 attempts. Sharman shook his head, told Magic how tough a score that was going to be to beat, shook his head again, squinted a bit, rolled the ball in his hands, and pumped in 29 of 30.

As an active player, Sharman set a new standard for dedication. The morning of every game he would go to the arena, at home or on the road, to shoot around and loosen up. On days when there was no game Sharman would find a gym and work out. This behavior was unheard of in the NBA.

When Sharman became a coach he introduced his day-of-game shoot-around as a team concept. Only by continuing to win, and thus proving his point, was Sharman able to get away with this bold usurping of his players' precious leisure time without starting a mutiny.

In his first season as Laker coach, 1971–72, Sharman led the team to the NBA title. The league's other coaches, in self-defense, instituted their own shoot-arounds. Today every NBA team works out almost daily throughout the season. The shoot-arounds have been expanded to often include scrimmaging and chalk talks. Thus every NBA player owes a debt of eternal ingratitude to Sharman.

Coaching and screaming the Lakers to the '72 world title, Sharman strained his vocal cords. Four seasons later, his voice gradually fading, he retired to the front office as general manager. Polyps on his vocal cords would keep that once-firm voice at a whisper, and make it impossible to consider a return to coaching. In 1982 Sharman's voice deserted him almost entirely, making it impossible for him to function even as general manager. He was moved to the position of club president, and West became the Lakers' general manager. So Buss would have to look elsewhere.

"Let me first tell you what I want," Buss said to West and Sharman in his first meeting with them. "I used to watch the UCLA–USC games in John Wooden's era. It was entertainment. That is my general feeling about going to sporting events. I hate those teams that play defense all the time.

"You know, a few months ago I read a newspaper article that reminded me that basketball was supposed to be the sport of the '70s. It has never materialized as such. The '70s are almost over and it never made it. Why not? The guy who wrote it had seven grievances with basketball. And one of the raps was—why see an NBA game when only the last two minutes are important? Skip it, turn on the last two minutes, and that's the game. That article wasn't a bad knock. It's just telling it like it is.

"My concept is, we should have as much excitement in the first quarter as we have in the third quarter, as we do in the second. You will have to see the whole game."

What Buss wanted was entertainers in shorts and sneakers. He knew that would mean a running game. When it became certain West would not return as coach, the top candidate for the job became Jerry Tarkanian, coach of the Runnin' Rebels of the University of Nevada, Las Vegas. In fact, Jack Kent Cooke had wanted Tarkanian for the Lakers and had been trying to lure him out of Las Vegas for three years.

Cooke's negotiations with Tarkanian were strangely and tragically interrupted after a meeting in the spring of 1979 between Cooke and Vic Weiss, a 51-year-old San Fernando Valley auto dealer and boxing figure who was acting as Tarkanian's representative. During the meeting, held in a Beverly Hills hotel, Weiss flashed a roll of bills that caused even Cooke, certainly no stranger to large chunks of cash, to gasp.

"That's an awful lot of money you've got there," Cooke said.

"Oh," Weiss said nonchalantly, "I always carry around $5,000 to $10,000."

The negotiating session was a promising one. It was to be the last session for Weiss, who disappeared after walking out of that hotel. His body was found nearly a week later, stuffed in the trunk of his car in a parking structure at a North Hollywood hotel. The wad of bills was never found. Police theorized that the killing was the work of organized crime, but no suspects were ever apprehended.

The murder put an understandable chill on the Tarkanian negotiations and they never really warmed up again, even after the UNLV coach got over the shock of losing a close friend. Tark, the target of an NCAA investigation at the time, was determined to stay and fight until he was vindicated. He also had a sweet financial deal in Vegas and was hesitant to leave.

So by the time Buss had taken over, the Laker search for a coach had pretty much moved on, though Buss was still interested in Tarkanian. It was announcer Chick Hearn, also the Lakers' assistant general manager and a man Cooke once described as possessing "one hell of an eye for talent," who first proposed Jack McKinney as a coaching candidate. Sharman and West agreed.

Jack McKinney was not exactly the coach you might expect a flamboyant owner like Jerry Buss to select. A protégé of longtime Portland Trail Blazer coach Jack Ramsay, McKinney was once described as "like Jack Ramsay, only without charisma." When a Philadelphia writer was asked for funny Jack McKinney stories, he said there were none.

But while the style was suspect, the substance certainly wasn't. McKinney played for Ramsay at St. James High School in Chester, Pennsylvania, then was reunited with his mentor at St.

Joseph's University in Philadelphia. A 6–2, 185-pounder, McKinney played for Ramsay for two years at St. Joe's, then became a coach himself, first for two years back at St. James High. He returned briefly to St. Joe's as Ramsay's assistant, then spent five years coaching at the Philadelphia College of Textiles and Science. When Ramsay left St. Joe's, McKinney replaced him. Eight years there resulted in a 144–77 record. After winning 19 games, the conference title, a berth in the NCAA tournament, and regional coach of the year honors in the 1973–74 season, with a team one sportswriter had predicted would win no more than three games, McKinney was fired the day after the season ended.

He turned his back on the collegiate game, moving into the NBA, where he spent two years as an assistant at Milwaukee and three in Portland, back under Ramsay.

When McKinney was first contacted by the Lakers, he couldn't believe it. This was a job among the most coveted in his profession. "My gosh," he thought, "will I be lucky enough to start at the top?"

As the negotiations with Buss entered the critical stage, McKinney found himself with a conflict. He was already committed to a two-week basketball clinic in Italy. No problem, Sharman told him, Buss is planning a trip to Europe. Maybe you guys can talk over there.

"Please," McKinney told Sharman, "if anything breaks, call me. I'll come home."

Something broke. About halfway through the clinic McKinney got a long-distance call. "It would be to your advantage to come home," Sharman told him. "Dr. Buss wants to speak to you."

What about the clinic? Who would finish it? The first person McKinney thought of, the first person he always seemed to think of, was Paul Westhead. Westhead played at St. Joe's when McKinney was an assistant there. Westhead had then been an assistant himself at St. Joe's under McKinney. Westhead coached one summer in Puerto Rico—a job McKinney got him. He went to Brazil for the State Department, thanks to a recommendation from McKinney. And now, while taking a summer break from his job at LaSalle College, where he had been head basketball coach for nine years, Westhead was about to get another call from McKinney.

Would he like to come to Italy to finish off the clinic and then take a vacation in Paris—all part of the clinic package? Westhead was on a plane quicker than you can say fast break. The two friends met in an Italian airport, one coming, one going, where Westhead got a two-minute briefing on the clinic.

Back home, McKinney found himself offered a one-year contract for $125,000 to coach the Los Angeles Lakers. He was thrilled, but not overwhelmed. He had hoped for a three-year guarantee.

"I don't know if you're even a good coach," Buss told him.

"I'm going to prove to you I'm a good coach," McKinney insisted, "and if I do, I want the opportunity to come in here and renegotiate."

"I like that attitude," Buss said.

And, he added, don't worry about having to come home early from Europe. When this season is over you're going to get that trip to Paris.

McKinney couldn't help but like what he saw when he came to training camp in Palm Springs in the fall of 1979. He was already familiar with his center, Kareem Abdul-Jabbar. McKinney had gotten a close-up look at the 7–2 center in his first year as a Milwaukee assistant, Abdul-Jabbar's last season with the Bucks. But for all of the court prowess of Abdul-Jabbar, a man destined to become the game's all-time leading scorer, McKinney looked at him and saw wasted talent. He saw an excellent but often unutilized passer who would be perfect as the trigger man of his new offense, throwing the outlet passes that could ignite the running game his new boss so desperately desired.

McKinney sat down with his center before training camp. "We've got the runners. We're going to run every chance we get," the coach told Abdul-Jabbar, "and we can't do that if you're in the backcourt."

"Okay," Abdul-Jabbar responded, "I'll run."

McKinney had to wipe away the saliva every time he gazed at his No. 1 draft choice—Magic Johnson. Sure the kid had just turned 20. Yeah, at 6–9 he was kind of big for a point guard. But McKinney never had a doubt he was looking at the quarterback for a running game that could, and would, revolutionize pro basketball.

McKinney had other weapons. Small forward Jamaal Wilkes had the sticky hands of a wide receiver, was an unorthodox and often unstoppable jumper, and had a knack for sneaking out of the pack early and streaking down the court for lead passes and uncontested fast-break layups. He was an ideal wing man.

Norm Nixon, who had been the point man, was extremely cooperative in that first training camp. "He made it so easy on me and Magic," McKinney later said. "He could have been real tough." Instead of resisting the change that moved him to the off guard and made Magic the point guard, Nixon, a two-year veteran, turned the controls over to the flashy rookie without any grumbling and moved to shooting guard. And, as the year evolved, Nixon still had plenty of opportunities to handle the ball. He finished the regular season with more assists than Magic, 642 in 82 games to 563 for Johnson in 77 games.

Nixon, who had played under Jerry West and would subsequently play under Westhead, Pat Riley, and then Don Chaney with the Clippers, recently called McKinney "the best coach I ever played for." Impressive considering that experience lasted only 13 regular-season games.

McKinney's big problem was the lack of a true power forward. The Lakers' last dominating force at that position for the Lakers had been Kermit Washington. But it had been nearly two years since Washington, in the midst of a seemingly harmless scuffle during a game against the Houston Rockets, had thrown a not-so-harmless punch that had left the face of Houston forward Rudy Tomjanovich a bloody wreck.

The result of the ensuing outcry was a trade that sent Washington, guard Don Chaney, and a first-round draft pick to Boston for guard Charlie Scott. It was a disastrous move for the Lakers. Scott made little impact and was traded at year's end, while the loss of Washington left a big hole in the Laker front line.

Who could fill the power void? Kareem? Abdul-Jabbar, never a devastating rebounder, now was not only being asked to be the power on offense and the intimidator on defense, but also the force on the boards. There was no alternative. The Lakers had two finesse types, two nonbanger types, at forward in Wilkes and Adrian Dantley. Wilkes was designated the power forward, but it was strictly an honorary title.

Lacking in muscle, the Lakers found themselves being shoved out of the playoffs by the Seattle Supersonics in '78 and '79. The L.A. media was merciless, blaming Abdul-Jabbar for failing to handle Jack Sikma and the rest of the Seattle front line, just as he had been lambasted a season earlier when, with Washington out injured, the Portland Trail Blazers, behind center Bill Walton, had knocked Los Angeles out of the playoffs. Abdul-Jabbar, a proud and sensitive man, felt it was futile to respond, to alibi about how in an elbow-throwing contest with these other front lines he just didn't have enough elbows. So instead he retreated even further into the mental shell in which he had hidden for much of his career.

McKinney took one look at the situation and knew he wasn't going far with a sulking Abdul-Jabbar. The problem was obvious. So the Lakers traded Dantley, one of their two small forwards, to the Utah Jazz for veteran power forward Spencer Haywood the day before the start of camp. A week before the regular season began, Dave Robisch and a third-round draft choice went to Cleveland for Jim Chones, another power forward.

Just one more key personnel move to be made. The final roster spot was down to two candidates—Ron Carter and Michael Cooper. Carter had become a personal friend of Buss, and would later work for him in real estate. Cooper was an unknown quantity. A skinny, 6–7 swingman out of the University of New Mexico, Cooper was a third-round draft choice in 1978 but appeared in only three games his rookie season because of a torn knee ligament.

McKinney sat down with Westhead, whom he had hired as his assistant, and asked his opinion—Carter or Cooper?

Westhead never hesitated.

"I think we should keep Ron Carter," Westhead said. "I am totally unimpressed with Michael Cooper's defensive performance. I've seen Coop play in the summer league. He comes and kind of flits around, you know, slam dunks three or four times, and lets any Tom, Dick, and Harry drive down the lane. He might want to try and block the shot once in a while. Very irresponsible.

"We know we have Magic and Nixon, who are two terrific offensive players. We're not so sure how tough they are going to be defensively night in and night out. We really need to get a guy that can come in and give us 10, 15 minutes a game, that can get after somebody and be reliable and be consistent. In my opinion, Ron Carter is a much more consistent player."

McKinney was good at sifting through advice, taking the good and ignoring the bad. In this case he nodded at Westhead, smiled, and said, "Okay, here's what we're going to do. I'm going to keep Cooper."

Despite the fact that Cooper quickly became recognized as one of the NBA's premier defenders, Westhead maintains it occurred only after the University of New Mexico star came to him and asked, "What do I have to do to get more playing time?"

"Defense can be your ticket into this league," Westhead says he told Cooper.

The first time Westhead saw that Cooper had the capacity to punch that ticket was the first time the Lakers met the Boston Celtics that season. Westhead, by then the head coach, put Cooper on Larry Bird and he shut the Celtics' superstar forward down—as much as anyone can.

Cooper remembers that season a little differently.

"It was McKinney who talked to me, not Westhead," says Cooper angrily. "I asked him what it was going to take for me to get some playing time and he said, 'Play defense, run like the wind, and hit the open shot.' That was fine with me because that's my style.

"I've always been a defensive player. I'm tired of this shit about people saying they *made* me a defensive player. I came from a defensive-oriented school. I don't know where people get the idea I couldn't play defense. What makes them think they made me? Fuck Westhead. And you can put that in your book."

There is no dispute about who installed the fast break that quickly became a trademark of the 1979–80 Lakers. McKinney knew what he wanted to do with this team even before he talked to Buss. Westhead was perhaps even more devoted to the running game than McKinney, and there were times when he would suggest radical additions to the new offense. McKinney would flash that relaxed smile of his and say, "That doesn't work here in this league, Paul." Some of the less radical stuff was put in.

And very quickly, even before the regular season began, it started to mesh. One night, while on the road for an exhibition game, McKinney bumped into a friend who had been an NBA observer for years. "Boy, I have not seen the Lakers play like this for a while," the friend said, shaking his head in awe. "They are playing like they know they are going to win."

Opening night, 1979, was the night of the Lakers' win over the Clippers on that last-second skyhook by Abdul-Jabbar, followed by Magic Johnson's ecstatic leap. Magic's reaction seemed a little extreme, with 81 regular-season games still to go, but Buss understood. He was feeling much the same way. His lifelong role as a fan had changed. The difference between rooting for a team you like and rooting for a team you own, he thought, is akin to watching your neighbor's kids versus watching your own.

The night of November 7 had not been the most pleasant for Jack McKinney. His club was blown out by the Golden State Warriors in Oakland, 126–109. But still there were plenty of positive things to talk about as he and Westhead stretched out in the midsection of a plane taking them on a late-night flight home. The team was 9–4, Magic Johnson was starting to make believers out of his doubters, most of the kinks had been worked out of a fast-break offense that was just starting to run on all cylinders, and besides, tomorrow was the club's first full day off in this young season.

By the time McKinney and Westhead reached the head coach's car, however, basketball had given way to a new topic— gas. It was a far more pressing matter at that moment, as the car's gauge hung dangerously below the empty mark. McKinney turned on the defroster and wipers before steering his vehicle out of its airport parking slot for the journey home to the Palos Verdes Peninsula, a 15-mile drive south. Both he and Westhead peered through the windshield, now streaked with the rapidly melting dew, trying to make out a friendly 76 ball or the red, white, and blue of the Chevron sign, or any other signal of an open service station. They finally settled for an all-night market/ gas station near home. By the time McKinney dropped Westhead off at his condominium, it was after one o'clock. Both men could think no further than their warm beds.

When Jack McKinney's eyes popped open on November 8 he sat straight up in bed and tried to brush away the cobwebs so he could remember what was on today's agenda. Was he home? Was there a game? A practice? A shoot-around? There hadn't been an idle day since before he had gone to Europe.

"Go back to sleep," said his wife, Claire, standing at the other end of the bedroom adjusting her clothes. "You've got a day off, remember?"

McKinney smiled and slipped back under the covers. Claire left in the family's only car, bound for a morning class on personal relationships she was taking with her close friend Cassie Westhead.

The next time McKinney's eyes popped open it was an hour later. The phone was ringing. He groaned as he reached over to pick up the receiver.

"Want to play some tennis?" It was Westhead.

McKinney grunted an affirmative.

"I've got the court for two hours. We can play singles at 10 and maybe some doubles with the girls at 11."

"What time is it now?" McKinney asked.

"Nine-thirty."

"Okay, give me a chance to get some coffee and I'll be over."

McKinney took a quick shower, poured his coffee, and then frowned as he unfolded the newspaper and glanced at the story about last night's loss. He read it quickly, then put it down. No basketball today, he told himself. He grabbed his racket and headed for the garage. He and Westhead tried to play tennis a couple of times a week, but it never quite seemed to work out that way; basketball kept getting in the way. But today was going to be relaxing.

Damn, McKinney muttered when he reached the garage. How stupid could he be? No car. Of course not, he thought, Claire took it to get to class. I totally forgot. How in the heck am I supposed to get over there?

The courts, in the condominium complex where Westhead lived, were about a mile and a half away. I could jog, McKinney thought, looking out at the quiet street. He stood there a minute, then crunched up his face in disapproval at the idea. Naa, I'll be too damn tired to play when I get there.

Then he saw it, leaning unobtrusively against a wall in the corner of the garage. It was his son John's bicycle and not something he, Jack, would normally ride. But he certainly knew how, and there weren't a lot of alternatives at the moment.

So he wheeled it out, shoved his racket into the bike's rack, and was off.

Day off or not, McKinney couldn't totally put the Lakers out of his mind. As he easily navigated the residential streets, clear of all but a few cars on this quiet Thursday morning, he ran through a mental checklist of things to be done at tomorrow's practice. Even on his day off he couldn't stop coaching, and why should he? He loved every minute of it. He was 44 and living a dream. This team was about to get hot. Good things were about to happen. He could just feel it.

As McKinney started down a long, steep hill, he wasn't going particularly fast. Robert N. S. Clark watched McKinney from his car as he waited at an intersection at the bottom of the hill.

"He was not speeding, as I remember," Clark said later. "He seemed to be going at a moderate speed, then he slowed down even more and looked at the corner. My impression was that he put his brakes on and something happened then."

What happened was that something seemed to lock as McKinney attempted to brake for the final run to the bottom of the hill. The bike came to a sudden, jarring halt, but McKinney's body kept going, straight over the handlebars to the asphalt beyond.

His hands, tightly gripping the handlebars, remained locked in position an instant too long. He couldn't use them to cushion his fall. Nor was he wearing a helmet. He hit the pavement headfirst, his arms, finally free, trailing underneath. He bounced with a sickening thud and slid on his stomach for another 12 . . . 15 . . . 18 feet before stopping.

A pool of blood formed under his head.

The only sound was the soft whirling of the wheels of the shattered bike as they slowly spun to a halt.

●

Westhead glanced at his watch with increasing frequency. He had gone out to the court to save it in case McKinney was late. But now it was 10:15, 10:20. Westhead laughed to himself. Jack was absentminded, but not this bad. He probably got a call from the office. He's on the phone with Bill Sharman or he's talking to some player, or maybe a couple of writers got him. No big deal. Westhead figured McKinney probably tried to call him but obviously couldn't reach him here at the court.

Westhead went back to his condo and sat around until Claire McKinney dropped Cassie off and drove on home.

"I don't know what the hell happened to Jack," Westhead told his wife. He was neither annoyed nor concerned, figuring Laker business had simply intruded. There would be no such thing as a true day off in this job.

Westhead and his wife played some tennis, and had some lunch. It was then that they got a call from Claire, who couldn't find her husband.

At the scene of the accident an ambulance arrived. One attendant kneeled down, looked at McKinney, shook his head, and told the other, "Too bad. This guy's not gonna make it." The other attendant, however, looking at McKinney's good physical condition, shook his head in disagreement. "Nope," he said, "I think he'll make it."

At 2:30 Claire McKinney again called the Westheads.

"I found him," she said, "in the hospital."

"I remember wondering if we were going to find someone on their deathbed," Cassie Westhead says. "It was total disbelief that this could happen."

It was a little after six when Westhead saw his closest friend, surrounded by nurses in the intensive care ward at Little Company of Mary Hospital in Torrance. Westhead had some difficulty getting in at all, but finally made it when Claire told hospital officials that Paul was Jack's brother.

In the first hours after the accident there was a question whether McKinney would survive. He had a severe concussion and had not regained consciousness. In addition, he had suffered a fractured cheekbone, a fractured elbow, and cuts and bruises all over his body.

Westhead looked at his friend and couldn't believe it was

the same man who had dropped him off less than 24 hours earlier. McKinney's face was not only bloodied, but contorted. He looked, Westhead thought, like he had been in a barroom fight against five guys.

"People were running around, monitoring all these life-saving devices," Cassie remembers.

The improvement was painfully slow. By Friday, McKinney's vital signs were stable and he was regaining consciousness for longer and longer periods of time. He was responding to voices and was able to say his name.

When Westhead awoke at 7 Friday morning he thought about the 10 o'clock shoot-around scheduled for that day in preparation for the evening's game at the Forum against the Denver Nuggets.

You know, he said to himself, if *I* don't go, *nobody's* going to go. I don't know what the hell I'm doing, but I might as well show up. It's like my days in school when the teacher was absent. If nobody shows up, they'll be breaking the windows and writing on the blackboards.

Few knew the extent of McKinney's injuries that morning. Some of them had glanced at a paper on the way to practice and knew their coach had fallen off a bike. Some didn't even know that much. It didn't sound too serious. How long could he be out, a couple of days?

Westhead went through the motions at the shoot-around and found himself on the sidelines at the Forum hours later coaching his first pro game. The Lakers, running on automatic pilot, managed to win when Wilkes hit a 20-foot jumper to send the game into overtime where his club prevailed, 126–122.

"Even if we go 71–0 the rest of the season," Westhead told a reporter, "it's still Jack McKinney's team."

The Lakers didn't do quite that well, but they didn't do too badly under Westhead. A three-game road trip was coming up and he had the feeling he was being sent as head coach simply because there was nobody else. At least there would be somebody there, he joked to a reporter, to make sure no more than five guys were on the court at the same time.

But as low-key as he appeared to be, Westhead must have

been doing something right. The club won three straight and five of its first six under him.

"We're really not so sure what we're going to do about an interim coach," Sharman told him, "but we'll keep this going for a while."

So instead of coaching hour to hour, it was day to day for Westhead, and then home stand to home stand.

While there were many in the Laker organization who remained optimistic that McKinney would soon be back, Buss was not among them. He figured he was looking for a replacement for the rest of the season, and the more he talked to people in and out of the Laker organization the more he became convinced Westhead was his man. If you are happy with what you've seen so far this season, he was told, Westhead is the guy to keep it going smoothly. He knows the system. He helped install it.

Buss liked what he saw. He would go with the status quo.

Having decided on Westhead as interim head coach, the Lakers needed a new assistant. The name suggested to Westhead was Elgin Baylor, who had coached the New Orleans Jazz for two and one half seasons and was now living in Los Angeles, working in private industry.

But Westhead had another idea. While waiting for a flight home from Denver following a game against the Nuggets, Westhead was seated in an airport bar with Pat Riley, the team's color commentator and sidekick to broadcaster Chick Hearn.

"Would you like to come down from the booth and join me?" Westhead asked.

Riley was shocked. Sure, he had been a pro player for nine years, five with the Lakers. Sure, he had thought about coaching. But he didn't expect the opportunity to come just now, in just this way. He was going to have to think this one over.

When Buss was first told Westhead wanted Pat Riley as his assistant, the owner was less than enthusiastic. Riley had no coaching experience, and the jump from a microphone to a chalkboard didn't seem very logical to Buss.

But Jerry West pleaded Riley's case. It's not totally unprecedented, West said. He pointed out that Billy Cunningham was a broadcaster before he became one of the game's top coaches with the Philadelphia 76ers. Besides, Riley had been a pro player for nine years, five with the Lakers, and was a very bright guy.

Buss still wasn't convinced. It seemed to him a coach should be either a former star player or someone with a lot of coaching experience.

It was Pete Newell, a former Laker and San Diego Rocket general manager, a former USF, University of California, and U. S. Olympic team head basketball coach, and still one of the most widely respected authorities on the game in the country, who finally convinced Buss that Riley was a legitimate candidate, that he had attended coaching clinics and was a serious student of the game who could develop into a good coach.

Riley himself had doubts, as did his wife, Chris. He was becoming intrigued with this strange new world of broadcasting, just beginning to learn about the production of shows and the editing of tape segments to form quality shows. He was not the here's-the-other-scores and here's-the-stats and now-back-to-you-Chick type. Riley had put together some creative pregame and halftime shows. He felt he had a future in broadcasting and he liked it.

Was he going to throw it all away for a few games on the sidelines, doing a lot more work, a lot more traveling as both assistant coach and scout, and then perhaps be out of work when McKinney returned? The Lakers planned to hire another former player, Keith Erickson, to take Riley's place. When McKinney came back what would happen to Riley? Would he be out of two jobs?

Riley asked Hearn's advice.

Give it a try, Chick told him. I think you can do it. And if it doesn't work out, or if Jack comes back and they don't need you, I promise you'll get your broadcasting job back.

That soothed his worries. What the hell. He'd give it a try.

McKinney continued to improve with the help of his wife, Claire, who was constantly at his bedside, helping and prodding and praying. Three days after the accident, Jack was able to recognize Westhead. Three weeks after McKinney's world came crashing down, doctors repaired the fractured bone in his elbow and surgically repaired and elevated a bone on the right side of his face. That was at Centinela Hospital Medical Center in Inglewood, where he had been moved. He was released December 1, after 23 days of hospitalization.

The body was healing. The healing of his mind was not so predictable. When, if ever, would he be capable of coaching again? Doctors couldn't say. McKinney, his family, Westhead, and the Lakers could only wait and hope.

McKinney's impatience was understandable.

Here he was, having reached the dream of a lifetime much sooner than he ever imagined, having put together a tremendous team far sooner than expected, and now someone else was running it.

Several weeks after leaving the hospital, McKinney wanted to meet with the team, but Westhead talked him out of it. He didn't feel McKinney was ready emotionally for such a meeting and he didn't want the players to see their coach in that state of mind.

"I couldn't even walk straight and I wanted to be out there," McKinney later said.

By mid-December, Westhead was experiencing a crisis of his own. His name was Spencer Haywood. Haywood, 6–9 and 225, had been a legend in the old American Basketball Association, a dominating scorer and rebounder. But by the time the Lakers got him, Haywood was 30 years old, working for his fourth NBA team, and was considered by some to be over the hill and a potential disrupting force.

Haywood was an eccentric. He played the piano and flute, was a jazz DJ, practiced yoga and fasting, and considered himself a deep thinker with a sensitive and poetic soul. He took a shower *before* every game to remove the pollen. And he could be absentminded. Abdul-Jabbar's girlfriend, Cheryl Pistano, planned a surprise birthday party for Kareem and invited all the Lakers. The morning of the party, at a team shoot-around, Haywood asked Abdul-Jabbar, "What time's your party tonight, Kareem?"

Haywood was friendly as a puppy dog, but could also be a world-class sulker. When a minor injury early in the season cost him his starting job, and when Westhead replaced McKinney, Haywood's playing time steadily decreased. He sulked and grumbled. At halftime of one game he stormed about the locker room fuming. "I don't need this shit," he said. "I'm independently wealthy."

During a game against the Pistons, Westhead looked down the bench and told Haywood to report in.

"Coach, I can't see," Haywood said.

"What do you mean?" Westhead asked.

"I can't see," said Haywood, who has some allergies. "But I'll be okay, I'll be okay." Increasingly angry about a lack of playing time, Haywood exploded after a game and labeled Westhead's reasons for not giving him more time "lies."

As Buss was holding a series of meetings to resolve the problem, McKinney stopped by the Laker offices, accompanying Claire to a Christmas party for Laker wives. It was one of his first outings away from home since the accident, but Buss welcomed him into his office to get involved, if he wished, in Spencer's fate. McKinney helped ease the situation and Haywood returned to the bench, placated for the moment. Buss was impressed with McKinney's ability to function in such a delicate matter.

But as the season progressed, the Haywood situation got stranger and stranger. Late in the season, with Haywood riding the pine, the Forum fans would break into a spontaneous chant: "Hay-wood, Hay-wood!" Why were they chanting for Haywood, by now a relatively minor character in the Laker drama, and hardly an object of widespread sympathy? Who knows? Said *Phoenix Gazette* columnist Joe Gilmartin, "The Lakers need two psychiatrist's couches—one for Haywood and one for all the fans."

Haywood responded to the chants by parading along the sideline during timeouts, waving a towel or his fist. He took to sitting cross-legged on the floor in front of the bench. In one crucial game, with Kareem at the foul line for two vital free throws and the crowd silent, Haywood screamed, "Kareeeeem! We neeeeeed these free throws!"

The other Lakers simply assumed Haywood had changed addresses and was now living on Venus or Pluto. But in the championship finals against Philadelphia, on the night the Sixers tied the best-of-seven series at 1–1, Haywood's bizarre Laker career culminated in the infamous Tape Cutter Incident.

His contribution to the series thus far had been comedic and dramatic relief—falling asleep in the film room, and then falling into a deep, coma-like sleep on a gym floor while in the hurdler's position during a team stretching drill. In the locker room after Game 2, Haywood snapped at Brad Holland, "Gimmie your tape cutters."

Holland, like most of his teammates, was losing patience with Haywood.

"If you say please," Holland shot back.

"If I have to say please, I don't wanna use 'em," Haywood said, his voice rising.

"Fine, then don't use 'em," Holland said, *his* voice rising.

By now the 6–9 Haywood and the 6–3 Holland had stood up and squared off, face-to-face, jaw-to-jaw. Jim Chones rushed across the locker room and pushed Haywood away.

"You crazy, Wood?" Chones asked. "Man, you're lettin' us down."

Westhead quickly convened a meeting of Haywood and Buss upstairs in the owner's office, and two hours later Haywood drove slowly out of the Forum parking lot in his Rolls-Royce, no longer a Laker. He was suspended.

After the playoffs the players voted him only a quarter share. "It's more than he deserved," Abdul-Jabbar said. Haywood was waived that summer.

Encouraged by his late-December outing to the Laker offices, McKinney went home and started talking about returning to duty in perhaps a month. By January he had convinced himself he was about ready to return. His doctors weren't so sure, and neither was Buss. Gone was the broad smile, glowing face, and easy manner of the man who had arrived several months earlier. Instead, he was a thin, nervous man, a look best described as desperation in his eyes, extreme fatigue written on his face. He tired easily and his mind still lacked its earlier sharpness.

He considered returning first as Westhead's assistant, but was talked out of that. "Someone else told me that it would not be good for the team," McKinney said, "that they might have trouble accepting me that way."

He couldn't accept that he wasn't ready. "He wanted to coach before he could drive," said his daughter, Sue.

By the last week in January, doctors told him he still wasn't ready. Sitting home was driving him crazy, so he went to the Forum and faced a full-court press for the first time, meeting the media in the press lounge. He told reporters this was to have been the week he returned to the sidelines, according to his own timetable.

"Fortunately, my doctors stopped me," he said. "They are taking in a lot that I overlooked. My job demands that I do my work in front of 16,000 to 17,000 people. I have to deal with the press and I have to deal with airplanes and travel. The question is, do I have the strength to do all that?"

The answer, even to the untrained eye, was obviously no.

By now the Lakers were 27–13 under Westhead.

"They have improved on little areas. I am envious of that. I wish I had been there when they went through that," said McKinney, sounding like a man watching his child being raised by foster parents.

But by then, McKinney had to admit, his enthusiasm about returning was tempered a bit by apprehension.

"No matter what happens, I may not look right," he said of his anticipated return. "If we keep on winning, they'll say, 'Nice going, Paul.' If we lose—well, that's just part of coaching. They'll probably think the dummy should have stayed the hell in bed.

"I don't think I can take two more months sitting home, watching afternoon matinees. When I came home I was wondering if I was ever going to be kneeling in front of those guys in the huddle again."

Over the ensuing weeks McKinney would call Westhead with the latest medical updates. "I talked to the doctors, and they're saying it's going to be a little longer," McKinney would say. "But I'm going to be ready one month from today."

That was fine with Westhead, but the weeks turned into months, and still McKinney wasn't ready.

Westhead tried to ease him back in by sending him on some scouting trips. But in the beginning Claire had to accompany him just to handle all the small details involved in traveling, details he couldn't handle himself.

In Portland, parking his rental car, McKinney banged into a Porsche.

Buss's concerns were heightened during one game McKinney attended as a spectator. Buss passed his coach in the stands. "Jack, how are you?" Buss asked. "How ya feeling?"

McKinney didn't answer. He hadn't recognized Jerry Buss.

With about eight games remaining in the regular season and a smoothly running powerhouse club cruising into the playoffs, Buss informed McKinney he was not going to make a switch for at least the remainder of the year.

What then? McKinney wanted to know.

"After we win the championship," Buss said, "the three of us—you, me, and Paul—will work it out."

McKinney was hurt, but admitted he still wasn't 100 percent. "I know it and I guess I just don't want to face it," he said. "I do have a constant improvement in sharpness, or lack of vagueness. . . . Certain words slip out of my grasp, but I can rephrase what I want to say, using other words. . . . There is a certain vagueness that doctors say only time can cure, and they say that it's not good for me to be under pressure at this time."

Shortly before the playoffs McKinney and Westhead sat down to discuss the situation.

"What do you think?" McKinney asked.

"I think you're going to get stiffed," Westhead said. "I don't like the way things are developing. In fact, I have the strong impression that if we are not successful in the playoffs and, in fact, even win the championship, I think you'll be gone first and I'll be gone second."

"Nah, if I can just get back into it," McKinney insisted, "I think everything will work out."

He'll never know.

With the Lakers blowing past Phoenix, then getting by Seattle and into the NBA finals, with a world championship on the horizon, the pressure on Buss grew, pressure unlike that any owner had ever faced. How are you going to make this decision? people kept asking him. Are you going to go with the guy who designed the team or the guy who won with it?

"The way I looked at it," Buss says, "was maybe McKinney would have won it. Maybe he wouldn't. This guy won it. I had a sure against a maybe. I'll go with the sure every time. Put me in that circumstance a hundred times and I would go with the guy that did it. I never thought there was a decision. It was never something I weighed.

"In my estimation I wasn't sure whether McKinney could really make a full comeback to coaching. Coaching requires such instantaneous decisions, intuition. To me, I think that's a very, very tough job for a guy that is not in the peak of health and in the full possession of his mental powers. I couldn't say he didn't have it, but I couldn't say for sure he did.

"My life was in that team. That was the bulk of everything I'd worked for all along. If I was ever going to make it economically, it had to be with the Lakers. It wasn't going to be with the Kings. All the money I had was tied up in this whole enterprise. And it had one flagship."

McKinney's obvious anger at not being handed back the reins of his team further solidified Buss's opinion that his former coach was not mentally ready to handle pressure.

Buss knew that McKinney was not thinking rationally. That should not have come as a surprise. He had been told that McKinney's ability to reason properly might be the last thing to return to normal. It was a difficult situation, and one that called for some compassion. But Buss didn't quite see it like that.

Why is this guy overreacting so much? Buss asked himself. He has had a very serious accident. The team is going beautifully. Why wouldn't he get behind us as part of the team? Why set himself aside and begin to criticize the team management? He should jump in behind us and say, "Hey, whatever you want to do, this is what I want to do. Whatever you think is best." I don't want to be associated with a guy that sees fit, at a critical time, to begin criticizing management. Everybody has to be working exactly for the same thing.

What further angered Buss was that he was hearing McKinney's criticism from others. He felt McKinney should have brought his criticisms directly to the boss.

So the decision was sealed.

●

Buss's next move was to call Westhead in and feel him out about becoming the permanent head coach. Westhead sat across from Buss in his Forum office and vehemently shook his head when the offer was made.

"No, no, I couldn't do this to Jack," Westhead insisted.

"Well, I understand that, Paul," said Buss, his easy manner growing firm, "but I can tell you, Jack is not going to be the coach. Jack will *not* be the coach of this team. Now, do you want the job, now that we know that Jack isn't going to be the coach? Do you want the job or do we get somebody else?"

Westhead felt hurt and disappointment for his close friend, but he had no doubt Buss was serious. Jack was gone. Period. It was silent in Buss's office. Westhead took a look around, took a long look deep down inside his own soul, then took a deep breath and said, yes, he wanted to be head coach of the Los Angeles Lakers.

McKinney suspected bad news might be coming his way, but he never expected to get it in a lonely phone booth on the Pacific Coast somewhere between Oregon and L.A.

He had been in Philadelphia with the Lakers for the first two games of the NBA finals, scouting the Sixers. On Sunday night, following Game 2, the team flew home while McKinney flew to Portland to pick up Claire, who had been visiting their daughter, Sue, at Oregon State.

In the meantime a story appeared in a Philadelphia newspaper that McKinney was officially out as Laker coach. Buss knew he would be questioned by reporters. He said he left messages for McKinney everywhere he might be, but they were not returned.

McKinney maintains that someone was at his home all that day and he never got a message from Buss.

When the reporters came knocking Buss told them the truth. No, Jack McKinney would not be back.

On their drive home from Oregon Monday night, the McKinneys stopped off at that phone booth to check in at home.

"Have you seen any TV?" asked McKinney's son, John.

"No," the senior McKinney replied, "we're on the road."

"Well, I was just watching the seven o'clock news and you've been fired."

Bob Steiner, Buss's director of public relations and a man who has been in sports more than two decades, defends his boss's decision but calls the whole McKinney affair "the most unfortunate thing I've ever been around, outside of somebody getting killed. Here's a guy who is an outstanding college coach, is a tremendous pro assistant, pays all his dues, gets his opportunity, and is doing a bang-up job. To me, that's the most discouraging thing I've ever been around."

McKinney finally met with Buss, got the news firsthand, then told the media, "I would say this is not a very stable time, but life goes on. You have to get ready to live it wherever it is or whatever it calls you to do."

Westhead tried to talk to his close friend, but there wasn't much to say. These men, who had once shared so many triumphs, now had trouble sharing a conversation. Westhead would speak but would have trouble getting a response out of McKinney.

"At that moment, he was totally crushed," Westhead said. "He felt that the world had fallen in. And that was the only time, I would say, that I had that awful feeling that somehow I was part of the world that had fallen in."

The bitter feelings spread to the Westhead and McKinney families. "They can't share our joys," Cassie Westhead said of the McKinneys, "and we can't share their sorrows."

On the night the Lakers, *his* Lakers, won the championship, Jack McKinney went to the movies.

Four days after he had coached the team to triumph in Philadelphia, Westhead signed a four-year contract as head coach of the Lakers at an annual salary that could go over $250,000.

His relationship with McKinney, who was packing his belongings to move to New Jersey, had worsened.

"At that time things really began to kind of break down," Westhead said. "All I know is that he wanted to get out as quickly as he could and leave anything and everything associated with the Los Angeles Lakers. I was not only associated with them, but I was like headlines. His approach was, leave me alone."

"Paul wasn't taking *his* job," Cassie Westhead says. "He was taking *a* job that was open. He bided his time to see if Jerry Buss would change his mind and bring Jack back. When it became obvious that wasn't going to happen, Paul became the coach. There was no guilt other than when he felt he was being judged harshly by others.

"But for Jack there was this wonderful future he had dreamed about and suddenly he was zapped. It was hard times."

Buss, not wishing to cast doubt on McKinney's ability to still coach and thus perhaps ruin his chances for another NBA job, told the media, "With Jack I had obviously disappointed the man and I felt my actions had perhaps strained the relationship and would not allow for the kind of enjoyable owner-coach relationship I want. I feel he was an absolutely adequate coach, but I don't see where he fits in with my idea of developing a situation for a lot of fun. Also, Paul is an excellent coach and I do have a lot of fun with him. I'm going to go with the guy I can run and chum with, and have a beer with, who I really feel at ease with."

Asked further about McKinney, Buss added, "I think he just felt it was unfair the way I had dealt with him. He was just deeply hurt. He felt, basically, it was his team. What had he done to lose it? I guess the answer is, he had an accident. It would be very difficult to win a championship under one coach and say, 'Thank you very much. I'll see you later.' This is not a public utility or a public company. This is my team, and if I feel comfortable dealing with one man and not the other, it seems extremely logical that I should choose the one I feel comfortable with."

Buss, though he wouldn't admit it at the time, helped McKinney get another job, convincing his friend Sam Nassi, then the Indiana Pacers' owner, to hire McKinney for the following season.

Saddled with a miserable team, McKinney wound up with a 125–203 record to show for four long years in Indiana. His last season there the Pacers were 26–56, worst in the NBA. In another of his seasons there, the club won only 20.

After being fired at Indiana, McKinney began the 1984–85 season as head coach of the Kings, then still located in Kansas

City. After a 1–8 start and tales of memory lapses by McKinney, he resigned, despite a four-year contract worth an estimated half a million dollars, and took his present position of scout for the club.

"Trying to do this has become extremely frustrating to me," he said of coaching at the time of the resignation. "The stress has given me many sleepless nights . . . until I reached a point of being burned out. Why not just release myself from all this pressure and let myself sleep at night?"

The relationship between the Westheads and the McKinneys was slow to heal.

The Christmas after he became Laker head coach, Paul and his family were knee deep in arranging holiday decorations in their Los Angeles home when the doorbell rang. It was John and Ann McKinney, two of Jack's children, both in their teens then. They were in town to visit friends.

Cassie Westhead threw her arms around them.

"We couldn't stay away," John said. "We are family."

"That was very healing for us," Cassie says. "Since then we [Paul and Cassie, and Jack and Claire] have talked on the phone, exchanged letters, and seen each other briefly. But we still need to get away together and talk it out. It needs to be done."

Contacted recently, McKinney took an honest look at his horrendous final days in Los Angeles.

"I thought I was fine," he says. "I thought Buss was being mean, but he knew what he was doing. I didn't know what I was doing. He was a businessman running a very successful business and he had to make a decision. It was not made as clearly as I would have liked, heaping more hurt on me. But it was a good decision, though at the time I thought it was horrible.

"I was very silly. I stupidly blamed him for my hurt. I was jealous of Paul. I couldn't see clearly. I didn't have good sense. All I knew was, poor little Jack was hurt and I thought everyone was against me."

6.

The Point of Contention

WITH the exit of Jack McKinney, one crisis involving close friends had been resolved, however awkwardly.

But there was another pair of close friends on this team, and their crisis was just beginning.

Off the court Magic Johnson and Norm Nixon were a familiar duo on the disco scene. On the court they could make pretty good music together, too, as a starting backcourt perhaps unrivaled in the league.

Magic was the point guard supreme. Nixon could also handle the ball. He had done so before Magic arrived. He did so when Magic was out resting, or injured, or double-covered, or simply happy to give up the ball to Nixon in a system that had been designed to let the pair be interchangeable. That's the way both liked it.

But it was Nixon who always had to make the adjustments, who had to step in or step aside, depending on the situation. It wasn't easy. But it wasn't anything new for Norm. He had been in that situation, it seemed, all of his career.

Norm Nixon just couldn't fall asleep. He tossed and turned, but the nightmare wouldn't go away.

Roland Jones, senior shooting guard for Duquesne University, was lost for the year, having broken a foot earlier in the day.

Until then life had been going real smooth for Nixon, Duquesne's junior guard out of Macon, Georgia. Playing the point, he had broken the school assist record as a freshman. With Jones carrying the scoring load, Nixon had provided additional offense when needed, averaging a little over 10 points his first year and just over 14 in his second.

But now Jones was gone and, with the season starting the

next day, there was only one place to shift the offensive load. I've got to carry this whole team by myself, Nixon kept muttering to himself in the darkness of his dorm.

That he did. But the nightmare turned out to be a dream.

Duquesne won that first game behind Nixon's 38 points. As the season progressed he learned how to be a big scorer while still dishing off the ball and keeping the offense flowing. He broke his own assist mark, then did it again as a senior in a year in which he also scored 661 points, one shy of the school record.

Nixon had learned to be a complete guard. Any doubts he may have had about his ability to make it to the pros were erased the summer before his senior year. The Boston Celtics were staging a summer league for their own top draft choices and selected undergraduates. The undergrads were placed in a separate group, but the Celtics, after watching Nixon perform, put him in with their own rookies. After a summer-ending scrimmage, several people, unaware of Nixon's status, came up and told him, "Hey, man, you are going to make this team."

He was only 6–2, and that meant detractors as well, people who wondered if he could stop anybody in a league where the guards kept getting bigger and bigger. But nobody ever questioned his quickness. Opponents often looked like Wile E. Coyote chasing the Roadrunner as they helplessly watched Nixon blow past them for an easy layup or pull up and hit a 20-foot jumper at the top of the key. He could run an offense and he could often run the opposition into the ground.

That was enough for the Lakers. Owners of three first-round picks in 1977, they used the third to select Nixon, after picking forward Kenny Carr and guard Brad Davis.

Nixon quickly moved to the head of the new class. He made the starting lineup in training camp. He set a team rookie mark that season with 553 assists and became just the second Laker rookie to score over 1,000 points, the first being Jerry West, who was now Norman's coach.

By the time Magic Johnson arrived two seasons later, Nixon was an established star. He was coming off a year in which he had shot 54.2 percent, second best figure in league history, had tied the league record for steals with 201, and had finished with

737 assists, including one game of 19 and another of 17. His assist total was ten short of West's club record.

So for Nixon to hand the ball to an untried rookie, even an untried rookie like Magic, was no small sacrifice. But Norm wasn't worried. His experience at Duquesne had taught him how to be a scorer. Besides, he wasn't really surrendering the ball. The Lakers would run a two-guard attack under Jack McKinney, with Magic and Norm sharing the point-guard role.

Nixon found the ball back in his hands in November of 1981, but not under circumstances that gave him any pleasure.

Magic had come back from the championship season with even more polish and poise. A year of experience had begun to refine his game. Oh, the flash and dash were still there, but it was more controlled now, more calculated. He picked his spots as his growing knowledge of the league made him even better at picking apart opposing defenses. Showtime and Winnin' Time had become synonymous.

In an early-season game at Kansas City, Johnson brought the ball downcourt and made an incredible pass, through three Kings defenders, into the waiting arms of Jamaal Wilkes underneath the basket. Dan Marino never drilled a sharper pass. That Laker–Kansas City game, coming in the midst of the Royals' World Series battle against the Philadelphia Phillies, drew little attention in Kansas City or elsewhere. The game was not televised. Yet those who watched that magical pass that night can still remember it years later.

Magic had that effect on people. So when he was snatched from the lineup it was a horrible shock to an organization that was already uttering the word *dynasty* in a collective whisper.

Johnson, who had taken some hard shots to his left knee in preceding games, was guarding Hawkeye Whitney of the Kings in the second quarter of a November 18 Forum contest. Johnson tried to cut when he heard something pop.

The diagnosis: a cartilage tear in his left knee.

Norm Nixon was back on the point. He wasn't Magic; nobody was. But Nixon was awfully good. He compensated for his lack of size with his amazing quickness, his deadly, springy, fall-away jump shot, his talent for penetrating enemy traffic in the lane, and his ability either to run the fast break or play off another guard's lead. Nixon was a steady-eyed, cold-blooded, often spectacular player.

He was an intelligent player too. Able to accurately analyze and react instantly to almost any situation on the court, Nixon could communicate his next move to longtime teammates like Magic or Michael Cooper with a certain look or a nod of the head. Theirs was a language of vibrations, formed through years of familiarity and superior court sense.

"We were the best three in the NBA because we read each other so well," Magic says. "We all made each other better. We could move around and play different positions, do different jobs. There wasn't a moment on the floor we didn't know what each other was doing. If Norm gambled [on defense], I knew I had to come over and cover his back, and if I gambled, they would cover me. It was just a nice situation, to have someone covering your back at all times."

They were also close off the court, where Norm was also known to make a fancy move now and then. Well-liked by teammates, Nixon dressed with style and was popular with the ladies during his bachelor days. He was known to teammates as Savoir Faire, eventually shortened to Sav, and to writers as Dr. Lipstick. He had one of the most awesome, though unofficial, streaks in sports history. You won't find in any NBA stat book how many consecutive nights on the road he found female companionship, but his record was ultimately ended only by his marriage to performer Debbie Allen.

"I'm not talking about anything," he told a reporter when asked about his streak. "Sooner or later, this stuff will wind up in print."

Not unless you start getting it in the locker room at halftime, he was told.

"Yeah," Nixon responded, that savoir faire smile on his face, "well, when I retire, I might tell you a story about *that.*"

There weren't a lot of smiles for Nixon when Magic first went out. Unfortunately for Norm and the Lakers, Magic's injury coincided with a period when Nixon was going through a prolonged bout with tendinitis in his left knee. Through the first half of the 1980–81 season, he could count on one hand the number of pain-free games he enjoyed. The tendinitis robbed him of his quickness, thus costing him much of his effectiveness.

With Magic gone and Nixon slowed, the Laker fast break was, at times, reduced to a slow trot. The team lost five of its first eight games after Magic disappeared.

"These are rough times," Westhead said. "It is a learning process in losing a few."

Guard Eddie Jordan was obtained in a trade with the New Jersey Nets, but he was a reserve at best.

Michael Cooper started in Magic's place at first. Then Westhead tried shuffling his lineup, replacing Cooper with Butch Carter and starting forward Jim Chones with Jim Brewer. The move was designed, according to Westhead, to improve his bench strength, but there was a lot of grumbling about it. Stories of dissension from unnamed sources began appearing in the papers, but Laker officials figured they knew the name of the malcontent.

"If he (Nixon) doesn't stop talking," one club official said, "he'll talk himself right out of Los Angeles."

And indeed, that statement didn't seem like idle talk. Trade rumors involving Nixon became daily bulletins. One story had him going to Seattle for Gus Williams. Then it was Nixon to Cleveland for Mike Bratz. Then to Denver for David Thompson.

The Lakers denied all the rumors.

And gradually they faded. As did many of the Lakers' problems. Cooper and Chones got back in the lineup, Nixon got his game back, the Lakers got used to working together without their magic man and if it wasn't winnin' time, it was at least survivin' time. After splitting their first 22 games without Magic, the Lakers won 17 of their next 23 to wind up 28–17 in the games Johnson missed.

In all, it was 101 days before Johnson returned. You might have to go back to General Douglas MacArthur's return to find a more celebrated comeback. "Magic Is Back" buttons sprouted up all over the Forum. Johnson's grand entrance on the floor was the type usually reserved for royalty.

Several of his teammates weren't impressed. They grumbled

about the inference that this was a one-man team. Hey, they hadn't done so badly while he was gone. The club was on its way to 54 victories, only six fewer than the year before. In less than a year this team had gone from winnin' time to whinin' time.

By the time Magic returned, the Lakers were playing pretty decently. But now, while Johnson went through on-the-court rehabilitation, his teammates had to go through some readjustments of their own.

There wasn't much time. Only 16 games remained until the start of the playoffs. As it turned out, that wasn't time enough.

The man who figured to have the biggest adjustment was Nixon. Once again he must share the basketball. Nixon handled the ball about 75 percent of the time in Magic's absence. That figure would drop to about 30 percent with Johnson's return. With that in mind, Mike Littwin, Laker beat writer from *The Los Angeles Times,* interviewed Nixon just before the end of the regular season.

The day before the Lakers began the playoffs with a best-of-three miniseries against the Houston Rockets, Littwin's story ran with a headline that read, "Norm Nixon Remains a Spectacular Talent Who Has This Nagging Idea That He Isn't Being Used Correctly."

In the story Nixon was quoted as saying, "I'm not one of the chosen people. . . . Playing with Magic, I'm the No. 2 [shooting] guard. I'm not a No. 2 guard. It's not what I do best. This is not the best situation for me personally. If I can play point guard, I can be an All-Pro. I could be that on a lot of teams. . . . I thought Magic would come in and have to adjust to our game, but we had to adjust to him."

The story quoted teammate Jim Chones on Nixon: "He's the best point man in the league. It's rough on him."

Asked what he would do about his situation, Nixon said in the story, "What can I do? Go to the coach? Go to Jerry Buss? I live with it. It's not that big a deal. A lot of people would like to have my problems."

Oh, but it was a big deal. To Magic. When he read the story he was infuriated. He felt betrayed.

He and Nixon had become very close.

"Me and Norm on road trips," he says, "I don't care where it was, we were out! Norm liked to party and, at that time, I was a young buck and I liked to, too, so we was *out.* It was fun."

But no more.

Johnson kept his hurt feelings to himself as the Lakers were beaten by the Rockets, 111–107, at the Forum in the series opener.

But on a plane flight to Houston the next day his anger burst forth like a broken fire hydrant in a conversation with Rich Levin, beat writer for the Los Angeles *Herald-Examiner.* Magic felt unappreciated. He felt his teammates were ungrateful. And jealous of him and his success.

He still hadn't calmed down by the next day when other reporters surrounded him after a shoot-around at Houston's Summit. Johnson stood outside the towering structure on an otherwise peaceful spring afternoon and again spewed forth his pent-up feelings.

"If Norm Nixon feels that strongly about having the ball," Johnson said, "we'll get him a ball, put his name on it, and he can keep it under his arm during the game. It'll be his ball. I just want to win. If it takes him having the ball, fine. If that makes him more secure, fine."

Pretty strong stuff. But there was more.

Johnson also indicated he thought some players were jealous of all the commercial endorsements he was getting.

"I turn down some," he said. "The point is, we are going to have one All-Pro on the team and that's Kareem. I don't care about being All-Pro. I don't care about steals. I don't care about being Rookie of the Year. We can't all be All-Pros, but we can all be champions. I want to be a champion."

Looking back now, Johnson is sorry he spoke out, but not sorry about what he said.

"It was probably wrong at that particular time," he says, "instead of going up to Norm myself.

"But I felt I hadn't done anything. I feel when you give your all—I just tried so hard to be accepted, not to do anything wrong. Just come in, blend in with them, just do whatever it took. Then, to get that on the back end after I'm trying to break my neck just to help the team win, you kind of be upset.

"If he wanted the ball and he wanted to do that, then he should have just said, 'Hey, I need it.' I could have played down low. I did anyway. I just felt bad. Bad and mad."

Nixon, too, was mad. He never questioned any of the quotes attributed to him. But he did question what he felt was the inference that he couldn't play with Magic. And he questioned the *Times'* timing, printing the story on the eve of the playoffs, two weeks after he made his remarks to Littwin.

"They took something and turned it all around," says Nixon. "I didn't even want to give it any credibility when it came out by spending a lot of time on it because it was such bull to me."

"I thought the idea was very innocent," says Littwin, now a columnist at the Baltimore *Sun.* "Here was a great player like Nixon who was being completely overshadowed and resented playing the off guard because he felt the team wasn't making the best use of his talents. I had no idea anybody would be that upset about the story. I know it was said I wrote it to provoke something. It did have an impact on the team, but it was not meant to. I thought my story was basically sympathetic to Nixon, but I think it sparked some of the friction on the team at that time. There was a strong undercurrent on the team.

"Norm was a great player. It's too bad he had to be in the shadow of an even greater one. Nixon was a very good guard, but Magic is one of the greatest, a player for the ages. I think Nixon didn't understand what he was up against."

He quickly learned what he was up against. It didn't take long for word of Magic's anger to reach Nixon. Norman confronted his teammate in the locker room before Game 2 of the miniseries. The other Lakers kept going through the motions of pregame preparation, but their ears were all pointed in one direction as they stretched their tall frames to hear the conversation.

"Listen, listen, I *hope* you don't let this article go and affect your game," Nixon said, "because you should know me better than that. You know what I would say and wouldn't say. Hey, man, just play your game."

Johnson looked at Nixon, nodded slowly, but didn't speak. He was still mad.

"Magic had been away from the team and he came back and we were trying to make the team thing work," Abdul-Jabbar says. "It takes a while to get it in synch and we couldn't make the adjustment in time to get ready for the playoffs. Everybody was real disappointed and I think it was the disappointment more than anything else that was the problem. Nobody ever disliked Magic. Nobody ever failed to appreciate what he has meant to this team."

While the team was still in Houston, Magic gathered his teammates around him during a bus ride.

"I'm not trying to come in here and do all this with the publicity and stuff," he told them. "It's just something that happened. Hey, I don't write what they [sportswriters] say about me, or the articles. I'm just here to win.

"Look, we're *all* gonna get something if we win the championship—new contracts, endorsements, everything."

Nobody disagreed.

Yet the cheers and smiles of 1980 seemed about to crack in this basketball cauldron, with the '81 playoffs barely under way, and no one, not Westhead, not Buss, appeared able to prevent this team-shattering collision of egos.

Westhead tried. He got Nixon and Johnson back together in front of the whole team in the locker room before Game 2 and told them, "This is a bad time for all this. I don't know what happened or what sparked it, but we're trying to win."

In a Houston restaurant a group of L.A. reporters were finishing dinner. Someone suggested mud pie.

"No," one reporter objected, "the playoffs could go on for six weeks. If we start eating this way now, we could gain 20 pounds."

"Let's have the mud pie," insisted Mitch Chortkoff of the Santa Monica *Evening Outlook,* a man who schedules his diets for the off-season. "The Lakers could be out of the playoffs this weekend. If they go on, we can always adjust later."

It seemed as if the Laker season might indeed continue beyond the weekend when they beat the Rockets at The Summit in Game 2, 111–106.

In Game 3, at the Forum, it came down to Magic. That was unfortunate on this particular Sunday afternoon because Johnson, still troubled by his recent knee injury and perhaps by his injured feelings, was having a miserable afternoon. He had just missed two of three free-throw attempts and was only 2 of 13 from the field when he brought the ball downcourt following a timeout, with his club behind 87–86 and just 15 seconds to play in the game, and maybe the season.

The play was designed for Kareem to get the shot. Johnson drove the lane but didn't see an opening to get the ball to his center and so continued on his way to what he hoped would be a game-winning drive down the lane.

Instead, he found the towering figure of center Moses Malone in his path. Johnson, forced to improvise, put the ball up. It twirled softly in the air in the sudden silence created by 17,505 spectators holding their collective breath and came down three feet short of the rim. In the hands of Malone. An air ball to end the season. Moses dribbled to the other end, was fouled, and added the final points to an 89–86 victory.

Kill the book. Cancel the movie. Perhaps the only story left to write about the Lakers' dynasty of the '80s was an obituary. Their reign had clunked to a halt one year into the decade.

Now it was Buss's turn to be angry. To this day he calls that his toughest defeat. He figures it cost him between $2 million and $3 million in revenue and he felt some of that blame should be placed on the media.

He equated his feelings with the furious reaction, years earlier, of President Harry S Truman when his daughter, Margaret, had publicly played the piano and been attacked in the press for the quality of her performance.

"I really felt there was a feud between Magic and Norm," Buss says, "but that it never would have reached the level it did had it not been written about. It's hard for a guy who loves his team. They're like your children and you don't want people picking on them all the time."

The silence in the locker room was broken only by the sound of running water in the shower and the rustling of clothes as the players dressed. When the doors were opened to the press, reporters and sportscasters moved in and went quietly to the individual stalls where they conducted their interviews in low voices, the players doing more nodding and shrugging than talking.

Chortkoff leaned over to a reporter and whispered, "Now aren't you glad you had that mud pie?"

Buss walked around, a beer in one hand, going from player

to player, speaking softly and offering a pat on the back or a consoling word or two.

The players dressed quickly and left. Soon it was just Buss, Bob Steiner, and a handful of local newspaper guys.

"What did you think of the stories in the papers the last few days?" one reporter asked.

It was like tossing a lit cigarette into dry underbrush.

"You can get anybody to say something controversial if you ask the right questions," bristled Buss, quickly warming up to the subject. "I'm not saying those stories are why we lost, but at least 200 people have come up to me, angry about those stories."

Buss's anger at the loss was compounded by a recent confrontation with a member of the L.A. media who was writing negative stories about Buss because he wouldn't give a friend of that writer a job.

Buss looked around at the five reporters surrounding him in the locker room, his face growing red, his hand tightly clenching the beer can from which he no longer sipped, and then he zeroed in on Littwin.

"Who's a better writer, Scott Ostler or John Hall?" Buss demanded.

"What kind of a question is that?" Littwin asked. "What's that got to do with anything?"

Hall, a longtime L.A. columnist, had recently left the *Times* to go to *The Orange County Register*. His column had been taken over by Ostler.

"Just answer my question," Buss insisted.

"I don't see the point," Littwin said.

"Just answer!"

"I don't know. I'll say Scott."

"See," said Buss, his eyes widening, "what if I ran to John now and told him what you said? I could create a feud, couldn't I?"

Moving his hands above his head as if he were pointing out the words in a headline, Buss, his eyebrows arched, added, "Littwin Says Ostler Better Than Hall."

While the reporters looked at Buss and then at each other in disbelief at this performance, Buss moved to Levin.

"Rich, are you a better writer than Mike?"

"I don't know," said Levin, laughing and shaking his head.

"Oh, but you must think you are, and if I can get you to say so, then I've started another feud. See my point, how easy it is to start something? I believe that's what happened with Magic and Norm. You guys live in this city and I think you should be a little more supportive of this team."

Buss's tirade went on for nearly 45 minutes. He kept repeating over and over how easy it was to start a feud and how this whole thing had been blown out of proportion. It was the only time the owner had ever let his temper flare in public.

"I had been boiling for several days," Buss says. "If you're an outsider, you say, 'This is news and I have the right to read it.' This is the whole concept about a newspaper, right? But if what they're writing is affecting something, and you're one of the ones being affected, it's very hard to look at that objectively."

"He lost his cool," says Steiner, who watched his boss's explosion from a nearby locker stall. "Gene Upshaw [the former pro football player] had a great statement. He said, 'You can't win an argument with people who buy newsprint by the ton.' The media are quotemongers. 'He said so-and-so.' You run over to this guy and say, 'So-and-so said this.' That's journalism. One of my Steinerisms that an old sports editor told me is that you have all sorts of freedoms, but you don't have freedom *from* the press.

"Watching Jerry in that locker room, I was thinking, 'It's Custer.' I'm sitting there at Little Big Horn. I can't believe he did it. I'm not against what he said. Except you can't win that argument. Strategically, that's a bad thing to do. It was his moment, but it cost him a lot. He was vilified across the country by the media."

Afterward, Buss said to Steiner, "I know you told me not to do this, but I'm glad I did it."

According to Steiner, another matter on Buss's mind that day was what he considered unfair criticism of Kareem earlier in the season by Levin and Chortkoff.

"I can't stand being defenseless," Buss had told Steiner earlier. "You've got to be able to strike back and defend Kareem."

"You do that and you're going to lose," Steiner said.

"How about if we don't give them any press seats?" Buss said of those sportswriters he felt were unfair. "They can buy tickets, or maybe we'll make a good seat available. But why should I give them tickets when they're hurting me? And they're not being fair."

"You're being logical in an illogical situation," Steiner said. "You can't win."

Nixon feels people handed him much of the blame for the Game 3 loss to Houston, blamed him for creating dissension.

"They put that on me," he says. "Nixon upsets Magic. He can't play. I went home and said, 'Oh, not again. Do I have to listen to this all summer about how I upset Magic and he couldn't go play his game?' That's what it was like. This *old* guy—here I am, I've only been in the league two years longer than him— this *old* guy comes in and upsets Magic and he can't play his game in the playoffs.

"There's another time when I had to try to block all this stuff out and just keep playing."

Even a few weeks after the locker-room confrontation the organization's anger at the media had not subsided.

"Jerry feels that if he lets all of you in the locker room to have access to the players," Steiner told a reporter, "and this is all he gets—the whole thing with Magic—he may not let you in there anymore."

"I don't think he could do that," the reporter replied. "That would be a violation of NBA policy."

"Well, the way Jerry feels right now," Steiner said, "he just might challenge that policy."

He never did. He realized that among his freedoms as an owner was not freedom *from* the truth.

Soon after the playoffs Buss took Magic and Norm to Las Vegas for a few days. He met with each man individually and asked if he could play with the other.

"At times Norman was the best point guard out there," Magic told his boss. "He's fast. He can shoot. He can assist, play good defense. It would be really stupid for us to get rid of him."

Nixon was just as enthusiastic about the backcourt combination, again maintaining the media had "blown everything out of proportion."

Over a large Sunday brunch in his Vegas suite, Buss got the two guards together and asked again, "Can you play together?"

No problem, both men said.

One crisis resolved.

But for Magic the biggest crisis of his life was dead ahead, just beyond the peaceful summer.

7.

On the Firing Line

There is a tide in the affairs of men, which,
taken at the flood, leads on to fortune. Omitted,
all the voyage of their life is bound in shallows
and miseries.

—From *Julius Caesar,* by
William Shakespeare

PAUL WESTHEAD has taken the tide and it has led him
to fortune beyond his dreams. It has also led to misery
beyond his comprehension.

When Westhead was a Shakespearean scholar at the University of Dayton, St. Joseph's University, and LaSalle College, he
never dreamed the juxtaposition of joy and sorrow among the
Bard's works would also serve as a road map for Westhead's
future.

Westhead did a great job of juxtaposing basketball and literature for a long time. He played under Jack Ramsay at St. Joe's,
graduating with a bachelor's degree in English. He got his master's in English literature from Villanova and immediately found
a dream position at the University of Dayton, where he could
teach English literature and Shakespeare and also be an assistant
basketball coach.

A year later he got a head coaching job at Philadelphia's
Cheltenham High School. Westhead spent four years there, then
returned to the works of Shakespeare at St. Joe's, where he
was an assistant coach under Jack McKinney, and finally to La-
Salle, where he was head coach for nine years. He took LaSalle
to two NCAA tournaments and one NIT, and was named NCAA
District Two Coach of the Year in 1975 when his club finished
22–7.

●

In a league where David Halberstam's *The Breaks of the Game* was about as far into the literary world as most ventured, Paul Westhead was a refreshing change.

Late in one game his first season, with time running out and the Lakers behind, Westhead, quoting from *Macbeth,* told his players in the huddle, "If it were done when 'tis done, then 'twere well it were done quickly."

Magic Johnson blinked once, twice at the remark, then, nodding at Kareem, asked, "You want me to get it into The Big Fella?"

"Right on," replied Westhead, grinning.

After losing to Seattle in the opening game of the 1980 Western Conference finals, Westhead quoted Benjamin Franklin to his team, saying, "We must all hang together, or assuredly we shall all hang separately."

After a victory over the Sonics in that same series, Westhead, facing an army of media people, was asked what Magic had said during a key timeout.

"What did he say?" Westhead repeated, " 'A horse! A horse! My kingdom for a horse!' "

The laughs rippled through the press area. Battered by the trite phrases of coaches who talked about having their "backs to the wall," playing "like there's no tomorrow," and facing opponents who "put their pants on one leg at a time," reporters were enchanted by this man who sprinkled literary references throughout his interviews and avoided clichés as easily as he did long losing streaks.

When Westhead was asked how the Pacific Division race looked, he said the difference between the contenders figured to be as imperceptible as "the trembling of a leaf," a phrase of William Somerset Maugham. Westhead once compared the smooth, slingshot jumper of Jamaal Wilkes to "snow falling off a bamboo leaf."

But while he may have spoken like a scholar, he didn't always act like one. Afternoon three-on-three games between sportswriters and coaches on the road could result in scratches and bruises for the man Westhead was guarding. He was a fanatical jogger, more unswerving than a mailman. On one afternoon run in Indianapolis, braving 26-below temperatures and a driving snow, Westhead turned a corner, heard a loud toot, and looked up just in time to avoid a head-on collision with an oncoming railroad switch engine.

Looking and acting a lot younger than his 40 years, Westhead seemed destined for a long run in this role fate had found for him. But just below the surface there were ominous ripples almost from the beginning.

The Lakers had overcome the loss of McKinney and appeared to be cruising toward the 1979–80 playoffs. But that's not the way the players saw it. It seemed to them that their smoothly running machine had downshifted, and they wanted to know why.

"By the time we reached 60 or 70 games," Nixon says, "we were almost at a point where we were just standing around, giving Kareem the ball."

This wasn't the system McKinney had installed in training camp.

"Our offense had been so great," Magic says. "Nobody could stop us. We had a counter for everything that you tried to do defensively. But he [Westhead] was trying to fit in and make sure he was the coach, and we were trying to do what he wanted. So what was happening was, we were trying so much, we weren't playing our game. We didn't want him to come in thinking he didn't have the authority, or we weren't going to do what he said. But after a couple of weeks it wasn't clicking like it was clicking before.

"See, McKinney made Kareem a decoy. We would never use him until that was our last option. First, it was look for Jamaal for the 'J' [jumper]. If he wasn't open, then we'd pin down [screen] for Norm. He'd look for his 'J.' If he didn't have it, then we'll pick across for Kareem and bring him to the ball. He [Westhead] wanted to change that somewhat. Not really the offense, but change it to look for him [Kareem] *first.* You know, when you look for Kareem first, everybody in the building knows that you going in to him."

So the players called a locker-room meeting. After speaking among themselves, they invited Westhead in.

Nixon stood up first.

"We all have something we'd like to talk about," he said. "We'd like to go back to our old system. Our offense has broken down to the point where we are just four guys around the horn with Kareem moving in the middle. At the beginning of the year, we had all this cutting and movement.

"In essence, what has happened now is that Kareem has to work so hard and none of us are getting any shots or getting involved in the game. We are standing around and giving it to him so much that when the game gets down to the stretch, nobody really wants to shoot. I mean, if I don't shoot the ball for 25 minutes, I don't want to shoot it when it's five seconds and we're down by one. Know what I mean? Don't put that on me.

"The way things are, [Jim] Chones ends up being in the corner and he's our power forward. I mean, he can't get rebounds from there."

It was quiet in the locker room. Westhead was listening and nodding, but not saying anything.

Magic stood up and echoed Nixon. Then both men looked back at Kareem. They needed his support to pull this off. They got it as he spoke up, siding with them.

And Westhead nodded. They had his support too.

"Westhead was receptive because he'd just stepped into the job," Magic says. "He'd say, 'Kareem, what you think we should do?' He was looking for help from guys, which was great because it could have really backfired if he went another route and said, 'We're going to do it just like this and I don't want to hear anything else.' It was good. That whole playoff he was always saying, 'Hey, what do you think?' Or we'd come to the bench and he'd say, 'What do you think we should run this time?'"

The time came, however, when Westhead had a plan of his own, and he didn't ask anybody's advice. It was December of 1980. Johnson was out with his knee injury and the Lakers, with Chones starting at power forward and Michael Cooper at guard, were struggling. Westhead decided to shake things up by starting Jim Brewer up front and rookie Butch Carter in the backcourt, leaving Chones and Cooper to come off the bench.

No problem. The concept made sense. More punch off the bench, perhaps a more effective distribution of the talent.

But Westhead didn't tell Chones and Cooper, two somewhat sensitive and insecure players, of his plan until the last possible moment.

Big problem.

During the pregame introductions Chones asked Westhead who he was to guard.

No one, Chones was told. You're on the bench. Brewer is starting.

"Maybe the move was necessary," Chones says, looking back, "but he shouldn't have done it the way he did. I was pissed off. I wasn't upset because of the change. I was brought here to be a sixth man. With the sacrifices I was making, the least they could do was to tell me about it, but maybe I was being naive. He [Westhead] was just not sensitive about the players' feelings. He was the coach and we were the players and that was it.

"I think maybe they were panicking early by making that change. What I really think happened was that they had made plans to get rid of me before the start of that season, but they couldn't justify it when I got in shape and had a great camp."

Says Brad Holland, "A lot of players were very disappointed and upset at the way it was handled. Right there, some started losing respect for Westhead."

When the game was over Westhead was surrounded by reporters. What about this change? they wanted to know. Why are Chones and Cooper not starting?

Westhead smiled and replied, "What we need on this team right now is a better balance of energy."

Balance of Energy. The media picked up the phrase and ran with it. Westhead had simply changed his substitution pattern, but he couched his move in terms worthy of a politician. B.O.E. It looked good in print and, to the casual fan, it made him sound like a coach with a hot new theory.

Chones, however, wouldn't buy it in the form in which it was presented. Embarrassed by being told of the change out on the floor, in front of his teammates, Chones never really got over B.O.E. His performance off the bench never reached the level of the pre-B.O.E. days, and he was traded at season's end, along with Brad Holland and some draft choices, for Washington Bullets forward Mitch Kupchak.

B.O.E. created Westhead's second player crisis, the first being The Curious Case of Spencer Haywood.

"I feel confident. I was not the culprit in the Haywood thing," Westhead says. "It was just where Woody was coming from at the time. He began to cut into the players and do things they didn't like. I remember him coming to me and saying, 'I need my minutes. I'm a star. I need my minutes, my minutes.' For me, especially from my college background, that didn't mean anything to me. What do you mean you need your minutes? I'm trying to win games. Like, you know, don't bother me.

"But after being in the league a few years, I had more empathy for that feeling. Not that I would have dealt with it any differently. Not that I would have said, 'Oh, you need your minutes? Sure, here's your minutes.' But I would have understood it a little bit more.

"In Chones's case, I'm not trying to knock him, but he was never the starter Haywood was. Chones was always a support player, at least when I got him."

Chones wasn't the only player with a complaint. While the literary offerings spiced up many a sportswriter's story, they didn't always go over so well in the clubhouse.

"Before the Houston series in '81," Nixon says, "we watched this film he [Westhead] showed us about Bum Phillips [then the Houston Oiler coach] holding on to a rope, talking about how everybody on his team carried their part of the line. Everybody on our team said, 'We don't want to watch Bum Phillips. We want to watch some championship team. Houston never won any championship.'

"I also remember this story he told us about a man in a boat, and how you had to throw the rope out to him, and how we all had to pull him in. All this was happening around the Houston series, all that Bum Phillips kind of shit, and the man in the boat. You're getting ready to play for a championship, you don't want to hear about no man in a boat. You can use metaphors about getting effort out, sticking together, pulling together. But really and truly, when you get to the championship, you don't want to hear no shit about holding on to no rope.

"You want to hear about going out, kicking some ass on the court. 'Norman, don't you let that motherfucker score on you, don't you let him beat you downcourt.' 'Kareem, block some shots, play some defense.' 'Magic, push the ball.' 'Kurt, damn it, push the ball every time.' You want to get guys fired up. You don't want to be sitting there hearing, 'You've got a man out in the boat. You got him the rope. Now all of us got to get together and pull the rope.' Who wants to hear that shit?"

Said one Laker of Westhead: "He was the kind of guy, if you had him give you a talk before the game, when you left the locker room you didn't want to play."

Nixon had earlier been angered by what he felt was Westhead's insensitivity over a serious injury the Laker guard had suffered in Game 5 of the 1980 NBA finals.

Kareem's ankle injury got the headlines that night at the Forum, but Nixon sustained a more serious injury. He tore ligaments in a finger while punching a ball out of the hands of a 76er. He played in Game 6 despite the injury, then underwent surgery and spent much of the summer with his injured finger in a cast.

After the cast had been removed, Nixon bumped into Westhead one afternoon at the Forum.

"I'd like you to come over," Westhead said, "and play with our rookies to get ready for the season."

Nixon, who didn't even know if his damaged finger would be healed by the regular season, was incensed. Veteran stars don't play in rookie leagues, even when they have ten good fingers.

Nixon told Westhead sarcastically, "Sure, have Kareem pick me up on his way out there."

Westhead didn't ask again.

When the sparks had finally burned out after the fiery loss to Houston in '81, it became clear the Lakers could not win without an effective power forward. They were disenchanted with Chones because of what they felt was his mediocre play and poor attitude following the B.O.E. affair.

"Mark it down," Westhead told Buss. "If we don't get a power forward, we probably won't win this year."

Yet when a good power forward was dangled in front of their collective faces early that summer, the Lakers looked in another direction. Larry Nance was available when the club's

In the beginning: The early Laker teams were led by Elgin Baylor (above, airborne against Seattle), and "Zeke from Cabin Creek"—future Laker coach and general manager Jerry West (below, driving against Oscar Robertson).

Three views of Kareem: relaxing at practice, sky-hooking over Moses Malone, and applauding one of his most persistent detractors, Wilt Chamberlain. (*Practice and Wilt, Andrew D. Bernstein photo*)

Magic Johnson and Norm Nixon: backcourt mates, rivals, friends.
(*Jayne Kamin/Los Angeles Times*)

It was Jamaal Wilkes's fate to be invisible. Even his finest hour, when he scored a career-high 37 against Philadelphia in the title-clinching game, was obscured by Magic's playing center and scoring 42. (For Jamaal's face, see below.)

Paul Westhead and friend. "'Tis not my speeches that you do mislike/But 'tis my presence that doth trouble ye." *Henry VI, Part II.*

Pat Riley: suave, debonair, bubbly.

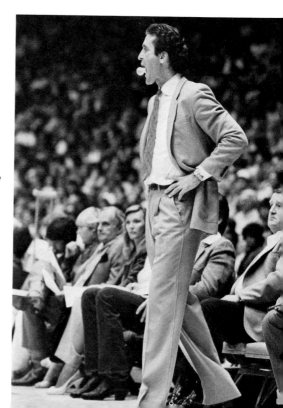

Jack Nicholson, a fellow Laker fan at his side, gives the choke sign to Boston fans during the 1984 finals. (*Andrew D. Bernstein photo*)

So you wanna be a basketball star? Magic Johnson meets the press during the 1984 finals. (*Andrew D. Bernstein photo*)

Michael Cooper (left) swoops down on the basket for one of his thunderous dunks. Kurt Rambis (below) in a typical pose—crashing to the ground against Philadelphia. James Worthy (below left) on defense against Larry Bird.

Jerry Buss, with the championship trophy after the defeat of the Boston Celtics in the 1985 finals. (*Andrew D. Bernstein photo*)

No. 1 pick, the nineteenth overall, came up. Instead, the team went for guard Mike McGee of Michigan. And after Westhead left, fingers were pointed at him as the man who insisted on drafting McGee over Nance.

As time went on it became an increasingly unpopular choice. While Nance became, at times, an awesome power forward for the Phoenix Suns—just what the Lakers had been looking for—McGee, who had set two all-time Big Ten scoring marks while at Michigan, never did become a full-time starter for the Lakers. He was instant offense off the bench, a good offensive rebounder, and eventually became a good defensive player, but it took him several seasons to adequately learn the Laker offense and he never really fit in.

One day, after a particularly frustrating session, with McGee stumbling through a team workout at New York's Madison Square Garden, Riley, by then the coach, threw up his hands as everybody was walking off the court and said loud enough for the whole squad to hear, "You know, I keep calling, 'Mike McGee, Mike McGee,' but there's never anybody home."

McGee turned and said earnestly, "I'm usually home, Coach. What time you been calling?"

In the summer of 1981 the player Westhead and others in the organization were pushing for was Mitch Kupchak, the Washington Bullets' tough and talented power forward who had leapt into the free-agent market.

Buss is philosophically opposed to signing free agents. "It's almost like kidnapping," he says. "I don't like getting involved in negotiations between another player and his owner." But Buss was desperate this time, so he agreed to pursue Kupchak.

Buss made him a then-astronomical offer—$5.6 million over 14 years, including seven nonplaying years—that Washington, it seemed, didn't have the resources to match.

"The moral vibrations from what I had done bothered me," Buss says. "I felt kind of bad about it. It left me with a bad taste in my mouth. So I compensated the Bullets more heavily then I probably had to."

He sent Chones, Brad Holland, a 1982 second-round draft choice, and a 1983 first-rounder to Washington in exchange for the 6–10, 230-pound Kupchak.

Buss had placed his money, and his prestige with his fellow owners, on Kupchak's large shoulders. He could have had Nance cheaper, and without having to dirty his hands and prick his conscience in the free-agent market.

Just before the start of the 1981–82 season a reporter asked Buss about the team's prospects.

"Is Westhead a real genius?" Buss said. "We'll find out. He asked me to get the talent. He wanted it this way. Now we'll find out what he can do."

It didn't take a genius to realize what was expected of Westhead. But he wasn't worried.

"That which does not kill me makes me strong," Westhead told his players at the start of preseason camp, quoting Victor Frankel, a World War II concentration camp survivor.

The first item in Westhead's overall plan to make his team stronger was to perfect its halfcourt offense. Houston had shut down his team's running game in the disastrous miniseries and the Lakers, forced into a halfcourt situation, didn't react well.

"That's partially because we were not ever as good in our halfcourt game, the Lakers are still not," Westhead says, "and also partially due to the rough edges of the return of Magic from his injury, and what that did to our timing.

"But I worked on the halfcourt game more to say, 'When we get into the next playoff, we don't want to get burned by the same problem we had last year.' Only a fool would do everything the way it was and then wind up in the playoffs and say, 'Oh gee, *now* what are we going to do? They're holding the ball on us again.' In my opinion the best time to correct that was on jump street, right from the very beginning.

"That was the sum and substance of this radical change that supposedly I was involved in."

To the players, and to Buss, it seemed a lot more radical. At the start of the 1981–82 season *Sports Illustrated* ran a shot of Westhead posing as the teacher in a classroom with the players sitting at student desks.

Some players resented the image presented by the photo. They were pros, they told themselves, they had played this game a bit. But the message they saw going out to the nation was that this brilliant basketball genius was going to teach *them* the game. They didn't feel they needed a teacher. And that's just the way some of them looked at Westhead, as a teacher, a college coach out of place in the pro game. They saw it in the pregame talks, which seemed too much like classroom lectures to some of them. And they saw it in the B.O.E. affair and other situations where they felt they were expected to simply follow orders, no questions asked. That was fine for college, but they were chafing at what they saw as an extension of that discipline into their pro careers.

So in this atmosphere, the introduction in training camp of what some players labeled the Paul Westhead Offense, with its emphasis on funneling the ball to Kareem in the middle, was not exactly greeted with enthusiastic high fives.

Says Magic: "Right at the start of camp, he [Westhead] said, 'We runnin' something new.' We said, 'Okay.' You know, you always get things changed. But this—it killed everybody. It killed Jamaal, Norm, myself. Took us right out. Here's Kareem averaging 30-something points a game and everybody else almost not even reaching double figures.

"Once we got down the court, it was four guys around the perimeter, and Kareem following the ball. That means Jamaal is standing now, Norm is standing, I'm standing, and Jim [Chones] is standing. No throwing. No making the defense move. We were predictable.

"Once he [Kareem] got it, he would kick it out with five seconds left on the [24-second] clock. Now we've got to make a move just to get the ball back up. It was throwing everybody off. If Jamaal didn't get it on the break, he didn't get it. And Jamaal, at that time, was at his peak. He was like, boom!

"We had so many options off that [old] offense. But now we *standin'*. Westhead structured us. You couldn't freewheel. We didn't get those easy hoops that we used to do. What we used to kill teams with was the fact either me or Norm could handle the ball. You couldn't do that no more. He just made me exclusively the ballhandler."

The many-optioned offense became a joke among some of the players and spread to the media. Before a Forum game a man came to midcourt to sing "America the Beautiful" and one courtside writer whispered to another, "That song was the third option."

Nixon was disgusted with the whole scene.

"If they cut Magic off," he says, "the whole offense broke down. Westhead wanted Magic to handle the ball *every* time, wanted Jamaal on the left-hand side of the court *every* time, and I was on the right-hand side of the court *every* time, regardless of what happens.

"I had never had anybody tell me not to ever handle the ball. Don't *ever* handle the ball? What do you want me to do? That was the part that stunned me. That was detrimental to my game because my future in this league wasn't at off guard. It'll always be at point, even though I could play off. And to play in a system where they were saying, 'Don't you *ever* handle the ball,' to me, that was career-threatening.

"I think he was in awe of Kareem more than anything else."

Yet Kareem, too, saw problems.

"He was establishing his thing with the team," Kareem says. "I'm always there, and it's a lot easier for everybody if they just use me when they have to and run most of the time. He had some other ideas. He wanted to set up a few more things. He had a whole lot of play sets, but the problem was, he left the ways that we were successful, and that made it hard for us to get things done. It was like wearing somebody else's suit. You're not going to look that great.

"I didn't say that much. I appreciated what Paul had done for us when Jack got hurt. I figured he had the right to try his own thing. He *was* the coach. They had the confidence in him. I'm just an employee. It doesn't matter what I think."

Magic tried to talk to Westhead.

"Hey, we best at just *going,*" Johnson said.

"This is what we run," responded Westhead firmly.

"Fine," Magic replied.

End of argument.

"This isn't the kind of business," Nixon says, "where you can sit down and run your coach through a bunch of questions and answers. You've just got to go out there and do what he says to do. You can question him, but you can't be telling the coach what offense to put in, what he better run, what he can't run. We knew what was happening, but what were we going to do about it?"

Westhead wasn't totally oblivious to his players.

"Paul was dealing with big egos," Jim Brewer says. "It was tough for him to decide whether or not to call traveling on a player in a practice. Sometimes he would just end the practice [rather than blow the whistle on one of the Lakers].

"The season before, we were loose. It was like, 'This is beautiful. You can say what you want.' You could throw in your two cents. Your input was accepted, sometimes even solicited. The next year, it was a tight ship. The lines of communication got closed."

Says Brad Holland of Westhead: "He tried to implement his own system. I sense he felt he had to prove himself. His attitude was, 'I'm gonna show everyone we can win my way.' Was it different [than the previous season]? No question. It was, 'I'm asserting myself. *I'm* the man.'"

Westhead had his own ideas about the problems at the start of the '81–82 season.

"Magic Johnson, it was very evident from the first stages of training camp, was not ready," Westhead says. "He was having trouble beating fourth- and fifth-round draft choices in summer go-abouts before training camp. I know Magic played that summer and got 48 points against Isiah [Thomas] up in Michigan and all that kind of stuff. But it was clear to me and, I think, to anyone who was around that Magic hadn't gotten his legs back, didn't have his feel back. He was a guy who was still in the hunt to return from his knee injury.

"My evaluation was, he was very, very uptight about the whole scene, any scene. You could say, 'We're going to use a no-play offense. Everybody do what they want.' Or you could say, 'We're going to call a play every five seconds and change it every five seconds.' Whatever it was, Magic was not ready and therefore nothing was going to work until he got himself through X amount of games and got his legs back in shape.

"Nixon, I think, is another story. Nixon was always kind of angry, about a lot of things. And if they change the play system, he figured, 'Hell, that's another thing I can be angry about.' He was angry about Magic's role on the team, his role on the team, Kareem was always a problem to him. Whatever you did.

"What Nixon was was a No. 2 guard, a shooting guard with Magic handling the ball. If you want to say you're forced on the baseline, a lot of shooting guards would give their right arm to be a shooting guard with Magic Johnson handling the ball and coming down for you."

Already unhappy with the new offense, the starters grumbled louder when they found themselves playing up to 40 minutes apiece in exhibition games. They'd be worn out, they figured, before the long season even started. Westhead, they decided, was determined to turn this thing around early, no matter the cost.

On opening night the Lakers had a perfect chance to begin vindicating themselves for the previous season. Their opponent was the party-spoiling Houston Rockets.

But again the Lakers lost, this time 113–112 in double overtime.

Up in his royal skybox, Buss was livid. And worried. "What's going *on?*" he muttered. "I just don't like this."

The feelings of frustration and anger came rushing back to Buss. Suddenly it was last spring all over again. He had spent a lot of money since then for Mitch Kupchak and yet here Buss was, back in his box, watching those damn Rockets celebrate another victory over his Lakers. The only thing that seemed to have changed was his payroll.

In the locker room Buss cornered Nixon, with whom he had a close relationship.

"Why are you playing that way?" Buss asked. "When you get down the court, why don't you go on in [drive the lane] like you used to? What's happening?"

Nixon smiled. "Well, this is the new offense," he told his boss.

It was definitely new to Buss.

"Will you diagram it for me and tell me what's different about it?" Buss said.

Nixon was delighted to do so.

From there Buss went to Pete Newell, West, Sharman, Magic, Dr. Charles Tucker (Magic's mentor from Michigan), and finally to Westhead. What Buss heard wasn't making him feel any better about the situation.

"The answers all seemed like double-talk to me," Buss says. "Theoretically, we were going into a more pure fast break, but nobody was fast breaking. And as I talked to people it was coming out more and more and more that this was just an entirely new offense.

"After talking to all these people I finally came to a conclusion, just myself without being told, that I thought explained what was happening. People had criticized Paul—he felt—so severely because he had used McKinney's offense in the world championship. And then, by winning that championship, he had been made the coach.

"So he went to a different offense which would be clearly recognized as his own. I felt that he was therefore proving *his* point with *my* team. I felt he was on a crusade. My life was on the line, he came in as an employee and I felt he was saying, 'I'm going to use this team to prove my point.' And he had done this without consulting me. I just didn't go along with it. I had specifically hired McKinney to begin with because that's the way I wanted my team to play.

"If Westhead had come in and said, 'Hey, I'm really thin-skinned about this criticism I'm getting. I'd like to try a whole new approach to this thing,' I probably either would have talked him out of it or gone along with it. I would have understood it better. But that's not what happened. What happened was, he just did it."

Westhead categorically denies that theory.

"Not true," he says, "not true because the Jack McKinney involvement was a year and a half earlier. It wasn't like it was the next season."

Pat Riley remains, to this day, Westhead's staunchest defender, just about his *only* defender in the Laker organization.

"I think he handled the [McKinney] situation beautifully," Riley says. "He directed and organized and prepared and did everything he had to do to keep the team on track while they were waiting [for McKinney's return].

"But by the time the second year comes around, you have to start developing who you are. You can't coach somebody else's system. You can't coach something you're not. Your philosophy and your personality will come out, and Paul's did. And mine did too after *my* first year. I started to change things."

But back in the fall of 1981, Buss didn't like the changes he was seeing. And the one man who didn't seem to get that message was Westhead.

"I tried to tell West and everybody about it, that I didn't like it," Buss says. "But as they kept talking to Westhead, it seemed he became very defensive, *very* defensive. According to my people, he would not take any criticism or direction from them at all."

Buss heard reports of an increasingly distant head coach, not communicating well with either West or Sharman. He heard reports of a man who demanded a personal secretary.

"He didn't want other people's secretaries knowing what his did," Buss says. "I guess he felt that someone was passing some information along the lines. Every coach that comes in ends up with the same old Laker secretary. I mean, you don't fire the secretary. Mary Lou [Liebich, the main cog in the administrative offices] has been here a million years. He wanted someone loyal to him. He began to box it off. He kind of isolated himself."

The lines of communication between Westhead and his players were also becoming garbled with static—from both sides.

Shortly after the start of the season Westhead went to Magic.

"Your rebounds are down," Westhead said.

"Yeah, I hear. I know," Magic replied. "You got me playing 30 feet from the basket. I got to stop the [other team's] break."

"I want you to go in and get the offensive rebounds."

"Coach Westhead, I can't run 30 feet in to try to get an offensive rebound, *then* try to be back on defense at the same time."

"I don't want to hear this," Westhead replied.

The Lakers flew up to Portland for the second game of the season and lost 102–100. Late in the first half, Abdul-Jabbar, seeking some operating room in the high post, inadvertently bumped into his new teammate, Kupchak, sending the power forward crashing to the floor.

That was the two-game season in microcosm—a team stumbling out of the starting gate, flailing around in search of cohesion.

In the locker room after the game no one wanted to point fingers. So they pointed reporters elsewhere.

"You been around long enough to know what's happening," Magic said, motioning sportswriters over to Nixon's stall for further elucidation.

Nixon just smiled and looked in the direction of Wilkes.

"It just doesn't feel right yet," Wilkes said.

At the team hotel Chick Hearn told reporters, "In a few weeks you guys might have a really big story to write."

The tension was everywhere.

In the hotel restaurant a group of sportswriters were discussing the team's problems when in walked Riley, the assistant coach. In the past he would frequently sit with writers and talk about the team off the record, supplying useful insight. On this particular night he had barely sat down and ordered a sandwich when the questions started. What is going on? How long are you guys going to continue with this new offense? Has Westhead lost control?

An instant later it was Riley who lost control.

"What is this?" he said, his voice rising in indignation. "We used to be friends. We could sit around and talk. Now I show up and I'm subjected to a grilling."

Bill Sharman had gotten married earlier that week on the Palos Verdes Peninsula to the former Joyce McLay. At the reception Cassie Westhead was speaking to a few of the other wives in the organization as they stood around the wedding cake.

"Next year on our wedding anniversary," Cassie said, "we want to celebrate by repeating the ceremony with our friends around.

"That is," she added with a weak smile, "if we're still here. You never know in this business."

Amen.

The Lakers hit a new low almost two weeks later in San Antonio. They were blown out 128–102, dropping their record to a shocking 2–4. In the locker room Magic stared at the sad story on the stat sheet, crumpled it in a ball, and slam-dunked it on the floor.

"I've never been on a losing team in my whole career," he told reporters, speaking softly, his voice filled with anguish. "I've never been beat like that. Never. I don't know what's wrong.

I'm just trying to keep myself together. People ask what's wrong. Nothin'. I ain't gettin' *any* shots. I can only take the shots if I get them. Tonight I got a lot of my points on rebounds and tip-ins."

He was asked again, for what seemed to him like the millionth time, about the New Offense.

"I do what I'm supposed to do, whether I believe in it or not," he said. "I do what I'm supposed to do."

The next afternoon the Lakers flew to Houston. At the airport most of the players boarded the team bus, its motor idling as the Laker traveling party boarded and the bags and equipment were loaded.

Johnson, still in a deep funk from the night before, walked slowly to the bus, wearing his stereo headphones, singing along with the music soothing his troubled mind. It was his only refuge. The laughing and joking with teammates was a thing of the past. Now some of the players weren't even speaking to each other. The days of players going to dinner or a show together were, temporarily at least, over. Everybody had retreated to his own world.

Instead of boarding the bus, Magic walked across several lanes of busy traffic, that slow off-the-court gait of his halting cars and busses, and stopped on a narrow traffic island, right in the middle of the main thoroughfare of Houston Intercontinental Airport. He plopped himself down right there, shut his eyes, turned his head skyward, and turned up his music, trying to let the warm sun and the cool sounds revive his flagging spirit.

"Man," Magic told himself, "we've only played six games. I've got to go through 76 more games like this. O-o-o-h man, it's going to be a hard season."

Westhead? He didn't notice Magic from his spot by the door of the bus where he was standing with Riley, waiting for the luggage to be loaded, intently diagramming plays, lost in his own world.

"I was hurtin'," says Magic, who couldn't have picked a more symbolic resting place for himself at that moment than an island. "You know, I can't be an individual. I feed off of everybody else. That's what gives me my strength. The only reason I can play is because the team gives me strength, being around the guys."

On November 14 the Lakers beat Phoenix for their third victory in a row and moved above .500 at 5–4.

One Laker, speaking off the record, told a sportswriter, "The only bad thing about winning is we're keeping him [Westhead] alive."

Not for long.

The following evening, a Sunday, Buss asked West and Sharman to come to his office prior to that night's game against the Indiana Pacers.

The owner folded his hands in front of him, looked each man in the eye, and said, "Let me start off the meeting by saying that I've reached a decision that I would like to fire Paul Westhead. However, there's three of us here and if the two of you want to talk me out of it, I'll let you talk me out of it. But you're going to have to talk. You're not going to be able to be neutral. You're going to have to stand up and say, 'That's the wrong thing to do.' And I'm going to need it from both of you, because if either one of you agrees with me, then that's the way it's going to go."

Says West now, "I don't really like to talk about that period. But I'll tell you, I don't like changes in teams. It was just something he [Buss] wanted to do. He felt the team was going to be better served going in another direction.

"Even though we had a winning record, we'd been struggling with our play. . . . It was early in the season when it's really difficult, I think, to make an assessment of the team. We [West and Sharman] expressed our concern about doing something that soon, because the season hadn't been going on very long."

"Let me ask you this," Buss said, "if I bring in Paul and say, 'Paul, let's let bygones be bygones and get your ass back in the original offense,' what do you think the effect would be?"

Neither West nor Sharman thought Westhead would agree to junk his own offense.

"Well, if neither one of you are trying to talk me out of it," Buss said, hearing what he wanted to hear, "I can only assume that you're in agreement with me. Should we fire him now and go with the assistant coach, or should we look around and see who's available?"

"Let's give it a week," Sharman said, "and I'll find out who's available. I'll make some overtures."

Both he and West felt a little relief when Buss agreed to give Westhead a little more time. Maybe it would still turn around.

The trio discussed possible successors to Westhead that night. Al Bianchi, a Phoenix Suns assistant, became their No. 1 choice, assuming he was interested and available.

At halftime of the Lakers–Pacers game, Bob Steiner went up to Buss's box.

"What happened in the meeting?" Steiner asked.

"Well, I told them I saw A, B, and C were wrong," Buss replied, "and they gave me D, E, F, G, and H as well. Essentially, there are too many things wrong to call Paul in and say, 'These are things we think you've got to change.' If it had been just a couple of problems, I'd do that and try it out. Everybody was of the opinion that I ought to make a coaching change."

"When?" Steiner asked.

"I'm not sure whether they've asked for five days or five games," Buss said. "And I don't know why I've agreed to that."

"Is anything going to change if we win the next five games?" Steiner said.

"No."

Down on the floor the Pacers were trotting back on the floor for the second half, led by their coach, Jack McKinney.

As the jetliner leveled off above the Los Angeles Basin, leaving LAX and banking toward the east, the view from every window was breathtaking. The sun had just set on this early winter evening, bathing the Hollywood Hills on the left and the Pacific Ocean on the right in a beautiful reddish haze.

But in his seat, halfway back on the left-hand side, Paul Westhead wasn't in the mood to enjoy sunsets. It had been two days since the Buss–West–Sharman meeting and Westhead still wasn't aware his Laker coaching career had been nearly terminated. Still, he knew things weren't right and that made him tense.

It was a two-hour flight to Salt Lake City, where the Lakers would play the Utah Jazz the following night. The sky was turning dark as the stewardesses started handing out snacks to each passenger. Paul Westhead had been on enough airline flights in his life to know large meals are usually served only on longer flights. For a two-hour hop you get a crummy pastrami sandwich and a little fruit cup if you're lucky.

Nevertheless, when the small sandwich was served, he whirled in his seat to face trainer Jack Curran, seated in the next row back.

"Is this all you get to eat?" Westhead asked in an exasperated tone.

Curran, who had about as much to do with serving the meals as he did with flying the plane, shrugged helplessly.

"If I had known it was going to be this small," muttered Westhead to no one in particular, "I'd have eaten at home."

Westhead got his large meal in Salt Lake City. He ate at the hotel restaurant, sitting alone in a corner.

The next night, at the Salt Palace, the Lakers were on their way to their fifth straight victory, but they still couldn't get the offense into high gear. It was still Slowtime instead of Showtime.

With seconds to play and the Lakers clinging to a slim lead, a timeout was called. Magic sat on the end of the bench and looked over to a team attendant for some water while Westhead was diagramming some new strategy.

Westhead looked up, saw Magic with his head turned away, and exploded. It was the second time that night the coach had noticed Magic looking elsewhere during a timeout.

"Damn it," Westhead said, "get in this huddle!"

"I am in the huddle," replied Magic, his voice rising a few octaves. "I'm right here."

"You are not paying attention!"

That's it, Magic thought, that's just it. I'm into the huddle, but I'm just not looking at him.

The Lakers hung on for a 113–110 victory, but almost blew it. As Westhead walked off the floor he was seething because he felt Magic had looked confused on the court in those closing seconds, a direct result, in Westhead's mind, of his failure to pay attention in the huddle.

Westhead stared at the large figure of Magic walking slowly

in front of him. What should he do? Westhead asked himself. He was annoyed, really annoyed, at his point guard.

"It was something that had a specific application to him and him alone," Westhead says, "and I felt that I should not wait for the next day or a practice session to address this.

"But also—and I felt very strong about this—he was such an important person emotionally and psychologically to this team that to address that in front of everyone immediately after the game would not be in his best interest."

Instead, Westhead caught up to his superstar as they entered the locker room and said, "Magic, I want to talk to you."

He led Johnson into an adjoining equipment room and shut the door. The quiet only heightened the tension. Only a few brooms and some dusty basketballs would be witness to the biggest confrontation of the night. Of the season.

Westhead, his eyebrows arched, his face red, his hands gesturing, looked up at Johnson. "You didn't pay attention one time-out," said Westhead in the stern voice he used to use to discipline his students, "and you did the *same* thing at the end of the game and almost cost us the game because you didn't know what we were doing. I don't want that to *ever* happen again."

"Hey," Magic said, "you might as well sit me down because I ain't being used anyway. Just sit me down."

"I don't want to hear that."

"Are you done?"

"Yes."

Those were to be the last words Magic Johnson and Paul Westhead would ever exchange as player and coach. The meeting had lasted 45 seconds.

Magic turned, stormed out, and marched back into the locker room, primed to explode with the accumulated frustration of the past few months. The other players were undressing and heading for the showers. None were aware of the Magic–Westhead meeting.

Johnson, staring straight ahead, muttered, "That's it. I've got to go."

No one heard him.

Magic seated himself at his locker stall and waited. He knew the next time he spoke those words, the entire basketball world would hear him. He didn't care.

Outside, the four L.A. beat writers—Randy Harvey of *The Los Angeles Times,* Steve Springer of *The Orange County Register,* Rich Levin and Mitch Chortkoff—were waiting for Westhead when a ballboy came by.

"The coach and Magic Johnson are in there," said the boy, pointing to the equipment room.

When the door of that room opened, however, Westhead walked out alone. Magic was already gone. The coach, fittingly enough, stood with his back against the wall and motioned the writers over to talk about the game.

One writer asked Westhead about the now-constant criticism of his new offense.

"The almond tree bears its fruit in silence," replied Westhead, smiling.

The L.A. writers turned and headed into the cramped locker room. Compared to the Forum, where there is ample space for players to dress, speak to reporters, and entertain a cast of Hollywood's finest, these were spartan quarters, barely room to tie your shoes, much less hold a private conversation. No secrets here.

Johnson was talking to Dave Blackwell, a Salt Lake City sportswriter who was unaware of the drama that was reaching its climax.

"Yeah, the key was Jamaal Wilkes's 26 points," said Magic, his voice soft, his manner polite. If he was a troubled man, he was also a good actor.

"Mag," Levin said, "what happened out there with you and Paul?"

"Just a minute, let me finish with this guy here first," replied Magic politely. Turning back to Blackwell, he asked, "Is that about it?"

"I think so. Thanks," Blackwell said.

As the Utah sportswriter started to walk away the four L.A. guys closed in. Blackwell now says jokingly that there are still skid marks on the floor where he made a sharp U-turn when he heard what Johnson had to say to the L.A. writers. Magic turned to them and, without a modicum of change in his voice, without a hint of emotion, made the blockbuster statement of his career.

"I can't play here anymore," he said quietly, staring straight ahead. "I want to leave. . . . I want to be traded. . . . I'm not happy now. . . . I haven't been happy all season. . . . I can't deal with it no more. . . . I've got to go in and ask him [Buss] to trade me."

"Earvin," Springer asked, "do you know what you're saying?"

Johnson never hesitated. "I know exactly what I'm saying. I haven't been happy all season. I've got to go. . . . Things haven't been . . . I don't know . . . I've seen certain things happening. I've sat . . . haven't said anything, but I've got to go. It's nothing toward the guys. I love them and everybody, but I'm not happy. . . . I'm just showing up. . . . I play . . . I play as hard as I can, but I'm not happy. . . . I'm not having any fun. . . . I just want to go."

Was Westhead the problem?

"Yeah, we don't see eye-to-eye on a lot of things. Me and him don't see eye-to-eye. It's time for me to go."

Go where?

"New York . . . Chicago. I'm going to talk to the man [Buss] tomorrow and see if a trade will happen."

By then Magic was the center of a scene that would have been comical had it not been so traumatic. The locker room had fallen silent and teammates were leaning over from their stalls, looking like actors in an E. F. Hutton commercial. When Johnson finished and the sportswriters turned to leave, the players turned back to their stalls in one fluid motion. No Laker fast break had ever been better choreographed. Some players acted as if they hadn't heard a thing and, when approached, feigned ignorance of the cause of Johnson's outburst.

"This was all about seven seconds after Magic and I had talked," Westhead says. "If he had walked into the shower first, he might have come out and said something entirely different."

But a shower wouldn't have washed away the problems. Magic was deeply disturbed over the situation. At least he had *finally* spoken his mind.

By the next morning everybody in the sports world would know the extent of those problems. One man would lose his job, another his innocence. It was a strange feeling for the writers, standing there in that locker room in the middle of the Utah desert with a story they knew would hit L.A. like an earthquake, shattering the image most fans had of the Lakers as a high-fiving, happy-go-lucky bunch of guys, one happy family, joking and jiving their way through the league.

As the writers left the locker room Randy Harvey, in his first season covering the team, turned to his colleagues and said, "I thought you guys told me nothing ever happens on this beat until the playoffs."

Once the writers were gone, a couple of players came up to Magic. "Man, you shouldn't have said that," he was told.

"Hey, I said it," Magic replied. "I'm going to take full responsibility myself."

He had to. Though several of his teammates shared his dissatisfaction and frustration, none of them would back him up publicly.

"They were scared to come forward," Magic says. "They wanted it, but they didn't say nothing. They were happy as long as they didn't have to say nothing."

Says Nixon, "I can't say nothing, cause if I say something, they would have probably thought I was behind the whole thing, that I *made* Magic say those things. When something like that happens, I just try to stay away from it.

"Let me tell you something—anybody else in the NBA had done what Magic had done, they'd have run him out of the league. He and Larry Bird at that time were probably the only two who could get away with something like that."

Was Magic wrong to speak out?

"For him, maybe not," Nixon says. "If he wanted it resolved, he knew how to get it resolved. Maybe he thought, 'If I say it, he [Westhead] is gone.' He said it and Westhead was gone. I couldn't say that. I mean, if it was me, I wouldn't have said that."

Would Kareem?

"No, I wouldn't have," Abdul-Jabbar says, "but I'm not him [Magic]. There were other ways to deal with it that could have saved him a lot of aggravation and embarrassment. He didn't want to talk to anybody about it until after the fact and, by that time, it was too late to keep any kind of lid on it."

The four writers found Westhead outside the locker room and told him what had occurred. He responded with a shrug of the shoulders.

Would he talk to Magic that night?

"Perhaps."

How would he feel about Magic being traded?

"I hope that would never take place."

Westhead then disappeared into the locker room. He didn't say a word to Magic.

"My opinion at that moment was that Magic Johnson was wrong in what happened in the game," Westhead says. "He obviously responded emotionally to what he thought was the embarrassment of being told off.

"I had no sense that my job was on the line. How would you have a clue? Why should I? Why would I? We had won a world's championship, we had won 54 games the next year, and here we are 11 games into the season. Why would you have any suspicion that you're going to get fired? What had you done to deserve *that*?

"Magic was very touchy, but that's nothing unusual when Magic's not feeling well. But there was never any real big problem between Magic Johnson and I, so I had no reason to think, 'Gee, Magic's having a problem and my firing will be the end result.'

"Obviously, in retrospect, I was very naive, but I was the last to know. It wasn't like I had two meetings with people at the Forum and they said, 'Hey, you better be careful as you proceed in the next week or two.'

"My opinion was, it was time to involve Jerry Buss and have Buss either privately and/or publicly set Magic straight and tell him, 'This is the way it's going to go. Don't make comments and blow up at what the coach is doing.' The time was appropriate that some standards of operation be established."

Westhead sat in the front of the team bus on the ride back to the hotel. The players, sitting toward the back, whispered among themselves, "He's gone now! Paul's gone now!"

In the darkness Kareem leaned over to Magic and said softly, "Hey, Earvin, I'm here to talk if you want to talk."

Magic didn't.

In L.A. the Kings were skating across the Forum ice when several phones on press row began ringing almost simultaneously. Hockey writers picked up the receivers, listened intently, then grabbed their notebooks and headed for Jerry Buss's box.

Bob Steiner wondered what all the fuss was about. Nothing was happening in the game.

The writers wanted Buss's reaction to Magic's outburst. Buss, fuming inside when informed of the Utah explosion, tried to maintain a calm exterior.

"I think everybody is very frustrated," he told the hockey writers. "The main thing you learn the longer you're in sports is, don't overreact, don't panic. Sit back and talk to everybody, then make the moves that are necessary, based on what you've discovered.

"I think there's a lot of frustration. It wasn't Magic's, it wasn't Paul's, it wasn't mine. Everybody's in the same boat. We're all unhappy with the same situation. We feel we should be winning by 10 to 15 points. We're not playing well."

What would he do now?

"An infinity of moves are possible. Which ones to choose, I don't know."

He knew one thing: He wished like hell he'd gone with his first instinct and fired Westhead after that meeting the previous Sunday.

Back in Utah, in a bar at the top of the team's hotel, an angry Pat Riley sat nursing a drink. He thought Westhead might be fired, and that would mean he'd probably lose his job too. And he didn't think it was fair.

"Things have really changed," Riley grumbled to a few writers. "In the old days a player just worried about playing, and never tried to get involved in coaching decisions, at least not publicly."

Riley lowered his head and stirred his drink.

A friend came over, put his arm on one of Riley's shoulders, and said, "Don't worry, Pat, you never know how things are going to turn out."

The friend was Utah Jazz assistant coach Bill Bertka. These two men would wind up leading the Lakers to their greatest glory.

Down in his hotel room, Westhead phoned Bill Sharman in L.A.

"Hey, we've got to get some things straightened out here," Westhead told him.

A meeting with Buss was scheduled for the next day.

In his room, Magic called his parents and then Dr. Tucker back in Michigan to tell them what he had done. He talked well into the night, getting the much-needed sympathy from home that he hadn't gotten from his teammates.

Reserve guard Eddie Jordan was the first one on the bus the next morning for the trip to the airport. The next man on was Springer.

"Hey, Steve," whispered Jordan from the back of the bus, "today would be a good day to lay low, wouldn't it? The shit's really going to fly, isn't it?"

"Right both times, Eddie," he was told.

At the airport Chortkoff ran over to his fellow writers in mock horror and said, "They've just made a horrible mistake!"

"What's that, Mitch?" asked one reporter.

Replied Mitch, "They just gave Westhead a boarding pass that says 'Coach.' "

In L.A., Steiner got a call from Pete Newell.

"For crissake," Newell said, "don't fire him now. You know you're going to put the burden on Magic."

Steiner didn't agree. "If we'd kept Westhead," he says now, "we would have been taking a bad situation and making it worse because you ultimately have to fire him. If you fire him anytime that year, the next year, whenever, unless you get rid of Magic, the onus is always on Magic whenever you make that decision. Sportswriters would have included it in their story if we'd have fired Westhead a *year* later.

"Jerry could have gone to Magic and said, 'Hey, Magic, for the good of the club, this doesn't work and I need you to say something like, "Yeah, I'm sorry what I did and I want to stay a Laker." ' I think Magic would have done that. But then you still have the guy you don't want being coach in the first place. We were disjointed at that time. We were winning, we were 7–4 and had just won five straight games, but they were all fucking ugly struggles."

Despite the huge mass of media people, television cameras, and microphones that descended upon the Lakers when they landed at LAX, Westhead blithely made his way through the crowd, drove over to his Forum office, and picked up some film of the San Antonio Spurs, the next night's opponent, unaware that Jerry Buss was picking his successor several rooms away.

Mary Lou Liebich told Westhead his 1 P.M. meeting with Buss would be delayed two hours. So Westhead called Monica, his 18-year-old daughter, and invited her and his wife, Cassie, to lunch.

Sitting at a Marina Del Rey restaurant, the peaceful, blue Pacific in the background, Westhead calmly, almost matter-of-factly, told his wife and daughter about the events of the night before and what he planned to tell Buss about how Magic should be brought under control. Just another day on the job.

Monica, then a freshman at Loyola Marymount University, listened quietly until Paul was finished.

Then she said, "Dad, you're going to get fired!"

As Buss grappled with his decision in the privacy of his office, he tried to gauge the reaction to his next move.

"If I fire Westhead, everybody will say it's because of Magic," Buss thought, "and that's bad. On the other hand, if I don't fire Westhead, it *will* be because of Magic. In other words, if I don't do what I had already intended to do, then I will have actually done what I will later be accused of doing—making my decision because of Magic. It's the damnedest thing. I'll be damned if I'm going to let Magic's reaction change my decision."

By the time Westhead had seated himself in Buss's office, he had gained new respect for Monica's insight. Buss had a stern look on his face, as stern as Westhead had seen. Buss laughed nervously to break the tension but it didn't work.

"Paul," he said, "we've decided to let you go."

Westhead was numb. Had it been only 18 months ago that he had sat in this same chair and felt hurt when Buss had told him Jack McKinney was out of work? Now another bombshell, this one an even more direct hit.

Westhead didn't argue. He could see it was too late for that. It's a done deal, he told himself, and I'm not going to beg.

"Well, you certainly have the right to fire me," said Westhead, speaking slowly, "but I would not like to get fired for the wrong reason. You are apparently firing me because of the offense. The offense is geared to run even more than we did last year."

"Maybe that's how it's designed, Paul, but that doesn't seem to me to be what's happening."

The conversation ended cordially. Whatever might have been wrong with him, Buss thought, at least Paul went out with dignity and class. Of the firing, Buss says, "He handled that in a more gentlemanly fashion than anybody I've ever, ever worked with at any level. It was an incredible testament to his integrity and ability."

For Westhead, there are no regrets.

"I did the absolute right thing," he says. "I would not have changed anything. If I had been losing and then got fired, I'd say, 'Maybe I ought to rethink this and get this pattern reshuffled, because it didn't work.' But it *worked.*

"There were other things going on around me, the whole Mitch Kupchak scenario where I was the prime mover to get him there. The Lakers had paid a lot of money and that put Buss on the line with the other owners. So the squeeze was on, and it had nothing to do with my offense."

But what happened to that offense? Wasn't he a running coach?

"Before, during, and after," he says. "Some coaches would have 63 options. I never coached that way. I am an incredibly simple running coach. I probably had less plays when I was fired than the year before. Jack McKinney would be an average NBA coach in number of plays and he had many more than me."

How many plays did Westhead have at the time he was let go?

"I don't know," he says, "probably a play series of maybe eight options and I'm probably exaggerating that."

Says Kareem, "We weren't winning the way it was fun for everybody. It was a slower game."

Westhead still insists that part of the problem was Magic's continuing rehabilitation from his injury of the year before.

"Literally, up until the day that I was fired," Westhead says, "he had still not returned to form. Seemed like maybe a month to six weeks after that, he finally got going. He did do well right after the firing, but that firing generated, I think, a little bit more emotional excitement for him."

The only player to call Westhead and wish him luck after he was let go was Kareem. Even though he was team captain, Abdul-Jabbar hadn't had any inkling of Westhead's impending doom. He was shocked by the falling ax.

"I thought Magic was going to get fined and everybody was going to get crazy," Kareem says, "but heads rolled real quick."

The public and many members of the media, locally and nationally, wanted another head to roll—Magic's. Columnists and national magazines ripped the upstart kid for having the nerve to fire his coach. Fans in the Forum and everywhere else the Lakers played booed Magic. The next time the team went to San Antonio a local paper ran a cartoon of Magic depicted as a baby, sucking on a basketball while Jerry Buss, as his nanny, tried to soothe him.

"He kind of fell from grace with the public," Kareem says. "He had always been a favorite and now he'd hear comments in the crowd like, 'Are you going to get *this* coach fired?' and stuff like that. Kind of a loss of innocence. Too bad, but that's the way things go."

"I was disgusted," Magic says. "I couldn't even listen to the radio no more. Nothin'. I dealt with it, but it was tough. But even tougher than all that was the booing of the fans. That just made me play. That made me have my best year. I figured, they booing, so I just got to go to work now.

"I didn't regret what I did or said. It made me a better person, made me mature. It made me grow up. That's the main thing. Some good can come out of something like that. I learned a lot from it, no question."

Nixon had his own interpretation of the boos.

"I don't think people were too concerned that Westhead got fired," he says. "It was just that a player could say that. That's what the establishment was more angry about. You've got people in the establishment who really detested that."

Bob Ryan of the Boston *Globe* offers this view from the East Coast: "It didn't look right. The propriety [of speaking out] might have been questionable to some, but certain people are entitled to exercise their obvious genius. Magic knows the game. He's one of those few who should be allowed to speak out. And he was right. He's one of the geniuses. The drift of the team was wrong. It was something the team couldn't live with."

Jim Chones also watched the furor from the East Coast as a member of the Washington Bullets.

"The team was playing like shit," Chones says. "You could see that. Don't forget, this guy [Westhead] had the most talent in the country. It's bullshit to say what happened was the players' fault. Anybody who knows Magic knows how easy he is to coach. I've never seen him get mad and disrespect anybody. If he can't speak up, who can?"

A sampling of letters to *The Los Angeles Times* that week:

"It has taken him [Johnson] only two seasons to go from Magic to Tragic."

"I just can't believe it. A winning coach is fired because an overpaid, spoiled-rotten superstar has a temper tantrum."

"I certainly hope Gerber's baby food signs Magic to a contract."

"Boycott the games until Jerry Buss, the real culprit, sells the team."

"Jerry Buss has lost the faith and confidence of thousands. He has given in to one of sport's all-time great crybabies, 'Glory-Hog' Johnson."

In the burst of criticism directed at the Lakers, however, the piece of shrapnel that hurt Buss the most was a column by Jim Murray of the *Times,* perhaps the most respected sportswriter in the country.

"Jim Murray said I was not fit to be an owner, and that really knifed me a good one," Buss says. "If there is anybody in the world you want to read, it's Murray. For 20 years you read him and enjoy everything he says and then, all of a sudden, you read that thing about you.

"I later had a great conversation with him at a dinner we attended. That was a really good feeling, because after that column I always thought he was so down on me."

Murray never knew until now how hard Buss had taken the words "unfit owner."

Says Murray, "The comment was tongue-in-cheek. It was more lighthearted than anything. I was talking about letting the inmates run the asylum. I do not feel he is an unfit owner. I don't feel there is such a thing as an unfit owner in sports. I don't even think George Steinbrenner is unfit.

"Like everybody, I was outraged that a basketball player got the coach fired. It looked like a clear-cut case at the time. Later on, it came to light that he was not the only one. The whole team was mutinous. I was wrong and what an awful thought that is. I like Jerry Buss. I'm sorry he took it so hard, but the cannon was aimed in another direction. I was wrong, but I had a lot of company."

There were to be cannons fired in Westhead's direction too. The following season he signed a four-year contract to coach the Chicago Bulls. He was fired after one year when the Bulls finished 28–54, then the second-worst mark in team history.

There were murmurs of a team mutiny during his season with the Bulls. Westhead, at one point, bought a case of mystical metal "energy bars," invented by a man who claimed the bars would beam power into the bodies of anyone who wore them around the neck. Westhead ordered his players to wear the bars in one practice session, and planned to make them a mandatory part of the game uniform, but was overruled by the team doctor.

Westhead is back coaching these days and, in one year, he has brought Loyola Marymount back to basketball respectability, landing the Lions in the National Invitational Tournament for the first time ever in 1986 after their first winning season in 11 years. Loyola was knocked out in the second round by the University of Wyoming.

Westhead says he is happy to be back on the job, any job, that coaching is coaching. His wife, Cassie, in looking at his roller-coaster career, is reminded of a game long ago at St. Joseph's in Philadelphia. She was sitting in the stands with Claire McKinney, whose husband was the losing coach that night.

The McKinney children, old enough to understand what had happened, started crying when St. Joe's lost.

"I see your kids in tears," Cassie said, "and I don't know if I want Paul in this business. When our kids get old enough to comprehend the game, I don't want them to have to go through this."

"If you don't feel the losses," Claire replied, "you'll never feel the wins."

Cassie never forgot those words.

"We've felt both sides," she says. "It's made us stretch as people and you know something, it's all worth it."

8.

Pat Riley:
From Turmoil to Triumph

IT WAS, to borrow a Chick Hearn phrase, nervous time. Jerry Buss had called a press conference to announce a new coach for his basketball team, but he wasn't sure who the new coach was. He was about to play straight man in an unintentional bit of vaudeville comedy that might be titled "Who's the Coach?"

The Forum press lounge was filled to capacity with media, lights, and cameras. The podium was in place, with its bouquet of microphones. Buss, normally very much at home in front of a crowd, didn't feel good about facing this one.

It was an awkward and embarrassing moment. The Lakers were riding a five-game win streak, yet earlier in the day Buss had fired Paul Westhead. Or was it Magic Johnson who actually fired Westhead? That's what the public seemed to believe, that the mighty Buss was letting a kid barely out of his teens call the shots.

Buss knew this press conference would be a tough one to escape unscathed. Everything had happened so damn fast. . . .

After firing Westhead that morning, Buss had summoned general manager Jerry West and president Bill Sharman to an emergency meeting at Pickfair. Buss offered West the head coaching job, or *thought* he did.

Buss felt West had been a sensational coach, and now he thought about how great it would be to have West back on the bench, even on an interim basis.

And now West had agreed to coach again, or Buss *thought* he had agreed at least to act as head coach, sit on the bench, help straighten out the offense, and slo-o-o-wly turn the reins over to Riley, when and if West felt Riley was ready.

But the discussion had been slightly fuzzy, the job titles vague.

175

All West knew was that he wanted to coach again like he wanted his nose broken for the tenth time by a flying elbow. He left Pickfair thinking Buss wanted to make Pat Riley the new head coach and wanted West to assist Riley for a while, help ease him into the job.

At 1 P.M., West and Sharman had met with Riley at West's Bel-Air home. They told Riley he was going to be the new head coach, with West helping out as needed. Or Riley *thought* that's what they told him, although the language again was sort of vague, almost as though they were discussing something unpleasant, like a social disease. Walking into the press lounge, Riley was under the impression *he* was to be the new coach, but he wasn't sure.

Buss stepped to the podium.

"Jerry Buss is an informal person," Bob Steiner explains. "I would guess that the president of a major corporation, before going into a press conference, is going to rehearse and be rehearsed. Jerry Buss doesn't do that. He has great confidence he's going to go out and say what he thinks, and then be able to field the questions."

This is one time Buss could have used a rehearsal. He announced that West had been appointed "offensive coach" and Riley would "stay as coach."

A silence fell over the room. Eyebrows knitted. Heads were scratched.

Riley was taken aback. That morning's promise of a head coaching job had just bounced like a bad check. He would be West's assistant. Or something. The only thing he could be sure of was that he still had a job.

Then Buss called West to the podium. West, too, was confused and surprised. He had approximately five seconds, the time it would take him to walk from his chair to the microphones, to decide whether he would return as head coach. Or semi-coach, or co-coach. Or no coach.

West had a brief conversation with himself.

"Do I want to coach this team again?"

"No!"

West would turn the reins over to Riley, but not in a few weeks or a month. Right now.

"I'm going to be working for and with Pat Riley," West told the press. "I feel in my heart he is the head coach."

Now it was Buss's turn to be stunned.

"I was dumbfounded," he says. "It was a total shock."

The press had more questions for Buss. Like, who is *really* the coach? Buss answered that West would be the man the press would deal with in postgame interviews.

"Wrong," West said to himself.

Okay, but who will be picking the lineup?

"Well," Buss hemmed, "obviously that's the job of the coach. I'm sure they should be able to get together and decide on that sort of thing."

One last question for Buss, just the right close for the proceedings. Had Buss spoken with Magic today? Logical question. A franchise was shaken to its foundations, a coach was fired, Magic and Buss were on the hottest of national sports hot seats. Surely Buss had contacted co-villain Magic on this day of panic and chaos.

"Well, actually I did, yes," Buss said, "but it was in a different context. I was checking with him about a birthday party I'm giving. I wanted to make sure he and Norm Nixon would be on time."

Nobody asked if Johnson and Nixon had been invited as co-guests.

When the press conference broke up, one question was still unanswered: Who's the coach?

Times sports editor Bill Dwyre went back to his office to write his story. He picked up the phone and called Steiner.

"What the fuck are you guys *doing*, Bob?" Dwyre inquired.

"Bill, we proved one thing," Steiner replied, "that we don't know how to run a press conference."

But how about a team? The Lakers had a game the next night at the Forum, against the San Antonio Spurs. Riley and West huddled, and West told Riley, I'll work with you, Riles, go to practices for a while and help iron out the offense and be there if you want any advice. But on game nights, don't look for me. My bench days are over. I'll be way in the background. You're the coach.

●

So it was Pat Riley's Lakers who faced the Spurs that Friday night, and it was a smashing debut, with the Spurs the smashees. Whatever problems had weighed the Lakers down the previous several weeks had disappeared as if by . . . well . . . magic. The Spurs, who had routed the Lakers by 26 points 10 days earlier, were run out of the Forum, 117–96.

It was just what the doctor ordered.

The Lakers didn't just run, they took off and flew. Whether it had been their actual running game that had been held under wraps, or their spirits, or both, the wraps were off.

"We were playing Laker basketball," Michael Cooper said with a satisfied grin immediately after the win. "We were loose and easy and running and having a good time. It was like the old days, and it felt damn good."

Magic Johnson, booed roundly during the pregame introductions and early in the game, had 20 points, 10 rebounds, 16 assists, and 3 steals.

Showtime was back.

"I saw a different look to the team that night," West says.

It may have been an optical illusion. According to Riley, the Lakers' return to form "showed that the offense wasn't the problem because we didn't change anything. You know, everybody's talking about how bad the offense was, but we ripped off 12 out of 13 running the same offense."

You didn't change anything?

"Nothing. Nothing. I had no *time* to change anything. When you come in and take a job there's gotta be a honeymoon period where you allow the players to show you that the system is bad. Usually all it is is a matter of attitude and effort and concentration. The offense was never the problem. It just was not. They [the players] used that as a crutch for whatever reason.

"I really think the players were looking for anything, subconsciously, to relieve the pain, whatever that pain was. Even though we'd won five in a row, there was a lot of negativity, there was second-guessing, unnamed sources. It was just an oppressive state. It had nothing to do with the offense. The whole team was beginning to get paralyzed. Every time we won a game, there was no joy, and every time we lost, it was complete misery. With finger-pointing. That's just the way it had developed. There was an immaturity on the team. Paul had not done anything to alienate anybody. He was good to people. He didn't yell and scream at people, and he treated people with respect and dignity. We had some negative people who had some strong voices on that team."

The Lakers kept running, and winning, 17 of their first 20 games under Riley. They had been winning before, but now the wins came easier. So did the points.

If Riley reestablished the team's image as a stunning, running club, he also solidified the Laker reputation as a team of Hollywood pretty boys. Since they had been in L.A. the Lakers' style had always featured finesse over muscle, and owners Cooke and Buss had both worked to give Laker games that Hollywood look.

And now the Lakers have a coach who is young (36 when he got the job), handsome, has a great tan, hangs out with movie people, has a TV background, lives in la-di-da Brentwood, has a beautiful wife and a beautiful wardrobe and a hairdo that appears to require a pit crew of stylists to whip it into shape for a game.

Riley's own story reads like a Hollywood script—kid from the wrong side of the tracks winds up on the right side of those bright lights of L.A.

Riley is the son of a career minor-league baseball manager, Lee Riley, who retired to Schenectady, New York, when Pat was six.

The youngest of six children—four boys and two girls—Pat Riley seemed determined to live up to the image of his film idol, James Dean, star of Rebel Without a Cause. He wore his hair in a greased-back ducktail and was thrown out of a Roman Catholic boarding school at age eight for being a general pain in the butt. In junior high he and some friends busted 50 windows at the school, then broke into the cafeteria and ate all the ice cream.

Pat would play pickup basketball in Schenectady's Central Park, nice games with nice, middle-class white kids. His father put a stop to that. When Pat was nine Lee Riley told his older sons to take the youngster across the tracks to Lincoln Heights, in the ghetto, to play ball with the tough black kids.

"I got my ass kicked," Pat says. "A guy chased me with a butcher knife one time. I begged my dad to let me go back to Central Park, but he wouldn't let me. He said, 'I'm going to teach you one thing—don't ever be afraid.' It took me another year, but I grew. Then I began holding the court."

He still had some emotional growing to do. In ninth grade Riley walked into his first practice for high school basketball with a pack of cigarettes rolled up in the sleeve of his T-shirt. The coach, Walt Przybylo, laughed at the kid and told him he wouldn't make the team without a change in attitude. The attitude changed, thanks largely to Przybylo.

In high school Riley was a fine basketball player—his team beat New York's famed Power Memorial High, led by a sophomore center named Lew Alcindor—and an All-American quarterback.

Bear Bryant wanted Riley to throw for the University of Alabama.

Instead, Pat opted to play for another legend, University of Kentucky basketball coach Adolph Rupp. On Rupp's Runts, Riley was an All-American who could shoot, leap, and bang.

The San Diego Rockets drafted him in the first round in 1967; the Dallas Cowboys drafted him in the eleventh round. They liked Riley's physique (6–5, 220), toughness, and athletic ability. Even though he hadn't played football since high school, the Cowboys offered Riley a guaranteed four-year contract, with a signing bonus.

But the Cowboys wanted Riley to play defensive back and he wanted to be a quarterback. The Cowboys had another rookie in mind for that position—Roger Staubach.

Riley turned down the offer and signed with the lowly Rockets.

His first day of camp in San Diego, five minutes into the first scrimmage, Riley was motioned aside by Jack McMahon, Rocket coach and general manager.

"I drafted you and my job is depending on you," McMahon growled, "and that is the *worst* five minutes of basketball I've ever seen."

"Jack, I've never played guard before," Riley said.

"You'd better learn," McMahon snapped.

Riley did, but the team was terrible. The Rockets finished 15–67 and had a cast of characters like John Q. Trapp, who once reported into a game and then pulled off his sweatpants only to reveal that he had forgotten to wear his basketball shorts.

Riley played nine seasons in the NBA, mostly coming off the bench, for the Rockets, Lakers, and Phoenix Suns. He spent five of those years in a Laker uniform after the team picked him up at the suggestion of Chick Hearn. Riley was a reserve on the great 1971–72 Laker team that had the best regular-season mark in NBA history (69–13) and won 33 in a row and the club's first NBA title in L.A.

Then he tore up a knee, and the Lakers shipped him to Phoenix. In 1976, at the age of 31, Riley couldn't pass the Suns' preseason physical. When nobody else wanted him, he was forced into retirement.

He didn't adjust well to the life of Southern California leisure. He spent most of his time at the beach, playing volleyball, reflecting, brooding, and filling several legal pads with his bitter observations on the NBA and life in general. He inquired about various coaching positions, with no response. He channeled his frustration into his home, tearing down a large garden cabana and rebuilding and remodeling much of the home.

Chris Riley would wake up to the sound of her husband's hammering and sawing, and would return home in the evening to find him still knocking out walls and ceilings. He wasn't working on the house, he was attacking it.

Riley's post-basketball funk hit an all-time low when he went to the Forum for a Laker game. He felt awkward about visiting his old teammates in the locker room after the game but figured he would run into some of them upstairs in the press lounge, a postgame hangout for every type of hanger-outer imaginable, most of them only loosely associated with the team.

But Riley, wearing a Laker championship ring, couldn't get in.

"Sorry, no ex-players," the press-lounge doorman told him.

Less than a year later Riley was rescued from a life of volleyball and assault carpentry by Hearn, who asked if he would like to be the Laker announcer's on-the-air sidekick. Riley still felt a strong loyalty to the Lakers and jumped at the offer. Typically, he jumped hard. He studied the game he already knew well, and he took acting and voice lessons, even though his broadcast role, working in Hearn's shadow, was minimal.

Riley gradually involved himself in the production end of the broadcasts. Instead of the usual grab-a-guest-and-kill-time halftime TV interviews, Riley conceived, taped, and edited a series of creative sessions with players that Barbara Walters would have been proud of, complete with highlight footage and music.

When Westhead offered Riley the assistant coaching job, he almost turned it down. He was starting to love this TV stuff. But now, five years later, the guy who couldn't get into the press lounge was running the team.

The players had been friendly with Riley when he was a broadcaster and then an assistant coach, so they felt comfortable when he took over for Westhead.

On a team bus ride after the first road game under Riley, Magic Johnson revived his "EJ the DJ" simulated radio broadcast, a show that had faded away under the Westhead regime.

Riley felt comfortable too. He knew his relationship with the players would have to change, but these were still his friends. There was mutual respect, mutual friendship.

Stepping into an elevator in the team hotel in Utah, Riley said hello to a stranger who had obviously just come from the hotel's basement disco, where several Lakers were doing some postgame unwinding.

"How's the disco?" Riley inquired.

"It's okay . . . if you like niggers," the man said.

"I get along with 'em okay," Riley said.

And he got along with the honkies okay too. But now he was no longer going to be one of the guys. He was *the* guy.

It wasn't all high fives and smiles after Westhead left. Three weeks into that initial joyride with Riley, the Lakers slumped, losing three of four. Buss called Riley in for a meeting.

"This is your team," Buss said. "Don't be afraid to coach it. There are no guarantees with that, of course. If you lose, you take the consequences, but if you win, at least you can take credit. Just make a statement. Don't let the team roll along by itself."

That day Riley met with Kareem and asked him to concentrate less on scoring and more on defense and rebounding. It was a plan that lasted only about two weeks, but it was Riley's first bold move.

Gradually he toughened up, took more control, began to coach.

"I was giving the players too much responsibility," he said weeks later. "The players have a responsibility to play, but I have a responsibility to coach."

Riley worked hard at coaching easy. When he was Westhead's assistant, Riley frequently attended coaching clinics and often was the only pro coach in attendance. He tirelessly watched game films, read books, studied other coaches, constantly analyzed the game, discussed psychology with his wife, Chris, at one time a practicing psychologist. Riley was a man in search of his own style. For starters, he copied.

"My first year coaching the Lakers' summer league team," Riley says, "everything Bobby Knight did, I did. I believed in his philosophy, in his defensive concepts. Defensively, and philosophically, I tried to implement—and still do, to a point—some of his theories."

The clinics and discussions solidified Riley's belief in himself, erased many doubts, convinced him that his coaching theories were basically solid, that he did have good instincts.

"I found out that it's really simple and basic," Riley says. "All the coaches I talked to told me one thing. You can read all the books you want, but don't coach Dean Smith, or Bobby Knight, or Pete Newell. Coach Pat Riley. Use these resources to add to your knowledge, but you can only coach who you are."

Riley's way is to give the players freedom, to step back and let them play, give what he calls "a hand ride," a jockey expression he stole from Westhead.

"I believe when you coach a great team, you put the players in a circle and you hang on to the perimeter," Riley says. "You don't step up in front and tell everybody what you did and how you did it. All of a sudden, it's as if the players didn't contribute anything.

"On a team that's struggling or rebuilding, I think a coach has to be more out in front. The players have to use you as a buffer, you have to do more coaching. Dick Motta in Dallas has done a hell of a job selling that five-year plan and being out in front of that team. It's Dick Motta's team. How he handled the Washington Bullets is light-years away from how he handles the Mavericks. With that team [the Mavs] you have to be more out in front. You don't have to do that with this team, but you've gotta be strong behind the scenes, really strong.

"I'm sometimes described as a laid-back, nice-guy coach. . . . But sometimes you've got to become temporarily insane. This team is rarely going to lose more than three in a row. After we lose two, I start tightening the screws. My personality doesn't change, I'm just demanding more. More practice time, my voice level changes, conversations with the players are more direct and pointed. There's not a whole lot of frivolity."

Riley wasn't running the team all by himself, of course. He was backed by West, the general manager, and Sharman, the president. All three have roots deeply imbedded in the Laker past. They make a strong team. All three are independent thinkers, strong-willed, intense, driven, critical, and analytical.

While the roles of West and Sharman have considerable overlap, the redundance is not due to sloppy management by Buss, but rather careful planning. West's elevation to the front office in 1979 was in no way a reflection on Sharman's abilities; Buss had confidence in Sharman, but wasn't comfortable with only one basketball adviser. The temptation would be, on any basketball matter, to do exactly what Sharman advised. That would take some of the fun out of ownership; Sharman would be calling the shots, not Buss. But if Buss also gave West a front-office post, it would give Buss a second opinion on any given matter. Then Buss could make the decision.

"I think the biggest thing I learned from Jerry [West]," Buss says, "is that the character of the player is nearly as important as his physical ability. So we really went after high-character people. We are one of the few teams that have not thus far had any [drug or discipline] problems, and I think a lot of that is due to his insistence on getting character people."

The Buss–West–Sharman–Riley collective philosophy is to

keep the roster stable, to pay star players a premium salary and avoid losing them to free agency (although there are recent signs of fiscal belt-tightening), to gradually infuse youth into the lineup, and to carefully select role players.

The team is built around Magic and Kareem. Everyone else is a role-player, even those who emerge as legitimate NBA stars, like James Worthy, Michael Cooper, and the now-retired Jamaal Wilkes.

Kurt Rambis is a perfect example of the role-player in the Laker system. Cut by the raggedy New York Knicks in '79, Rambis played one season in Greece and was playing in a summer league in San Francisco when he caught the eye of Mike Thibault, then a Laker assistant coach, who invited Rambis to training camp.

Rambis said no thanks. The Lakers had just signed Kupchak, and they were the defending NBA champions. What did they need with a Greek League power forward? Going to Laker camp would be a joke. But Westhead phoned Rambis and convinced him the Lakers would give him a legitimate shot at making the team if he could play defense, rebound, and bang.

For a while it didn't look like Rambis was going to be doing much banging. Kupchak was off to a slow start with the Lakers, but he started to get hot in late November. He was beginning to get used to his new teammates. He finished a game against the Spurs on November 20, 1981, with an 11-for-11 shooting night from the field. The Lakers' long search for a worthy successor to Kermit Washington at power forward appeared over.

On December 19, Kupchak sat down for breakfast in San Diego's Sheraton Harbor Island Hotel, took a deep breath, inhaling the ocean air wafting in through a window, and told a reporter eating with him, "I feel great. I slept well last night for the first time in weeks. I'm really relaxed with things now."

It was to be the last good night's sleep he'd enjoy for months.

Twelve hours later Kupchak and his teammates were facing the Clippers at the San Diego Sports Arena. Early in the second quarter Kupchak took a pass from Magic Johnson. He spotted an opening and drove the lane. Several feet from the basket, he went down as if he'd been shot. No one had touched him. His left knee had simply blown out like a cheap tire.

The damage was severe—a broken bone, cartilage damage, and a shattered ligament that would eventually dissolve in his bloodstream.

Six months later, while the Lakers were looking up into the glare of TV lights after winning another world's championship, Kupchak was recovering from the glare of the operating room after additional surgery on the knee, which still hadn't healed properly.

It would be nearly two years from the day of the accident before he'd return to action, and even then only on a very limited basis at first. In the meantime the Lakers were worse off than ever. They'd given up Chones for Kupchak and now they had neither.

They went to Jim Brewer, but he wasn't the answer. They went to Mark Landsberger, a reserve forward who also served as the team's resident Yogi Berra, the subject of countless jokes within the organization. Everybody had a Landsberger story.

The most famous one involved the time he and Lon Rosen, team director of promotions, went to a shopping mall for an autograph session.

A youngster approached Landsberger and asked for his autograph. Landsberger smiled and signed the piece of paper handed to him.

Could he jot down his number next to his name? the youngster wanted to know.

Landsberger again complied, writing down his *phone* number.

There was an apocryphal story people loved to tell about Landsberger's reaction when you asked him how many rebounds he'd gotten. Rather than speaking, Landsberger, who rarely strung together more than two or three sentences at a time, would stomp his feet like a horse, once for each rebound.

On the court Landsberger (6–8, 215) specialized in rebounding, often leading the team in rebounds per minute. But much to the dismay of his coaches, the Laker forward, whose moves never reminded anybody of Dr. J, would often put the ball right back up and have it blocked in his face rather than tossing it out to teammates.

On a January night in Indianapolis, less than a month after Kupchak was lost, Landsberger missed his first five shots, several of them blocked by Herb Williams.

Riley went to Rambis, and he responded with 14 rebounds in 25 minutes and some tough defense. With his black-rim glasses, Rambis looked like Clark Kent, and thereafter he was nicknamed "Superman." He had been handed a spot in the starting lineup and all the pushing and shoving of the NBA's finest has not been able to budge him since.

Rambis is an NBA oddity. His standard dress is T-shirts and jeans. He looks like an oversized hippie. Or maybe a biker. The first time Kareem saw Rambis he said he wondered where the guy's Harley-Davidson was. Rambis doesn't shoot from beyond 10 feet and has no flashy skills. Playground superstars look at Rambis and believe in their hearts they could beat him out if given a chance.

"I'm sure they think that," Rambis says, "and in a lot of cases it's probably true. But I've always held the belief that an NBA team can't just go out and get talent. You have to get players who can do certain jobs, fill a role."

Says Jim Chones, who played the role of Laker power forward for two years, "Rambis has the least physical ability of anyone who had the job. Everyone else could do more. But they just want you to do the shit. You're asked to limit your scoring, do the garbage stuff. You're paid well and you get to be with a winner. They sell you that shit, but you're the only guy banging, getting gashes upside the head. Nobody mentions that. Over 82 games, you are abused. It's tough. The only one you can talk to about it is your wife . . . and the wall. It's a hell of a spot to play, but they got it down to a science here in L.A."

The job requires subtle skills—setting picks, trailing on the fast break, playing tough defense—and an unsubtle style. That's Rambis. He dives for loose balls. He falls a lot. He has landed in dozens of courtside laps.

"It jacks the team up," Rambis says. "If one player is really hustling, it pulls everyone else along. If no one is hustling, the team looks ridiculous out there."

So Rambis becomes another piece of the Laker puzzle.

Another brilliant acquisition was Bob McAdoo. The Lakers rescued him from the NBA's junk pile, and he helped lead them to two championships.

When the Lakers got McAdoo there were some serious ques-

tions about whether he would fit in. The Lakers' inner circle—
Kareem, Magic, Silk, Norm, and Coop—zealously guarded the
team's personality. Winnin' time was a state of mind as much
as a collection of talent. Losers need not apply. Nor head cases.
Spencer Haywood had discovered that.

Despite being a former NBA MVP and a three-time league
scoring champion, McAdoo, coming to his sixth team in a decade,
had the rep of being somewhat of a malcontent and malingerer,
and the Lakers were wary of him at first. They were pleasantly
surprised to find, behind McAdoo's sometimes detached manner
and silent stare, not only a good nature but a competitive fire
that could burn as brightly as any on the team.

McAdoo not only wanted to excel at basketball, but at any
other sport known to man. On one Laker flight McAdoo, Nixon,
Magic, and a sportswriter were arguing about which of the four
was the best tennis player. Then they started to talk baseball,
and McAdoo launched into an argument with Kareem over which
of the two was a better first baseman.

Finally, Magic stood up and ended the debating.

"If you do it," yelled Magic, "Doo do it. But Doo do it better."

Someone asked McAdoo how well he bowled.

"Don't bowl," McAdoo replied.

Norm and Magic looked at each other in mock amazement.
"Doo don't bowl?" they cried in unison.

McAdoo paused, then added, quite seriously, "Yeah, but give
me a week and I'd bowl 300."

McAdoo once lost a Ping-Pong match to a sportswriter at a
Richfield, Ohio, hotel, outside of Cleveland. McAdoo played a
lot of Ping-Pong over the next year. When the team returned
to Richfield the following season, McAdoo got his rematch and
his revenge, beating the sportswriter easily.

Still, the Lakers never let McAdoo get too cocky. They teased
him mercilessly. As Magic told him once during a bus ride,
" 'Fore you came here, you never been on national TV, didn't
know what national TV *was*. Teams you'd played on had only
been seen on *regional* TV. You ought to bow your head and
thank us for putting you on *national* TV."

Certainly, McAdoo proved he was ready for prime time. He
was another important member of the Showtime cast constantly

being assembled by West and Sharman and Riley. And when the cast was ready to perform, when the stars and supporting actors were in place, the only guy who could screw it up was the coach. It was Riley's show to blow, and he didn't.

Despite the Lakers' long run of success under Riley, the belief persists in some quarters that Riley is a lucky stiff who happened to fall into the most glamorous coaching job in all of basketball.

Larry Brown seems to be of this school. In fact, he's the school spokesman. Brown, the former ABA and NBA coach now at Kansas University, once said he never considered Riley or Billy Cunningham true coaches because they inherited their teams. When the Lakers won their first championship under Riley, Brown made disparaging comments about the sorry state of the coaching profession when a broadcaster can step in and win a title.

"Probably a lot of other coaches look at this as a situation where I got lucky," Riley says. "If I did, so be it. But I'll never apologize for the talent I have on this team, or for the way I got this job. It's what I've done with it since I came here.

"Five years ago they were telling me I was the luckiest son of a bitch alive, and I believed 'em. I used to be affected by it a little bit, but it doesn't bother me at all anymore. It's almost humorous.

"I think the one thing I did accomplish with this team is to maintain its excellence. We didn't break it down, and screw it up, and overcoach it. We maintained."

That first season under Riley the Lakers maintained like crazy.

The Lakers had lost another head coach under weird circumstances. . . . Magic Johnson and Jerry Buss had been publicly roasted and embarrassed following the Westhead affair. . . . Mitch Kupchak had been lost to a possible career-ending injury. . . .

There had been a midseason Kareem crisis when his teammates questioned his worth. . . . Riley had thrown Kurt Rambis into the starting lineup, causing one NBA coach to say, "Any team with Kurt Rambis in the lineup can't win the playoffs." . . . The Lakers had waited for a rookie coach to find himself and take charge. . . .

Through it all the Lakers kept drawing the right cards from

the deck. The acquisitions of the aging McAdoo and Grecian refugee Rambis proved brilliant in the playoffs.

After being embarrassed in their brief postseason appearance the previous year, this time the Lakers rode through with a vengeance. They swept Phoenix and then San Antonio, both 4-love, to face Philadelphia in the NBA finals.

Philly fell in six. Magic was the series MVP, with 13 points, 13 rebounds, and 13 assists in the title game. Jamaal Wilkes added a quiet, sneaky 27 points.

When it was over Riley stood in the Lakers locker room, champagne blending with the Dippity-Doo in his hairstyle, cascading off, then mixing with his tears before ruining the razor creases on his Italian slacks.

"It seems like a millennium since I took over," Riley said in the din. "Yeah, a millennium. I've got brain drain right now, mush brain. I dug down for everything I could find. I need four months just to rest up."

The Lakers would need more than that. This was no happily ever after. It would seem like another millennium, and then some, before they would be back on top.

PART III

PART III
Feudin' Time

●

*The world the Lakers inhabit is a world of
big stars, big salaries and big games.*

To perform in that world requires a big ego.

And when such egos collide, watch out!

9.

Nixon and West

A S Norm Nixon came out of his Baldwin Hills home one day in the summer of 1983, several kids from the block raced up behind him. They were breathing heavily, obviously bursting with news.

What now? Nixon thought. What else could go wrong? His team had lost its world championship in an embarrassing sweep at the hands of the Philadelphia 76ers a few weeks earlier, and he, Nixon, had finished the year injured.

"Hey, Norm," one of the neighborhood kids said, "somebody is going to get robbed."

"What do you mean?" Nixon asked.

"There's been cars parked at both ends of our street with telescopes, guys looking into houses," another of the kids said excitedly. "People are setting somebody up."

Sure enough, Nixon started to notice the cars. Maybe they *are* watching somebody, he thought. It's got to be a drug dealer.

It wasn't too long before Nixon discovered who they were watching. He had pulled up in front of his house at 2:30 one morning several days later and was heading for his front door when a figure stepped out of the shadows.

"Hey, man," said the figure, whom Nixon to this day won't identify, "I have to talk to you."

"Whoa," replied Nixon, holding his hands up, "what the hell is going on?"

The man said he'd be right back. Nixon went into his house and woke up his brother, Ron, who was staying with him. Minutes later there was a knock at the door. With his brother by his side, Norm cautiously opened it.

The man from the street walked in, looked around quickly, shut the door, and said, "Norm, I just want to tell you that we've been following you for the last two weeks. We were hired by . . . Jerry West."

195

At first Nixon didn't believe it. But he became convinced when the man told Nixon every place he had been for the previous two weeks. That summer Nixon had been learning the banking business. The detective told him where the banking office was and when Nixon had arrived and left.

"If you still don't believe me," the man said, "I'll tell you where we are parking. We are at either end of the block. I've got a job to do, but I like you and I felt an obligation to tell you. Now I've got to go back to work."

With that he disappeared out into the night, leaving Nixon and his brother to stare at each other.

Any lingering doubts Norm had were removed the next day. As he drove away from his house he looked in his rearview mirror. One of the mysterious cars pulled out from the curb and followed behind him at a safe distance.

This is like the shit you see on TV, Nixon thought. This is *unbelievable.*

Finally, Nixon had had enough. He walked outside with his Doberman a few days later, marched down the street and right up to one of the stakeout cars. He didn't recognize either of the men in it.

"What are you guys doing?" asked Nixon in an angry tone.

"Oh, we're watching somebody's house for them," one of the men said. "They've been having trouble."

Before Nixon could answer, his dog darted into the street, directly into the path of an oncoming car. The car barely brushed the dog, but it was enough to send the animal scurrying in fear back to its own backyard. Nixon looked at the car, then the dog.

"Damn," he muttered. He had been planning to come right back with his brother and some friends to shake these guys up so they'd leave him alone. But his dog came first. By the time Nixon assured himself the animal was okay, the car was gone.

He never saw any of the mysterious cars or their occupants again. But Nixon was still mad. So he confronted West.

"You've been hanging out with some drug dealers," West said. "And we know that you do a lot of drugs."

"Jerry, I'm not going to admit that for you," Nixon replied.

"I don't care where you say you saw me, or what you say you saw me doing. I'm not going to simply tell you just for your personal satisfaction that I do drugs."

"That's the first thing drug users do is deny, deny, deny," West said. "That's the first thing they do."

Nixon just shook his head.

"If I did a lot of drugs," Nixon says, "people that would know better than anybody else would be the coach and the trainer. I don't miss practices. I don't miss busses. I don't miss planes. I'm very rarely hurt, very rarely miss games, averaging more minutes than anybody on the team. So I should be the *last* one that should have to deal with something like that."

When questioned recently, West refused comment on the whole incident.

Nixon and West were never the best of pals. Norm's rookie season, West was his coach. And, Nixon felt, his frequent tormentor.

"I was playing with veterans," Nixon says. "I was playing with Kareem, A.D. [Adrian Dantley], Jamaal, Lou Hudson, and guys like that. I felt like I was the only one on the team that he [West] felt like he could argue and not mess up their game that bad. He could do it and I would take it. I don't think the other guys would have taken it. I mean, you don't know how A.D. and all of them might react to it.

"So I was like his whipping boy my rookie year, but I understood it. It used to go in one ear and out the other. I didn't come into this league with a lot of problems. I felt if I played one year in the league, then I would be able to get a job somewhere else."

According to Nixon, in one game his rookie season he got trapped with seven seconds left in the half and flipped the ball to Kareem. The Laker center shot and missed, and the opposition used the remaining time to score. Someone was standing in front of West, preventing him from seeing Kareem shoot.

West stormed into the locker room, marched right up to Nixon, and yelled, "Damn it! Damn it! Who in the hell took that shot?"

"I did," said Kareem, seated next to Nixon.

West looked at Kareem, then back at Nixon, and told the rookie, "How could you *pass* him the ball with seven seconds left?"

Another time that year the Lakers, in Atlanta, watched the Hawks pull off a 14–0 run early in the first quarter.

West called a timeout. Nixon, standing in the huddle, sweat pouring down his face, had half his team's point total.

"Damn it, Norm," West yelled, "would you fucking guard somebody?"

Says Nixon, "I told myself, after my first year I just wasn't going to take that abuse. I wasn't going to go through that again. Especially when it was uncalled for. He was just *always* messing with me, in front of the players, just all the time."

Ernie DiGregorio, a veteran guard on the squad, would reassure Nixon. "You can play," Ernie D. would tell him. "Don't let anything take you out of your game."

Stormy days for Nixon? Not according to West.

"I wouldn't say stormy in the sense of my relationship with him as a coach," West says. "He was a young player who I think needed direction other than where he was going. For him to prosper as a player, he would not have gotten to the point where he is in his career unless he added some discipline to his game, particularly being careless with the ball in situations where you had an advantage. At that time you don't need to be spectacular. You do the simple things. And I thought defensively he needed a lot of work.

"There were times I know he wasn't enamored with me, and he probably isn't enamored with me today, which is fine. But my feeling about him is, I liked him a lot. I still like him a lot. He was a tremendous player for us."

West proved his feelings before Nixon's second year when the decision was made to cut a guard. Who would it be, Nixon or Brad Davis? Davis, who had been drafted higher than Nixon, was put on waivers.

"I made my feelings known to Mr. Cooke that he [Nixon] would play quicker for us than Brad Davis would," West says. "Again, from my perspective, those are things Norm Nixon will never know or never understand."

Nixon's feelings about West never changed. In the 1983 NBA finals, Norm, facing writers from all over the country at an impromptu press conference, was asked to compare himself with West as a guard.

"I never saw Jerry West play," Nixon said. Then, after pausing, he smiled and added, "And I never saw him *coach,* either."

The Lakers' 1983 season ended in disappointment while Nixon's ended in the trainer's room.

He had company there. The Lakers, with the first pick in the draft the previous spring, had selected North Carolina forward James Worthy. They brought Worthy along slowly, but he appeared ready to kick himself into a higher gear as the 1983 regular season wound slowly to a close.

Instead, Worthy's season ground to a sudden and horrifying halt a week short of the playoffs. Going up to tip in a missed shot against the Phoenix Suns in a meaningless regular-season game at the Forum, Worthy came down awkwardly on his left foot, fracturing a bone below the knee.

The Lakers reached the NBA finals for the second straight season, but Bob McAdoo joined Worthy on the sidelines, missing two of the four games and part of a third with a pulled thigh muscle.

And Nixon, suffering from a partially separated left shoulder injured in Game 1, as well as a strained tendon in the left knee and four stitches in his chin, all from Game 3, spent Game 4 of the finals watching from the bench as the Sixers swept the Lakers off their throne to give Julius Erving his only NBA championship ring.

With center Moses Malone at his peak, Erving still able to soar to the basket, Andrew Toney and Maurice Cheeks in the backcourt, and a tough stifling defense designed by coach Billy Cunningham, Philadelphia would have been awfully hard to beat, even by a healthy Laker club. But with three key performers ailing, it was no contest.

As the Lakers prepared for another run at the top in the summer of 1983, Nixon's name kept surfacing in trade rumors. And in other rumors. In NBA front offices around the country they whispered, *Nixon's on drugs. Nixon's got a bad case of tendinitis in the knees. Nixon's lost a step. Nixon's a troublemaker.*

Norm heard them all. And he knew what the bottom line was going to be.

"When I came to training camp and West threw his arms around me and told me not to worry about all the trade talk," Nixon says, "I knew I was gone."

His teammates tried to assure him it wasn't so. They felt he'd be awfully difficult to replace.

But he *was* replaced in 1983 on the mid-October day before the Lakers broke training camp in Palm Springs. Eating dinner with Magic and Michael Cooper, Nixon got the word that he and Eddie Jordan had been traded to the San Diego Clippers for center Swen Nater and the rights to San Diego's still unsigned No. 1 draft pick, guard Byron Scott.

Does he think West's suspicions or the fact that Nixon learned about the detective may be the reasons he was traded?

"I'm not sure those are the reasons," Nixon says. "I just think you peep somebody's hole card like that, it might not make for a great relationship. It's just like if somebody is doing something, and I found out they're doin' it, they might not feel that comfortable having me around anymore.

"Or hey, maybe they were just trying to make a business move. Who knows why I was traded?"

One reason might have been Nixon's tendency to second-guess Laker coaches and the front office on everything from strategy to trades, both openly and behind the scenes. During the Westhead crisis Nixon was one of the most vocal critics of the foundering coach, although he never went public with his complaints. It's possible that West and Riley saw Nixon as a potentially disruptive influence and thought it best to unload the popular guard, especially when the opportunity came up to get a hot-shooting replacement like Scott, six years younger than Nixon (28 at the time), along with a needed backup center in Nater.

The final farewell came a few days later at a surprise birthday party for Nixon thrown by Debbie Allen, then his girlfriend. The players, front-office people, and their wives and girlfriends all showed up at a swank Beverly Hills restaurant.

Near the end of the party Cooper called Norm and Magic into a rest room for a private farewell. This tight trio was about to be reduced to a duo.

They hugged there in the middle of the rest room, and cried.

"That was deep," Magic says. "That was a deep time."

It was the end of an era. The Lakers had broken up their winnin' chemistry. Would the new formula do as well?

10.

Kareem:
Center of Controversy

KAREEM ABDUL-JABBAR, the 7–2 center of the mighty Milwaukee Bucks, was standing at his dressing stall in the visitor's locker room at cozy Cobo Hall in downtown Detroit. The Bucks had just beaten the Pistons and Kareem was slipping into his street clothes. For him it was just another locker room, another forgettable game in a long NBA season. But for one young man standing in a corner of the locker room, this was the opportunity of a lifetime.

The boy was about 11 years old and tall for his age, but very shy. He and a friend had sneaked into the locker room when the guard wasn't looking. They had come from Lansing for the game, a 90-minute drive, and seeing Kareem this close up was even more exciting than the game.

Kareem was the league's MVP, the greatest center since Chamberlain and Russell. The two 11-year-old basketball junkies were praying they wouldn't get thrown out. They were just trying to act cool.

"Go ahead, go ask Kareem for his autograph," the tall boy's friend whispered.

"No."

"Yeah! Go on! He's about ready to leave."

"I can't."

"Go on, he won't bite you."

"No, I *can't.*"

"You *got* to! When will you get a chance like this again? Go on, go get his autograph."

And so Earvin Johnson screwed up his courage, walked across the locker room, and very respectfully asked Kareem Abdul-Jabbar for an autograph. Without a word, Kareem signed.

"I was goin' *crazy,*" Magic Johnson says, smiling broadly as he recalls carrying the priceless piece of paper with Kareem's signature to school. "I was like the *man* of school that whole *week!* Yeah! Ka-*reeeem!* Everybody's saying, 'Let me *see* it!' It was great."

Eight years later Kareem and the tall kid met again, this time as teammates on the Los Angeles Lakers.

The kid was really tall then, grown to 6–9, and known to every basketball fan in the country as Magic. He was the NBA's No. 1 draft choice, and the Lakers' hope for the future. The present, too, for that matter. Kareem was 33 years old, and the Lakers were hoping to get one or two more productive seasons out of him.

The pairing of the great but fading veteran and the hotshot teenage rookie raised some interesting questions.

Magic was a take-charge player, a natural leader. He was accustomed to being his team's main player, the focus of the offense, but the Lakers already had one of those in Kareem. How would the two of them handle this situation?

Would Kareem resent this kid and all the publicity he was sure to get? Would the veteran accept the rookie, or would the Big Fella consider the kid's rah-rah, high-fiving style an affront to the dignity of the game?

It turned out, of course, that their talents and playing personalities were wonderfully compatible. It took about five minutes for them to establish a working relationship on the court, a partnership that would launch one of the two dominant teams of the '80s, the other being the Celtics.

It took about five years, though, for Kareem and Magic to establish a relationship off the court.

Since the day he came into the NBA in 1969, Kareem had been The Man. To say he was expected to be an instant franchise-maker for whatever team landed him would be vastly understating the case.

At Power Memorial High School in his native New York, his teams were 95–6, including a 71-game winning streak.

As a freshman in college, not eligible for varsity ball, he

led his UCLA *freshman* team to an easy exhibition game victory over coach John Wooden's varsity club, which was ranked No. 1 in the nation in the preseason polls.

Lew Alcindor, as he was named then, frightened people. The nation's college coaches took one look at his ferocious dunks, his armpits rim-high, and passed legislation outlawing the dunk in college basketball.

The anti-Alcindor rule barely slowed him down. He toyed with collegiate competition for three seasons, leading the Bruins to NCAA titles each year. He was the championship tournament Most Valuable Player all three times. He was College Player of the Year in '67 and '69. During his stay in Westwood, the Bruins were 82–2.

He had the same kind of immediate impact when he was drafted by the Milwaukee Bucks. His second season Alcindor played on a team that didn't have a glorious supporting cast, with the exception of an over-the-hill Oscar Robertson. Still, Alcindor led the Bucks to the NBA title and was named the league's MVP.

From then on nothing less was expected of Kareem each season than powering whatever team he played for to the top. When he succeeded he was given the lion's share of the glory and credit. And when his teams failed to win a title, the blame was usually placed squarely on Abdul-Jabbar's shoulders.

He had already won three of his record six league MVP awards when he asked to be traded prior to the 1975–76 season. He was tired of living in Milwaukee, where he felt deprived socially and culturally. He also felt commercial endorsements would never find their way to him so far from the media centers. He wanted to come home to New York.

When nothing could be worked out with the Knicks, the team he had dreamed of playing for since boyhood, he agreed to return to Los Angeles in exchange for Elmore Smith, Brian Winters, Dave Meyers, and Junior Bridgeman.

When he went to L.A. at the age of 28, Kareem was still a young giant in the game, a graceful and dominating superstar. But he was not an instant hero in town. The respect and adulation accorded to many players of lesser ability was slow coming to

Abdul-Jabbar. On the popularity scale, Kareem was knee-high to Steve Garvey.

Kareem often chafed under the burden of greatness. He resented the media for their expectations and their preoccupation with one man in a five-man game. His aloofness with the press and the public made him an easy target for criticism. When he was with the Lakers, Kareem and his girlfriend, Cheryl Pistono, had a son and named him Amir. One L.A. sportswriter cracked—not to Kareem—"Is that Amir, as in 'A mere six rebounds'?"

Other than those at Kareem's expense, there weren't many laughs for the Lakers or Abdul-Jabbar during his first three seasons in Los Angeles. The team was winning, and Kareem was scoring. He was even rebounding, leading the league in that department his first Laker season. He was voted the league's Most Valuable Player each of his first two seasons.

But the Lakers weren't winning *championships.* What was the use in having the world's greatest center, of paying him $600,000 a season, if he doesn't bring you the big banner? Especially when he seems so joyless, when he's a wooden Indian in public, and when he sometimes seems to be going through the motions on the court? One writer referred to him as Kareem Ab*dull*-Jabbar.

In those four seasons the Lakers, in order: missed qualifying for the playoffs; were swept 4–0 by Portland in the Western Conference finals; lost to Seattle in the first round; and lost to Seattle in the conference semifinals, 4–1.

Kareem believes it was a matter of him receiving too much credit when the team won and getting *all* the blame when the Lakers lost. The team did have obvious weaknesses, especially in the frontcourt muscle department. Kareem was carrying a heavy load.

Still, he had passed his thirtieth birthday, and it was widely speculated that he was nearing the end of his career.

"He is clearly discouraged and doesn't have confidence in his new teammates," Steve Hershey wrote in the Washington *Star* during Abdul-Jabbar's first Laker season. "The Lakers have the worst collection of forwards west of the Virginia Squires.

There's not a consistent performer in the lot . . . and Kareem knows it. The truth is, he has lost his enthusiasm."

An anonymous NBA coach was quoted as saying, "Kareem is just tired of being surrounded by a bunch of turkeys."

Enter Jerry Buss. Enter Earvin Johnson. Exit several turkeys. Cue the new age of Kareem and the Lakers.

When Buss immediately obtained twin towers Chones and Haywood, Kareem was ecstatic. With the addition of Earvin Johnson, Kareem was beyond ecstatic. Let the new kid have his publicity, Kareem thought. Let him have some of the spotlight, it's bright enough and hot enough for both of us. So what if he's got some hot dog in him. If he can play like they say he can, he's going to make us all look better.

As Jamaal Wilkes said that season, "Kareem has been a consistently great player every year, but he's getting old. He hasn't won a championship in L.A. and let's face it, winning a title in L.A. or New York isn't like winning it anywhere else. The man definitely wants another ring on his finger."

He got one, quickly. In one season the Lakers went from struggling also-rans to World Champions. Forum attendance jumped nearly 3,000 per game. And Kareem came out of whatever funk-slump he had been floundering in. As early as the first day of training camp, he recognized the Lakers now had the ingredients—new coach, new guard, new forwards—for a winner.

Above all, literally above all, the Lakers had themselves a new center. Kareem felt like a kid again.

"All the pieces were there," Kareem says. "I was satisfied when we got Chones and Haywood. I knew we'd be competitive. The year before in the playoffs against Seattle, we've got Silk [Wilkes, 6–6 and 190] playing Jack Sikma [6–11, 250]. Now, all of a sudden, we've got Silk dancin' around the outside like he can, and killin' 'em. Everything opened up. And Magic's game definitely complemented Silk's abilities, and Norman's abilities, and mine; and Chones fit right in.

"If we'd kept on the same way [as the previous season], I would've just got worn down by the criticism and the constant physical attrition I had to deal with. McKinney's system was— I don't want to call it genius—but he made some brilliant adjustments. He was perceptive and understood what our potential would be with someone like Magic running the offense. He tailored the offense to Magic's talents.

"In camp, McKinney told me, 'Look, you're gonna get a lot more easy shots this year, because Magic is always gonna be breaking down [beating] his man and loosening up the defense.'

"Before Magic, we had Norman [6–2, 175], and they'd kind of get in front of him and I couldn't find him all the time. I didn't have any problems finding Magic [6–9, 220]. A lot of times he was right next to me, because he went to the boards all the time.

"Because of that, they couldn't really cover Norman. So if they decided, 'Well, we're gonna commit ourselves to stopping Magic,' I'd get the ball out to Norman, and he's a great point guard or off guard because he shoots so well and handles the ball so well. We had a lot of talent in the backcourt. Their understanding of the game is so great."

Abdul-Jabbar's stats didn't increase dramatically, although his field-goal shooting improved to a career-best 60 percent. It was the *way* he played—his style, his enthusiasm—that was different.

"It seems like the game is more fun to him," said Lucius Allen when he saw the change in Kareem, his old playing partner from UCLA and Milwaukee. "It's the most relaxed I've ever seen him. To me, he's become the Kareem he was wishing he could be at all times the last four, five years."

And the Lakers had become the kind of team everyone in L.A. had wished they could be the last four, five years, and more.

"The dramatic difference was Magic," Kareem says. "He just had so many skills that we didn't have and were crucial to the success of any team. It was like night and day as far as what we were capable of doing. . . .

"Magic did so many things in a combination, the effect was amazing. He just changed everybody's attitude. . . . It was a big contrast, that season and the one before, when we were just struggling in the middle of the pack. Now we're beating everybody, beating Seattle—they were the world champs—and that was a good feeling."

●

But there would be bad feelings too. The first crisis arose in the summer of '81, just after the embarrassing playoff loss to Houston. Johnson was talking to Buss one day and suggested he (Magic) would like to see his contract extended, to cement himself to the Lakers for a long time.

"How about for a lifetime?" asked Buss, who proceeded to draw up a 25-year, $25-million contract (it was subsequently reworked to $2.5 million per year for nine years), which included provisions for Magic to have some management duties when his playing career was over.

News of the contract, revolutionary in dollars and years, created a stir, especially in Bel-Air, at Kareem's hideaway. He read the newspaper reports of management provisions in Magic's contract and hustled to the telephone.

Kareem knew Buss and Magic were fairly tight, that Magic hung out at Pickfair sometimes, shooting pool and shooting the bull, and that Magic and Buss occasionally attended sporting events together and frequented the same Westside discos.

But now it seemed to Kareem that the two had become too chummy, that Magic had been promoted one notch too high, that now he might even have a say in team matters. What was he going to be? A junior coach or general manager while still in uniform? Abdul-Jabbar phoned Buss's secretary and requested an audience with the boss.

Kareem told the press, "In many ways a basketball team is like a family. If you pick one person out and put him in front of everyone else and say, 'This is my favorite child,' the other people in the family are going to be affected by it. . . . Some members of the team [Nixon and Wilkes also expressed concern] wondered if their value lay in competing for the affection of the owner rather than what they do on the court."

There was some suspicion that Kareem also chafed at the amount of money Magic was to get. Kareem was making $1 million a year also, but his contract was for 23 years fewer than Magic's.

Magic was perplexed that his contract had created such a stir. There were rumors that the disgruntled Abdul-Jabbar would wind up with the New York Knicks, and Johnson certainly didn't want to go down in history as the man who drove Kareem out of L.A.

"We got to have the Man," Magic said at a press conference. "If the Man ain't right, the Lakers aren't right, the Lakers are in trouble. I can tear up my contract right now if it causes problems on the team. I just want to win. . . . We had enough problems last year. We definitely don't want any problems with The Big Fella."

Magic called Buss.

"We could just forget it," he told his boss, referring to the new contract. "Here it is now all the guys wondering, am I management? I didn't need it. We can forget this thing. I personally don't need it."

"No," Buss said, "it's gonna blow over."

"But if I see any problems coming up," Magic said, "we can just forget it."

"All right," Buss agreed.

"I'd been through enough," Magic says now. "It was like one thing after another. And I didn't want to start no more problems. It's just like saying, 'Hey, I *give.* Forget it.' Really."

After Buss met with Kareem the problem seemed to be smoothed over, although Buss still wasn't sure.

"I had felt Kareem would be *happy,*" Buss says. "What I was trying to say [by signing Magic] was, it's gonna be my position while I'm running the team that I'm gonna try to provide some management positions for players after they retire. I did it with a lot of players in different ways. Kareem read it to say Magic would begin to participate in management before he retired. He wanted to know if that was true. I said, no. He was upset about it, very upset. He didn't seem like he was totally satisfied when he left."

Says Kareem, "I thought they put a lot of pressure on Magic with that. Obviously Dr. Buss realized that to tie Magic up for a long time was a wise move. I didn't have any qualms with that. But Magic put a whole lot of pressure on himself and he didn't have to do that. I just wanted to help him deal with it. I didn't want it to end up to be like Pete Maravich, where they gave him all the publicity, talked about all this money they were giving him, he had the ball all the time, and all the pressure was on him to win. It just drove him out of the game.

"Well, this is a team game. Magic is a team player. To put him out front like that I didn't think was wise."

For all the heat they generated on the court, the relationship between Magic and Kareem was surprisingly cool in these first few years.

"At that particular time it was hard to get through to Kareem," Johnson says. "It was hard to talk to him then. I guess it was just him, that's just the way he was. Certain times you just couldn't talk to him, and we respected that. *Now* you can go up and say anything. It's a lot different in the last couple years.

"Back then everybody respected his territory. Some mornings, some afternoons, you *knew*, don't say nothing to him. You could just see the look on his face when he came in— 'Don't talk to me.' So nobody would talk to him. It was just that way.

"Everybody could see that we wasn't favorite pals or buddies the first three or four years. I think I wanted him to know I wasn't trying to get into his territory; he was the man. But things came so fast for me that maybe he thought I was intruding. I don't know."

Kareem could see Magic holding back, but that was okay with Abdul-Jabbar. He wasn't the type to rush into a personal friendship, either.

"Magic was very distant," Kareem says. "Not unfriendly. He just didn't really approach anybody [on the team] his first couple years. I didn't really know him, other than superficially. He kept to himself. Oh, when we'd go to Michigan [to play the Pistons], we'd hang out, we'd go around places together, but I never really got to know him until recently.

"I held back because he had to make the adjustments coming into the league and dealin' with all of this. I guess *he* held back because of my stature in the game, the whole aura around me. There was never any conflict or anything like that, it just took a while before we got to know each other."

That distance between the Laker superstars wasn't helped by the debate that sprung up in the early days of the 1981–82 season.

The debate topic: Do the Lakers really need Kareem?

When he went down with a foot injury early in the '80–81 season, the Lakers ran off six straight victories and upped their scoring average. The question arose among Laker players, and members of the media: Are the Lakers a better team without Kareem?

Such a question seems utterly ridiculous now that he is recognized as perhaps the greatest ever to play the game, but five years ago there was a genuine debate. Some actually felt the Lakers would be better at center with Jim Brewer, who was more adept at running the court. They argued that Kareem's rebounding had slipped considerably. And they said his defense was not overpowering.

Hold it just a minute, said his supporters. What about his intimidating presence in the middle, his brilliant passes, his leadership, and, of course, the skyhook, the most devastating weapon the game has ever known? "When games really got funky," Jim Chones says, "Kareem was always there, under control, shooting on-balance. He was our stability."

When Kareem missed the six games with his bum ankle, the other players had a hell of a time. They respected Kareem, but loved that extra juice in their running game. Publicly they all talked about how the team needed Kareem. Privately some Lakers felt they could do without him. Trade the Big Fella, God bless him, to another team and get a younger, faster center. Kick out the jams.

Mitch Chortkoff of the Santa Monica *Evening Outlook* and Rich Levin of the *Herald-Examiner* gave voice in print to the Kareem-less–Laker scenario. Levin, as a joke, handed out matchbooks stamped with the words "TRADE KAREEM."

"Yeah, there was some ridiculousness going on," Riley says. "We won six in a row with Jim Brewer playing center, and I think everybody was getting carried away with just how great Earvin Johnson was, and his impact on the team, and how it would be best to run for 48 minutes and not have to throw the ball into the center. That kind of stuff was going on, and we had lost a couple games by dropping the ball down inside to Kareem at the end, being too predictable. Players were actually doing some moaning about it in the press."

Riley conceded that, yes, the Lakers could blow away teams like Kansas City and Cleveland every night using the smaller, no-Kareem lineup. But in the playoffs you had to have The Big

Fella. Game 6 in Philly had been a happy fluke—one game. You couldn't win a championship without Kareem.

What also bothered Riley, newly installed as coach, was the players voicing their criticism to the media.

"I don't like that kind of behavior," he says. "You don't ever criticize a teammate in the press, ever! I was at that point establishing our policies and our ground rules, that that stuff just doesn't happen. They were wrong, and the media was wrong about needing Kareem. Let's be realistic."

But realism had more than one side. During the course of the controversy Magic was having lunch in an Indianapolis coffee shop with two Laker beat writers. They asked Magic how he really felt about Kareem.

"When he leaves, you'll be able to see the *real* Magic show," he said. "I've had to change my game because of the Big Fella. I'm just waiting my turn. My time will come."

Not long after, those comments, or a reasonable facsimile, were printed in the *Herald-Examiner.* By now Kareem was well aware of the debate. In a TV interview he angrily stated, "I'm not dead yet. The reports of my demise have been greatly overrated."

Riley, who had been steaming since the debate started, had had enough. He called a team meeting.

"You 'unnamed player' [the way a critic of Kareem's was identified in a newspaper story], stand up," Riley said in firm, angry tones.

Nobody stood.

"Who here thinks we can get along without Kareem? Whoever it is, maybe *you'll* be the one to go. If you've got something to say, say it here and we'll discuss it. If you're gonna start giving information like that to the media, allowing them to use it against us, then we're on our way down."

Riley swept the room with his glare. Nobody spoke. Nobody stood up.

It was time to get back to business.

The debate was just one in a long series of thorny entanglements with the press that have dogged Kareem throughout his career.

"He has the art of keeping the world at arm's length down to a bittersweet science," Ted Green wrote in *The Los Angeles Times* in 1979, before Magic Johnson and Jerry Buss had appeared on the Laker scene. "At this point in his career, he may be quoted less than any major athlete at the top of his profession. He himself admits to a 'mysterious' public image."

Kareem's high school coach had kept him isolated from the press, as did John Wooden at UCLA. It was a policy endorsed by Kareem and his parents. In the NBA, Kareem broke no records for cordiality toward the press. In interviews he seldom made eye contact, seldom offered anything more than perfunctory answers. Often he would conduct an entire postgame interview with his back to the reporters, his head buried in his locker like a man looking for a place to hide, his voice coming out in monosyllabic mumbles. Sometimes, even later in his career, Kareem would shower quickly after a game, dress without even toweling, and be striding out the locker-room door before the press was allowed in.

In his autobiography, *Giant Steps,* Kareem says his impression of sportswriters in NBA cities was that they were, for the most part, "wheedlers, little guys who derived great satisfaction from tweaking the tiger's whiskers. . . .

"Sitting by my locker after a game, I started to feel as if a swarm of flies was buzzing around my head; they couldn't really do me any harm, but they annoyed the hell out of me."

He felt the writers were trying to con him, work him, make him look bad, so he worked them back.

"I tried to keep my responses minimal, direct, removed," he wrote. "It would be hard to take quotes out of context if there was no context. I was making their job difficult, and they no doubt began to dislike me for it. But I didn't care, these hurtful little guys couldn't touch me; in fact, I kind of had fun pissing them off."

And some of them had fun pissing back. The result was a largely negative public image for Kareem despite the deep respect for his basketball talents.

His longest-running feud was triggered by an incident in 1978 when a female representative of a youth organization phoned Kareem's business manager to ask if Kareem could speak to the group. This was during the season, and the business manager explained that Abdul-Jabbar simply didn't have time. The woman persisted, and finally Kareem's agent said, "Look, Kareem can't do it. And even if he could, his usual fee for an appearance is $5,000."

The woman became angry. She phoned Rich Levin, who responded with a story, the basic theme of which was, despite his awards and heroic deeds, Kareem wasn't a hero even in Los Angeles. Levin offered the story of the spurned youth organization and Kareem's so-called demand for $5,000 as an example of why he felt the Laker star hadn't dented the public's affection. The man was too cold, too aloof, and didn't care, wrote Levin.

Now Kareem was steamed. Nobody had contacted him for *his* side of the story. He felt he had been wronged and unfairly chastised and characterized for what he saw as a minor misunderstanding. Kareem demanded a retraction; the *Herald-Examiner* refused.

Levin covered the Lakers for six more seasons, but Kareem never spoke to him again after announcing to the sportswriter, "I have nothing to say to you." Kareem claims Levin was antagonistic to him even before the offending article, that the story was simply the last straw.

A vow of silence toward one reporter might not seem like a big deal, but consider: Kareem was the Lakers' one superstar, the league's No. 1 player, and Levin was representing one of L.A.'s two major newspapers. Levin was in the position of continually reviewing Kareem's performance for a large segment of the huge city's sports fans.

"When it came time in a game story to evaluate his play, I took advantage of the opportunity to rip him, when normally I wouldn't have," says Levin now. "It was easy to take shots at him. I know now it was unfair, that it was immaturity on my part, on both our parts.

"I honestly regret the whole thing. It wasn't much fun covering the team all those years without being able to talk to the No. 1 guy. But I honestly think things like that eventually prompted him to reach out, be more expansive."

The feud reached ridiculous extremes on occasion. At the team's hotel in Indianapolis one day, Levin got on an elevator on the sixteenth floor to come down to the lobby. He was alone until the elevator stopped again at the fourteenth floor. The doors opened and there was Kareem. The two men looked at each. Kareem got on and the elevator continued down the remaining 14 stories, the two standing back to back. Not a word was spoken.

On another occasion Kareem got onto the team bus in Seattle, dragging his travel bag behind him. It was noisy on the bus as was usually the case. About halfway down the aisle, Kareem felt a tug on his bag. He looked back. The bag was stuck under a seat—Rich Levin's seat.

The two men stared at each other. The noise ground to a halt. All eyes were on the middle of the bus. Nobody was going to lift a finger to help. They all wanted to see who would give in first. Kareem tugged. The bag would not move. Finally, Levin reached down and pulled the bag free. Kareem yanked on his end and kept walking. The noise level slowly picked up. Again, no words had been exchanged.

Riley referred to the traveling media as "buzzards" because, he said, "you guys are always hovering around, waiting to pick somebody's carcass."

As a joke a group of writers went to a hat store on the road one day and bought identical caps with the word "Buzzard" and a picture of one on the bill.

After Riley got a good laugh from the stunt, two writers were eating lunch in a coffee shop, still wearing their "Buzzard" hats. Kareem walked in, leaned over as he passed them, and muttered, "There's only one buzzard among you and he's not here right now."

No one had to ask who he was referring to.

Prior to the 1985 NBA finals against Boston, Kareem motioned to Ted Green, now a sportscaster, to come over to his locker. Abdul-Jabbar reached into his bag and pulled out a yellowed 1978 page from the *Herald-Examiner*.

The headline at the top read, "Is Kareem Over the Hill?" Kareem had been 30 at the time. The story was written by Levin, now an official with Major League Baseball.

Kareem cackled and asked Green, "Where's he now?"

In the late '70s, Abdul-Jabbar wasn't exactly receiving bouquets from Green, then the town's other major Laker beat writer as a member of *The Los Angeles Times* staff. Green had no ax to grind, but he saw Kareem as a gifted superstar who didn't always seem to be getting the most out of his considerable talents.

Green wasn't alone. Around the league there was almost as much talk about what Kareem should do as about what he did do.

"The Lakers [staff and front office] weren't happy with him, but they couldn't go public," Green says. "He was a proud and sensitive person, and they were paying him a lot of money. So they'd vent their feelings in private. He was a great star, had all the talent in the world, they were paying him a lot, but it seemed like he wasn't always playing up to his potential."

Of Green, Kareem now says, "Ted wasn't too bad. Ted would at least talk to me. I didn't have any lingering complaints against him. Sometimes Ted was off the mark, but we got along."

Kareem now admits that his rapport with the press and public wasn't what it should have been, and that he wasn't trying very hard to make friends. Then, with the urging and encouragement of girlfriend Cheryl Pistono, with whom he has since parted ways, Kareem started to reach out.

"Once I started to give people a chance to be decent," he wrote in his book, "I found to my ultimate surprise that quite a few of them *were* decent."

He took a giant step toward changing his image with his famous speech in the movie *Airplane*.

Abdul-Jabbar played himself, disguised as an airline pilot named Roger Murdoch.

A young boy invited into the cockpit immediately recognizes him as the basketball star.

Kareem keeps denying his identity.

The boy persists, telling Abdul-Jabbar how much he likes him, then adds, "My Dad says you don't work hard enough on defense and he says that, lot of times, you don't even run downcourt and that you don't really try, except during the playoffs."

That does it.

Kareem angrily grabs the kid by his shirt and replies, "The hell I don't. Listen kid, I've been hearing that crap ever since I was at UCLA:

I'm out there busting my buns every night. Tell your old man to drag [Bill] Walton and [Bob] Lanier up and down the court for 48 minutes."

The movie cameo helped chip away some of the ice between Kareem and his public. They saw he could laugh at himself.

The transformation of Kareem as a person is an ongoing process, but most observers—media and others close to the club—now see a dramatic difference in the way he relates to people.

"I just think my maturity has helped me to see the way through all that [trouble relating to the public], to make better decisions, not to put myself in a position where I can't communicate or where I don't see what's going on around me," he says. "A lot of times you just shut yourself away from everything, and I just stopped doing that. I took the time and made the effort to understand what's happening, and I think I've benefited from it.

"The media guys don't feel like I've got a chip on my shoulder now. I'm more approachable to them, and they kind of write it up that way. I think they're a lot more open to giving me a fair break, as far as what they report. And that definitely helps as far as the way people perceive me, 'cause the media interprets me to the public.

"It's all a natural process, and once I saw a little bit of improvement there, I said, 'Hey, maybe this could work.' "

During those years when he was tuning out the outside world, Kareem was nowhere near as aloof to his teammates. He had his quiet moments, but there were times when Kareem was the life of the party. There were times when he would dominate the conversation, initiate the fun. He would tell from-the-heart stories of painful moments in his childhood, growing up in a world over which he towered awkwardly. He might talk basketball, or baseball, or politics, or take his turn making fun of his teammates.

"Kareem is just a nice guy, a very intelligent guy," says Jim Brewer, a Laker power forward from '80 to '82. "I found him to be very open. He has a lot of insight, a lot of wisdom."

Brad Holland was a rookie in 1979, a first-round draft pick (selected after Magic Johnson) and a local L.A. hero, having played at UCLA. When Holland reported to training camp he was nervous and apprehensive.

"Scared to death, actually," Holland says. "I thought, 'What will I say to Kareem? He may not even speak to me.' I was totally intimidated.

"I got to the gym early and was shooting around, and I felt a hand on my shoulder. It was Kareem. He said, 'Glad to have you with us, Brad.' Jamaal Wilkes did the same. You don't know how much I appreciated that.

"Kareem and I got to be pretty close. He would save me a seat next to him on airplanes and buses. Everyone else would be talking hoops all the time. We would talk religion, or politics, or horses. He could talk about anything. He's the most well-read person I've ever met."

Holland is Mr. Clean-cut, an All-American-boy type, religious, polite, hardworking, humble. Kareem took to calling Brad "Kemo," short for Kemo Sabe. That's what Tonto called the Lone Ranger, who was certainly the All-American guy in his fictitious world.

"We had a system of fines," Holland says. "If you were late for a bus or to a practice, you'd get fined. Kareem was the instigator of that. He was the official timekeeper. You'd get on the bus late and he'd be all over you, and then the whole team would get on you. It was a lot of fun. . . . But if *he* was the one who was late, you waited to see what kind of mood he was in before you got on him. If he was stoic, you'd just keep quiet."

Not anymore.

"Now," Magic Johnson says, "if Kareem comes on the bus late, they [the players] *own* him. They're all over him. It's easier to talk to him, get to know him. Everybody is real close to him now. Now it's great."

When Kareem is having fun he usually takes the whole team with him.

Jamaal (Silk) Wilkes walks into the locker room wearing a new Hang-10 shirt and Kareem cries out, "Silk! You got your back-to-school threads!"

Spotting the rookie Magic toting a huge portable stereo, Kareem asks, "What's the weather on Mars, Earvin?"

At a team shoot-around in Holland's rookie season, during layups, something dropped out the bottom of his sweatpants as he shot a layup. His wife, Leslie, had washed Brad's practice sweats with the family laundry, and a pair of her bikini panties got hung up inside Brad's sweats. Now the panties were lying on the gym floor.

Kareem swooped over and picked up the tiny garment in mock surprise and horror.

"Where did *these* come from, Kemo?" boomed the captain, stopping practice cold.

Holland blushed furiously and stammered something about how it must have been a laundry mix-up. He tried to take the panties back, but Kareem held them away. He stretched them out and put them on his head like a French beret. He did a five-minute routine with the panties while Holland hid his face and the rest of the Lakers rolled on the court, convulsed with laughter.

Fun-loving teammate or aloof giant? The greatest player of all time or a one-dimensional scorer? The questions surround Kareem more than any other living legend in any sport.

Kareem's own neighbor and fellow 7-foot L.A. legend has been his harshest critic through the years. Wilt Chamberlain lives on a hilltop high above Kareem's canyon, so Wilt looks down on Kareem literally and figuratively.

Chamberlain rarely misses an opportunity to belittle Kareem. Wilt's favorite statement seems to be, "I could outrebound Kareem in my sleep." And, no doubt, Chamberlain has done just that many times.

The two are acquaintances from way back, from the East Coast, when Wilt was a young NBA superstar and Kareem was a high school kid. They eventually had a falling out, partly due to Wilt's political support of Richard Nixon, and they haven't been party pals since. In his book Kareem tells of receiving two used silk suits from Wilt's wardrobe back in the old days.

"He had probably been out dancing in them for days," Kareem wrote. "They were all pitted out, with huge stains underneath the arms and halfway down the back. And they smelled! God, they were awful. . . .

"I thought about keeping the clothes anyway, just as a souvenir, but my mom said positively no, they'd just stink up the closet. She threw them out."

It's difficult to imagine why anyone about whom Kareem would write so sensitively in his book would turn on him, but Wilt has. Chamberlain showed up to help honor Kareem when he broke Wilt's all-time scoring record, but that was merely a momentary détente in the ongoing cold war.

"For Wilt, it's the kind of thing where he has to knock me to make himself look good," Abdul-Jabbar says. "That's the name of that tune. There's nothing anybody can do about it, and at this point, whatever he says falls on deaf ears as far as I'm concerned."

That doesn't stop Wilt. On a CBS halftime show during the '85–86 season, Chamberlain was asked, for the millionth time, his opinion of Kareem Abdul-Jabbar.

"I have to be blunt," Wilt said. "The weak link on that team is Kareem. His transition game is the worst I have *ever* seen. Surprisingly, though, at the end of the game, he's the best."

The man who is now the greatest scorer in NBA history, the man who has dominated the game for nearly two decades, has had to spend much of that time defending himself against critics.

He can now shrug it off by saying, "People think I'm going to lead them to heaven or they think I'm going to lead them to hell. It's got to be black and white with me. That's because people expect so much from me."

And when he's needed most, he usually delivers. Kareem has the most dramatic playoff overdrive gear in NBA history. No one has ever been able to jack their game to a higher level the way he has. His defense hardens, his rebounding becomes more of a factor.

No sports figure has ever made as many encores as Kareem. Every year he is supposed to be the old man, ready to surrender to the new fast gun in town. And every year he shoots 'em down. It was supposed to be the Ralph Sampson Era, the Akeem Olajuwon Era, the Patrick Ewing Era. But at age 39, Abdul-Jabbar is still living the Kareem Era.

He is no Pete Rose, hanging on for a record; no Muhammad Ali, boxing as a mere shadow of himself; no Willie Mays, stumbling in pursuit of fly balls. Abdul-Jabbar, though several years older than anyone who has ever played the game, still seems at or near his peak. A great sports story? Yes. But maybe even a greater story for medical science.

Perhaps Kareem could best sum it up by borrowing a phrase from former President Herbert Hoover.

When asked what happened to all his critics, Hoover replied, "I outlived the bastards."

PART IV
Showtime

●

It has all the elements of a scriptwriter's dream.

Take one slightly aging living legend and rejuvenate him with the infectious spirit of the new kid in town.

Put the two of them in a sparkling showplace under the gaze of the rich and famous.

Have them do battle with the tough guys from the other side of the tracks.

And then have them do it again.

It's High Noon.

It's Star Wars.

It's Showtime.

11.

The Hollywood Lakers

ON Wilshire Boulevard, about two miles before it dead-ends at a row of cliffs overlooking the Pacific Ocean in Santa Monica, there was a nightclub named The Horn. The club featured live entertainment, big names, and new faces—singers, musicians, and comedians in an intimate setting, a small stage surrounded by 150 or so patrons in cozy booths.

Back in the early 1960s The Horn attracted an upscale clientele, L.A.'s hipper Westside set. Jerry Buss, a budding financial superstar, was a Horn regular.

The club's shows always opened the same way. The lights would dim and a singer planted at one of the tables would stand up and begin to sing the establishment's signature tune, "It's Showtime." Another singer at another table would rise, then a third, all harmonizing.

Buss loved that opening. It gave him goose bumps. It was dramatic and theatric; it created a mood, charged the room with electricity and expectation. He loved to sit back, a pretty woman at his side, light a cigarette, sip his rum and Coke, and let himself be swept up in a fantasy of lights, music, and entertainment.

When he bought the Forum and the Lakers in 1979, Buss knew exactly what he wanted—a grand-scale version of The Horn. He wanted atmosphere, ambience, entertainment. He wanted Showtime.

This meant that the main act, the Lakers, had to be flashy, slick, and talented. Buss figured the purpose of a basketball team was the same as that of a nightclub act—to entertain. Once you had your talent booked, you set the mood. Buss dumped the Forum organist and brought in a 10-piece band of young musicians from USC to pump the crowd. He hired a new public address announcer with a livelier voice. He commissioned the recruitment and training of a team of top female dancers who became the slick, sexy Laker Girls.

Not a mere collection of cleavage strutters and leg flashers, like most pro sports cheerleader groups, the Laker Girls were hired strictly on the basis of their dancing ability. Buss swears it. His players perform at a higher level than do college players, and he wanted a correspondingly higher caliber of sideline talent. He wanted big-league cheerleaders. If any of the Laker Girls also happened to be attractive, why, that was merely a happy coincidence.

Next Buss mapped out a strategy of packing the house with the right sociological blend of fans. He wanted to make his show available to the working-class fan, the loyal beer-and-popcorn folks, who would make a lot of noise. And, for a dash of glitter and glamour, Buss wanted to attract the Hollywood crowd, the rich and the famous, the city's powerful and beautiful people.

Sprinkle in such touches as hokey mascots, improved media accommodations, an updated owner's skybox, and a stack of current soul and disco tunes to blare over the P.A. system when the band needs a rest—then throw in the basketball team—and you've got Buss's version of Showtime.

The term wasn't new to basketball. The Harlem Globetrotters were the original showtime team, and college superstar Pistol Pete Maravich came to the NBA in 1970 preaching and practicing the gospel of Showtime.

But Buss took the concept to new heights, or to tackier depths, depending upon your viewpoint.

"Buss seems to have perfectly mated a product to an environment," says Bob Ryan, Boston *Globe* sports columnist and a respected NBA analyst. "Try this in Cleveland, or Kansas City. His emphasis is on entertainment, the whole package. The Lakers *stand* for something now—the break, the instant basket, the blitz. They are a team of the future, the embodiment of speed and dazzle. That's exactly what Buss wants 'em to stand for. They are the vision of an owner. Buss isn't everyone's idea of a classic owner; his dress [very casual], his chicks [very young, often very slick]. But everyone recognizes him as one smart, intuitive sonuvabitch."

Buss wasn't the Lakers' first Hollywood-leaning, Showtime-loving owner. Bob Short knew the value of showcasing his spectacular superstars, Baylor and West, so he lured Doris Day, the First Fan, to the Sports Arena with free courtside tickets.

And under Jack Kent Cooke the Lakers solidified the glitter image that would come to inspire some basketball fans and nauseate others. Cooke, the former Canadian bandleader, certainly appreciated a good show and despised dullness. He didn't just set the stage for Showtime, he *built* the stage, the Fabulous Forum.

And Cooke, who loves to be surrounded by the bright and the beautiful, by the *crème* of society, instilled in his Forum the Hollywood party ambience. Along with Wilt, Kareem, Magic, and other in-your-face players, Cooke gave L.A. fans the chance for in-your-lap thrills with the courtside seat.

First, however, Cooke had to relegate the working press to the cheap seats and he bounced Doris Day into the street. All in the name of money.

In Laker Days BC (before Cooke) the working press sat courtside, as they do at all NBA arenas. But it occurred to Cooke, ever mindful of details, that the press doesn't pay for those choice seats. So when the Lakers moved to the Forum, Cooke created a press section high up in the western stands, in the cheap-seat zone, and sold the courtside seats to paying customers.

When Buss bought the team he moved the press back downstairs, courtside. A common knock against the Lakers and the NBA at the time was that they were boring. Buss theorized that the writers might find the game more exciting if they could hear and see what was going on down there on the court. A football game is more exciting when watched from the 50-yard line than when viewed from the Goodyear blimp.

When Cooke bought the team from Short he took Doris Day off the comp list. Indeed, he did away with the comp list entirely, except for the working press. Day's husband reportedly was indignant.

"The hell with it," he told Cooke. "We've never had to pay for tickets. Doris is a hell of an attraction for your team."

"I'm sorry," Cooke said, "that's the way it's going to be."

Day was an attraction, a veritable Laker institution, but as Cooke says now, "We didn't need it. We were *selling* seats."

Cooke did sell two choice courtside seats, next to the visiting coach, to Jack Nicholson, Day's successor as First Fan.

"Nice guy," Cooke says of Nicholson. "It was often said that in the early photographs of me, he and I look very much alike. [Movie producer Mike] Frankovich often said he was going to do the Jack Kent Cooke story and use Nicholson."

Before every single Lakers and Kings game Cooke hosted a lavish dinner party at his exclusive round table in his exclusive Forum Club for 15 to 18 invited guests.

The guests would then repair to Cooke's exclusive skybox. When the Forum opened he tried sitting courtside, then moved several rows up at midcourt, but there were too many distractions, so Cooke blocked off a section of about 13 seats high in the northern end of the Forum stands. The skybox was born.

On March 8, 1973, shortly before the start of a Kings game, Cooke was almost ushered to the great skybox in the sky.

He had undergone a complete physical exam earlier that day and his doctor promised to phone Cooke that evening at the Forum with the results. The doctor did phone, and Cooke took the call on his skybox phone.

"Keith [Dr. Eggar] told me, 'Jack, it's the most marvelous results from your physical examination. Gee whiz, [you have] the heart of an ox'—didn't say a lion, he said an ox—'and the body of about a 25-year-old man.'"

Cooke said to Eggar, "Here, tell Bob the news," and handed the phone to Dr. Robert Kerlan, Cooke's close friend and a noted orthopedic surgeon.

Finally Cooke took back the receiver, told Eggar, "Thanks again, Keith," and hung up the phone.

"At that moment, my whole jaw was paralyzed," Cooke says. "I had had, just at that *instant,* believe it or not, a massive coronary thrombosis. That *instant!*"

The hockey crowd was streaming into the building. Cooke didn't want to cause a scene, so he walked to his office. Paramedics loaded him onto a stretcher, wheeled him out a seldom-used back exit, and whisked him to a nearby hospital.

Cooke recovered and soon the nightly partying resumed. Karl Malden attended almost every game, sitting behind Cooke and to his left, because that's the direction to which Cooke was most inclined to turn. Glenn Davis, Walter Matthau, Rhonda Fleming, and even the deposed Doris Day were regulars or sem-iregulars in the Cooke skybox. Lorne Greene, Shelly Berman, and Don Rickles would keep the conversation lively. Assorted doctors, lawyers, and titans of industry padded out the nightly guest list.

When Jerry Buss bought Cooke's sports empire he merely expanded on Cooke's party-a-night theme. Buss knew that when L.A. people have friends or relatives visiting from out of town, often the visitors will ask if it's possible to see a real movie star.

Says Buss, "I thought, 'Wouldn't it be great if I could always have movie stars, consistently, at the Forum?' Eventually every-one would know if you really want to see a movie star, there would be one place you could do it—Jerry Buss's box at the Forum."

So Buss set out to stock the Forum with stars. He convinced the Forum concessionaire that he could bring in bigger crowds and create more excitement if he could lure stars. He asked for an entertainment allowance. The concessionaire gave him $50,000. Buss began to compile a list of celebrities—movie and TV people, athletes, celebrated authors and scientists. He searched for and found every Nobel Prize winner living in the L.A. area. They all went on his invitation list.

Over the years Buss has expanded Cooke's original 13-seat skybox to 63 seats. The expansion solved a thorny protocol problem, that of accommodating all Buss's friends and business associates who demand great tickets near the court when none are available. What Buss essentially says is, "If you want to watch a game, you can sit with me. I *own* the joint, and if these seats are good enough for me, how can *you* complain?"

Some come to the skybox. Some stop coming. But Buss's skybox remains SRO for every Laker game. He saves eight seats for the night's designated celebrities and ten for a regular group of friends. The rest of the seats are used by the Forum advertising department and by original Mariani–Buss partners.

On many evenings the best show, for celebrity watchers at least, is in the seats. With Buss's deliberate cultivation of the rich and famous, the team's artistic success, and the NBA's gradual upgrade to big-league status, Laker games have become the place in L.A. to see and be seen, especially during the late rounds of the playoffs. It's not uncommon on any given night to get a glimpse of a dozen or more of the following (in alphabetical order, so as not to offend): Ann-Margret, Jimmy Buffet, Christopher Cross, Michael Douglas, Buddy Ebsen, Darryl Hannah, Veronica Hamell, Bo Hopkins, Rob Reiner, Lionel Ritchie, Kenny Rogers, Mr. T, Dionne Warwick, Raquel Welch, and Debra Winger.

Many other athletes are regulars. Dodger third baseman Bill Madlock and former baseball manager Frank Robinson are season ticketholders. John McEnroe shows up often with Tatum O'Neal.

After the game Buss usually drops by the Lakers' locker room to chat with the players and coaches and to introduce his famous guests to famous Lakers. It's an arrangement that guests and players both seem to enjoy. An ancient axiom of show biz is that all athletes yearn to be entertainers and all entertainers wish they could be great athletes.

After any game you can count on an appearance by two or three stars off this partial list of one-time or regular locker-room guests: Sammy Davis, Jr., Tom Selleck, James Garner, Joe Namath, Don Rickles, Henry Winkler, Tina Turner, Scott Baio, Muhammad Ali, Henny Youngman, Don King, Stephen Stills, Stevie Wonder, and two or three of the Jackson Five, including Michael.

Michael Jackson visited the Laker locker room once, very quickly. He had choreographed a Laker Girls routine and had come to the game to see it performed. He arrived late and missed the routine, but decided to stay around and say hello to his buddy, Magic Johnson, after the game.

Magic himself is now as much a part of the show-biz glamour as any of the stars who come to see him play. This was true from the start, especially in his first two or three seasons in L.A., when he spent more time in discos and at parties than he does now. These days, though still a showstopping dancer, he prefers quieter pursuits—the beach, movies, or hanging out in his new home, alone or with a small group of friends.

Late in 1984 he became a year-round citizen of L.A. when he moved into a two-story, six-bedroom Tudor-style home located at the dead end of a winding private road in exclusive Bel-Air. From his backyard he looks at a complete wilderness, a canyon stretching miles into the distance with no sign of civilization. There is a theory that the canyon hillsides were once covered with homes but they were all blown away by the mega-volume music Magic blasts out of his wall-of-thunder disco.

A selling feature of the home was a barn-sized room Magic quickly converted into the disco, complete with one entire wall filled with sound equipment, a setup that resembles the control room of the Starship Enterprise. He can roll out from the wall a desklike disc-jockey console from which he spins records, controls the room's multicolor, multieffect lighting, and keeps a hundred or more guests—or himself, alone—partying for hours.

Adjoining the disco is a full-size racquetball court, which Magic has converted to a basketball court. He'll shoot for hours by himself, accompanied by disco music, or play HORSE until sunup with teammates who stop by, or with friends or kids from the neighborhood. The hottest HORSE games are with his close friends Isiah Thomas and Mark Aguirre, who spend time with him in the off-season and when their respective teams pass through L.A. Those three have been known to battle at HORSE until dawn in search of a shot the others can't make.

Magic likes people and, though he doesn't drink or take drugs, he does love to party. He fancies himself a master chef, and will host a barbecue at his home where he personally cooks for as many as 200 guests. Every year when he arrives at the team's training camp at Palm Springs, Johnson buys a couple hundred dollars worth of pots and pans and kitchen equipment. Once or twice during camp he'll invite the entire team to his hotel bungalow and cook dinner in the kitchenette, usually fried chicken. Cooking talent runs in the family. Johnson's mother turns a mean skillet; every time the Lakers play in Detroit she bakes about 20 sweet-potato pies for the players and coaches.

Johnson throws himself a birthday party every year in Lansing, and in '85 he also threw a West Coast party. He rented a huge hotel ballroom and sent out 600 invitations to close friends, like Sugar Ray Leonard, Jim Brown, the Jacksons, DeBarge, John Matuszak. . . . The event was black tie, with Magic's favorite disc jockey flown in from Michigan to provide the dance music.

"I got calls for two weeks before the party from people wanting to be invited, probably 70 or 80 calls," says Lon Rosen, a Laker employee and a friend who helps coordinate Magic's schedule.

Magic doesn't shrink from the spotlight in L.A. He was leaving a movie theater in Century City two years ago when he was suddenly surrounded by about 300 high school girls. He chatted with them for several minutes, asked them where they went to school. They were all from a Catholic high school near the Forum, and Magic asked if he could come to the school to speak. He did so and later was invited to attend the school dance as honorary prom king. He stayed for the entire dance, wearing a cardboard crown. And the following year he attended one of the school's plays.

On a vacation in Hawaii one recent off-season, lounging poolside, Magic was accosted by a steady stream of autograph seekers and well-wishers. Finally he got up from his deck chair and walked to the Jacuzzi.

"C'mon, everybody," he called out, easing himself down into the hot bubbles. "You want to ask questions, c'mon over."

Soon he was surrounded by about 100 people—assorted hotel guests—and he fielded questions for 45 minutes.

At an Eddie Murphy concert at Universal Ampitheater, Marvelous Marvin Hagler walked to his seat, was recognized by the audience and accorded a nice round of applause. Then Magic walked in and received a standing ovation.

But Magic isn't always available.

When Josh Rosenfeld first became the Laker's public relations director a few years ago, he received a request for an interview with Johnson and scheduled it for a Sunday.

"I don't do interviews on Sunday," Magic told him.

The next day Rosenfeld approached Johnson after practice.

"Sorry about that mix-up," Rosenfeld said. "I'll have to learn the habits of all you guys. I didn't know you were religious. I certainly won't ever ask you to do anything on Sunday again."

"Sunday," Magic replied, "is my football day."

There is one Laker fan, of course, who needs no introduction—Jack Nicholson. He sits courtside, immediately to the left of the visiting team's head coach, in a seat comped him by Buss. When Dick Motta coached the Dallas Mavericks he and Nicholson got into a courtside altercation. Nicholson claims he merely asked Motta to sit down. Motta claims Nicholson goosed him. Motta responded by offering to make Nicholson an assistant coach so he would at least work for his seat.

Certainly Nicholson is an enthusiastic fan. He attends every home game unless he is shooting a film out of town, in which case the Lakers ship him videotapes of the games he missed. During the playoffs Nicholson frequently travels to road Laker games. In Boston for the 1984–85 finals, he stirred up Celtic fans and was even accused of mooning the Boston Garden crowd. Although taped replays are inconclusive, the mooning has become part of Laker–Celtic legend.

Nicholson does not visit the Laker locker room after games with the rest of Hollywood, but he does socialize with the players. They are frequent guests at his private club on the Sunset Strip, On the Rox, and he has hosted team victory parties at his home.

Cooke almost never ventured into the locker room. Buss almost never misses a postgame visit. Being around the players and around the stars is an extension of Buss's life-style. Considering that he attends about 250 sports events a year, counting college and pro football, stars and jocks *are* his life-style.

After his locker-room visit Buss often shuns the more upscale crowd in the Forum Club to hang out in the smaller, more spartanly appointed press lounge. Eventually he, his date of the evening, and the rest of his entourage are whisked off in his baby-blue limo, either back to Pickfair or to one of Buss's home-away-from-home Hollywood discos.

Buss almost always has a date. He is famous—or infamous—for his female companions, almost all of whom seem to be from this mold: 18 to 20 years old, blond, and attractive. In his early days as Laker owner, Buss would proudly show friends and acquaintances his bulging scrapbook, page after page of snapshots of his many dates, mostly models and assorted former *Playboy* centerfolds. He never dated the same woman two nights in a row, although a few rated repeat invitations. Some days he would have one date for lunch and another for dinner.

To some it seemed as if Buss was cashing in on his newfound

fame, his sudden high visibility, by harvesting a lion's share of Hollywood's available young women. According to Buss, it was simply a matter of business—or pleasure—as usual.

"The trouble with that [believing he dated frequently because he was suddenly a big wheel] would be," Buss says, "that it would seem to indicate I started that when I started this [owning the Lakers and Forum], and that's not true. I was doing that when I was 17. Starting even at 15 or 16, I was really one of the top students around, and then at the University of Wyoming I was really very well known as being an exceptional student.

"In a college atmosphere that makes you one of the heroes. So I wasn't an athletic hero, but I was a campus hero because I got the awards. Girls are attracted to the cheese in whatever game you're playing, so I was a star in that system. As a result, I had a great number of girls that I had a choice of.

"Later, after the Ph.D., I went to work for a consulting company where I had an unlimited expense account, and I traveled. I was 24, and I was one of the few guys around who could say, 'Hey, let's go to Perinos,' and sign it off. So again I was kind of a hero. Now I go into the missile industry, which has its own mystique, and I have the doctor's degree. I'm 26, 28 years old, I'm a missile scientist, so again, it was easy for me."

Buss describes his marital status during these years as "married and separated, and separated and married, going back and fourth. . . ."

He continues, "By this time, I'm getting into a money situation, I'm owning a hotel, a big apartment house, a couple of shopping centers. Women are attracted to power, the guy that's leading the pack in whatever game it is. So just because the way my life has gone, it's always been easy for me. It had nothing to do with suddenly owning the Lakers and Kings.

"But I'm past 50 now, and I'm slowing down a great deal in that category."

Buss became officially engaged in 1979, but the marriage plans were broken off by mutual consent.

"I think I will get married someday," he says. "I think I'll be married in the next two or three years. When I go to discos these days it's more to talk and joke and have fun. I'm not seriously writing down phone numbers."

But he hasn't stopped dating and shopping around.

"At one time I tried pretty much to have a different date every night," Buss says. "The reason for that was, I think that a lot of guys mislead girls. They date the same girl time after time when they know they're not going to marry the girl or get into a permanent relationship. To me, that was always kind of chicken. You're misleading this girl, absorbing her time, where she could move on to the next guy, theoretically thinking her objective is marriage. Unless I feel there's a chance for a permanent relationship, I cut it. I usually can feel that after two or three dates."

Buss has dated numerous members of Hugh Hefner's *Playboy* flock, many of whom he met through his close friend John Rockwell, who lived at Hefner's mansion for some time. Now Buss frequently meets young women on his rounds of Beverly Hills and Westside discos. When he and his entourage arrive at a night spot, they are always escorted to a centrally located table, which quickly becomes the hub of activity in the room, especially if a Laker player or two happens to be discoing at the same place and happens to drop by Buss's table.

If the conversation lags, Buss has a repertoire of sure-fire party tricks. He has been known to set his chest hair on fire for laughs. And in college he saw the movie *Red River*, in which Montgomery Clift puts out a cigarette by grinding it into the palm of his hand. Buss thought this a splendid gesture, and taught himself the trick. You can do it by icing your palm first, which is cheating, or simply by the mind-over-matter method, which Buss prefers.

But whether it's the tricks, or the conversation, or the lure of power and fame, Buss's corner at the disco is almost always well-populated.

"Wherever I go we always get a real good table," Buss says. "We grab all the great girls, and that corner becomes like paradise. You know if you sit with us, you'll get to meet the 15 prettiest girls in the place.

"I sit there and just droves of people, men and women, will come up to me and ask questions and want to talk. Girls come by and they'll say, 'My boyfriend thinks you're sensational, and he would never forgive me if I didn't get your autograph.' Other girls come up and say, 'I love the Lakers.' You start talking to them and say, 'Well, would you like to go to a Laker game with me?' "

Not that Buss ever lacks for company. He has an entourage, the Seven Dwarfs, nicknamed by *Herald-Examiner* columnist Doug E. Krikorian.

It's an unusual, eclectic group. Buss is Doc, naturally. The other six regulars sit in Buss's skybox at each home game and frequently travel with him to out-of-town events and on the disco and banquet circuit.

The oldest dwarf is John (Happy) Rockwell, a pal of Buss's for 20 years. Buss helped Rockwell bankroll a Hollywood saloon, and Rockwell helped Buss land the Phoenix Playboy Club. Both ventures went under. Obviously, Rockwell isn't kept around as an investment adviser. He's a buddy.

One time in Las Vegas, Buss was down to the last $500 chip of his gambling budget.

"We're going to make a comeback," he told Rockwell, and they left the table hours later with a pile of chips worth about $140,000.

Another time they were at the end of their line at the tables when Buss and Rockwell rallied, Rockwell walking off with over $5,000 and Buss with $70,000.

Another key dwarf is Miguel (Sleepy) Nunez. Miguel is a black man in his mid-20s who dresses slightly less conservatively than Michael Jackson. But he pays his way by selling $100,000 or more worth of season tickets each year for Buss.

"They're all bright, upbeat people," Buss says. "They help make the evenings interesting, and they're very loyal. They're with me 125, 135 games a year. I come to so many games, it would get boring if I didn't have my friends."

Some nights Buss stays home and reads, the king alone in his castle. Pickfair is a 42-room mansion on 2.7 hilltop acres in Beverly Hills. It is the former home of movie queen Mary Pickford and the swashbuckling star Douglas Fairbanks. Buss bought the estate in 1980 at a probate auction for $5.4 million. He put $1,025,000 down and signed up for 20 years of mortgage payments of $37,261.77 per month.

Prior to Pickfair, Buss lived in the penthouse of the Sunset

Tower in Hollywood. He loved it, but his live-in girlfriend at the time wanted a tennis court and swimming pool, and she persuaded him to buy a home in Bel-Air. The girlfriend moved out, but two of Buss's four children moved in, so he bought Pickfair. At one point all four of his children were living there.

But now Buss is alone there and he rattles around the mammoth castle like a ghost. He decided Pickfair wasn't his style or his size, and he went penthouse shopping.

"People are impressed when they go to Pickfair, but when you take a girl to a penthouse at night," Buss says, "with all the plush furniture and the view, some soft music, it's automatic. Believe me."

Buss is never lonely at Laker games. Attendance has risen steadily during his seven-year reign, and last season topped 16,000, the highest since the Wilt–West–Baylor seasons of '71–72 and '72–73.

This is surely due to the quality of the floor show, starring the Lakers, but it's also a measure of the success of Buss's ticket-pricing policy, sort of a Robin Hood master plan.

Under Cooke there was only a $2 difference between the price of the worst seat and the best in the house. This was pretty much the pricing philosophy throughout the league. Buss's theory was that by jacking up the price of the good seats and lowering the cost of the not-so-good seats, he would bring more people in. The rich folks can afford to pay more, and the masses—including senior citizens, kids, the military, and the handicapped—need inexpensive tickets.

Buss also remembered a theory he had heard years before, that entertainment tickets should be priced at the equivalent of two hours' income of the fan you're aiming to attract. For minimum-wage workers, this would mean $6 and $7 tickets.

Buss knew the Lakers also attracted many professional people who would be willing and able to pay much more for a real nice seat. As a result the 100 courtside seats for a Laker game are the richest tickets in sports, having soared from $15 under Cooke to $60 under Buss the first season, on up to the current $150. The rich price tag has given that golden rectangle of seats an aura of its own. It is the toughest ticket in town for a regularly scheduled event. Michael Jackson tried to buy courtside season seats and was turned down, as is everyone who applies. There are simply no vacancies.

When Buss bought the Forum he owed favors to several bankers and financiers, and he had other friends to whom he had promised courtside seats. He needed to free at least 10 of the 100 front-row seats to meet those personal obligations. Buss figured the best way to do so would be to raise the courtside prices steeply. He planned to bump the cost to $45. When he got $45 checks in the mail from people, along with notes thanking him for keeping the increase so reasonable, he realized it was going to take more than that to scare fans away. So he decided to charge $60 and, expecting a mutiny of angry courtsiders, he called a meeting of the 100 ticket holders to explain the hike. When Buss arrived at the Forum for the meeting there were already about a dozen Rolls-Royces parked near the Forum Club entrance. Buss realized he didn't need to feel guilty about squeezing these particular patrons for more ticket money.

"I notice many of you people drive the finest cars," Buss told the assembled group. "Those cars cost $120,000, and the average car costs $12,000. So you're willing to pay 10 times as much as the average person for luxury. And that's what I intend for you to do here. Ultimately, you'll pay 10 times as much as the average person for your seats."

One man approached Buss afterward and said, "This is the most outrageous situation I've ever heard of. It's ridiculous. However, I want my seats. And I'll tell you something. It's really a bargain when you get down to it. Every major deal I close, I close by taking a client down to the floor. It's the cheapest part of doing my business."

In seven years, through all the price increases, Buss has had only two cancellations of courtside season seats, and those two were for medical reasons. One man hoping to buy his way into the golden rectangle offered to write Buss a check for four seats for five years in advance, over $100,000. Buss had to decline. Nothing open.

Buss and his staff also devised a plan of selling 2,000 prime-location seats on a year-round basis for all Forum events. The price was $4,000 a year per seat, and is now up to $6,000.

Buss's rich-and-poor ticket-pricing concept has spread throughout the league and, no doubt, has been a factor in the NBA's overall attendance boom.

Most of the other teams have also copied other aspects of the Lakers' showtime package, but no team has matched the Lakers' complete tinsel-glitter extravaganza. The Laker girls, for instance, remain the league's definitive dancing girls.

Not all the sideline entertainment has been of such slick and professional quality. For the first two or three seasons of Buss's reign, Rex the Peanut Man danced nightly. Rex, a regular Forum peanut vendor who appeared to be about 80 years old and to weigh about 70 pounds, would prance out to center circle once or twice each game during a timeout and dance to the band music. Sometimes the Laker girls would join him and the result would be one of the more bizarre spectacles offered at any sporting event since the Roman Colosseum was open for business. Rex even got himself a Hollywood agent. One year he was treated to a birthday party at Pickfair before he was quietly retired from the dancing business.

The Forum's current resident eccentric is Dancing Barry, considerably younger and somewhat more versatile a hoofer than Rex. Barry started out by paying his way into games, donning a tuxedo, and dancing through the aisles during timeouts to incite the crowd. Now he's on the Laker payroll, and is still a popular late-in-the-game feature of most home games.

He is also, for those who prefer a more basic approach to an NBA game, the No. 1 symbol of all that is garish and schmaltzy and—if hoops are your religion—downright sacrilegious about Laker games at the Forum.

This view is neatly articulated by Boston sportswriter Ryan, who says, his voice rising with emotion, "I just want a game. I don't need, above all, Dancing Barry. If he could *dance,* that would be one thing, but he's absolutely and thoroughly untalented. He's such a jerk, without any redeeming social or entertainment value."

Another Eastern view of Showtime was offered by Alan Greenberg, columnist for the Hartford *Courant.* Writes Greenberg, "You go to the Boston Garden and you get a basketball game. You go to The Fabulous Forum, and you get a basketball game in between lounge acts.

"I call it trash. But out here, where they take their garbage and turn it into TV shows, they call it entertainment."

Showtime at the Forum begins, naturally, with the national anthem, performed over the years by a long list of the great and near-great in the recording industry. The most famous Forum rendition of "The Star-Spangled Banner," and one of the most controversial in sports history, was the Marvin Gaye version, performed before the 1983 NBA All-Star game.

Lon Rosen, the Forum's director of promotions, booked Gaye, the legendary Motown singer, to sing the All-Star anthem. Gaye came to the Forum the day before for a live run-through. He was an hour late and accompanied by five sinister-looking aides/bodyguards. He had his own prerecorded musical accompaniment, which was the pulsating rhythm track to Gaye's hit song "Sexual Healing."

Rosen timed Gaye's anthem with a stopwatch. It ran more than four minutes.

"You've got to cut it down," Rosen told Gaye. "CBS will allow us only two minutes for the anthem."

"No problem," Gaye said. "I'll be here at 11:30 tomorrow and we'll run through it again."

The anthem was scheduled for precisely 12:33 the day of the game. Gaye entered the building at 12:25, strode to center court, and delivered a two-minute "Star-Spangled Banner" that had the fans clapping to the unorthodox beat and screaming and whooping.

The Forum crowds can get excited and noisy, but for sustained decibel level, Laker fans are nowhere near the league's loudest. This is no doubt due to West Coast style, which is less frantic and energetic than in most other big-league cities.

But Chick Hearn is another reason for the respectful quiet that sometimes descends upon stretches of a game. Hearn is the radio and TV play-by-play man, and a good number of fans hold down the cheering in order to listen to Chick's "word's-

eye view" on their radios. This in-house audience is a phenome-
non unique in all the league.

Hearn, hired by owner Short at the end of that first L.A.
season, 1960–61, is one of the most recognizable and beloved
figures in the team's history. Chick brings to the game the enthusiasm of a ringside wrestling announcer, the knowledge of an
insider, and the regal bearing of a member of Parliament.

Every game is World War III, every injury potentially career-
ending, every play crucial to the franchise, not to mention the
future of Western civilization.

He has invented basketball terms that have become part of
the game's vocabulary. He peppers his broadcasts with silly say-
ings, grandiose pronouncements, outrageous opinions, and col-
orful, accurate, detailed accounts of the action. He created such
phrases as "faked him into the popcorn machine" for brilliant
moves on the court and "the mustard is off the hot dog" for
not-so-brilliant moves. He has captured the rhythm and pace
and spirit of the NBA better than anyone who ever sat behind
a microphone.

When the Lakers play, Hearn is like a proud or indignant
father watching five of his kids run around. He brags about
their feats on the air with gushing praise, but scolds them harshly
for their mistakes.

Jack Kent Cooke recognized Hearn's hold on Laker fans.
When games were televised Cooke hated to deprive the TV
audience of Hearn's "word's-eye view," and he couldn't take
Chick off radio without risking a fan uprising. So Cooke invented
the simulcast. Hearn would do the radio *and* TV play-by-play.
Hearn has missed only two games in the last 26 seasons, a re-
markable statistic, especially considering he once quit.

That incident occurred when Jerry West was involved in a
bitter contract dispute with Jack Kent Cooke. Cooke's secretary,
Rosemary Garmand, phoned Hearn at his home one morning
and asked if he would please contact West and instruct him to
come to Cooke's office immediately.

"Gee, I don't know where Jerry is," Hearn said, wondering
why he had been called in as a go-between.

"Well, find him," Garmand said. "Mr. Cooke said you could
find him."

Hearn phoned West and relayed the message. West said he would not go to Cooke's office.

Hearn relayed that message to Cooke.

"What do you *mean*, he won't see me?" Cooke demanded. "You call him back and you get him!"

So Hearn phoned West again, but West held firm. Hearn phoned Cooke.

Cooke was getting madder.

"Get him here to my office!" Cooke commanded. "You're going to do it!"

"What I'm going to do is *quit!*" shouted Hearn, and slammed down the phone.

Minutes later Cooke called back, there were mutual apologies, and Hearn was rehired, or unretired.

Under Cooke and Short, Hearn's official title was Assistant General Manager, and he was a trusted adviser on player personnel matters. That title and function were dropped when Buss bought the team. Now Hearn is simply the announcer, the voice and the heart of the Lakers, on the air and off.

Hearn provides for the Lakers' traveling party constant commentary and quips on bus rides and plane trips, in hotel lobbies, restaurants, and in airports.

Chick was riding up a hotel elevator when it stopped and a man got on wearing a Superman costume. The man rode up one story and got out. "Silly son of a bitch could've jumped that high," Hearn whispered indignantly.

Chick controls any situation he's involved in, with a few exceptions.

Ten years ago, on a team flight to Cleveland, an oil leak grounded the airplane for repairs in Akron. Hearn, broadcast partner Lynn Shakleford, and trainer Frank O'Neal headed for a lunch counter for hamburgers. There weren't three open stools in a row so Hearn asked a customer if he would mind moving down one. The customer scooted over without a word. A few minutes later there was a screeching of tires outside as three police cars pulled up near the front door. Several officers walked into the tiny restaurant.

"All of a sudden," says Hearn, "I feel something pointed and hard sticking in my back, and someone is saying, 'Get 'em

UP!' I leaned over to Shakelford and said, 'Listen to that silly son of a bitch.' "

The policeman repeated the command, and Hearn realized it was directed at him. He dropped his hamburger and threw his hands into the air.

Guns drawn, the policemen frisked Chick. Just then the waitress got the attention of one of the officers and nodded at the solo customer. It turned out that the man had entered the diner just before Chick and his friends and had ordered a meal, growling, "And get it out here fast, or I'll kill you."

The waitress called the police and reported that the man was sitting on the second stool from the end of the lunch counter. Which is where he *had* been sitting until Hearn asked him to move. The police then arrested the correct suspect and let Chick off for good behavior.

Hearn, who rules every broadcast with an iron hand, has seldom been upstaged. At the conclusion of one TV interview, however, Chick was presenting Elgin Baylor with the standard gift provided by the show's sponsor.

"Take this gift certificate to any Harris and Frank men's store and get yourself some nice clothes, Elgin," Hearn said.

Still on camera, Baylor handed the certificate back to Hearn and said, "Here, Chick, you need this worse than I do."

Hearn always seems to have a one-liner handy for any occasion.

One night in Indianapolis he shouted on-the-air instructions for the camera to zoom in for a shot of the beat writers sitting courtside. Misunderstanding Hearn, the cameraman zeroed in, instead, on a couple of *waiters* serving drinks to fans.

Another announcer might have been flustered, but not Chick.

"No," he said calmly into his mike, pointing toward the writers, "these guys serve up a lot of baloney, but they are not waiters."

On another occasion a writer traveling on the team bus was annoying Hearn by talking too much.

As the bus pulled up to a Denver street corner, Hearn noticed construction work going on immediately outside his window where the sidewalk was being torn up with jackhammers and picks.

"Hey," Hearn yelled to the writer, "want to make some extra money?"

The writer, playing the part of a good straight man, nodded affirmatively.

"Then get out there, put your chin on the sidewalk, and keep talking!"

On trips to Cleveland the Lakers used to stay outside Richfield, Ohio, in a desolate area not only far from the city lights but away from even street lights.

When it snowed heavily, as it did on this day, there was no point in leaving the hotel grounds unless a walk down a deserted highway in zero-visibility conditions was your idea of a good time.

After eating lunch in the hotel restaurant, most of the Laker traveling party sat down in a row of chairs, stared at the ceiling, and agonized over the thought that the game against the Cavaliers was still 30 hours away.

Finally, Rich Levin of the *Herald-Examiner* stood up and announced, "I'm going to my room to kill myself."

He left and no one spoke for several minutes.

Then Hearn stood up and asked, "Which way is Rich's room?"

Hearn's style has always been the rapid delivery, the verbal equivalent of a fast break, and under Buss's Laker ownership Chick has been paired up with a team with foot speed to match his lip speed. Since the beginning of the Buss–Magic era the Lakers, if not always the best team in the NBA, have consistently been the prettiest. Their fast break, when cranked to maximum RPMs, is considered the most devastating running game in the history of basketball.

And that, the running game, is the most vital component of Buss's grand Showtime design. All the girls and mascots and music and courtside glitter would be meaningless decoration if not for the trademark fast break.

Buss tends to work in the background, to let his coaches and executives and advisers do the work and make the decisions, with his final approval. But if there is a message that rings down loud and clear from the owner's skybox, it is this: Run.

Running is a Laker tradition, ever since Jerry and Hot Rod and Elgin.

"The Lakers brought racehorse basketball to the West," says Celtic announcer Johnny Most, "and it became a thing of beauty. Other clubs in the West had to change their styles to keep up with the Lakers, and now everyone out there is galloping. It's racehorse basketball, and L.A. does it better than anyone."

Buss was determined to continue the tradition, accelerate it even, especially now that he had Magic and Nixon in the saddle. Buss hired McKinney because he was a running coach and he fired Westhead because he thought he had slowed the team down.

The Lakers must run because Buss demands it and because the coaching staff and front office believe in fast-break basketball. To Pat Riley the lightning transition game is anything but a theatrical gimmick. It is the direction of modern basketball, essential to the team's success.

"Whether it's for Showtime, or whether it's for marketing, or it's for his [Buss's] whim, that's how I like to play," Riley says of fast-break basketball. "That's how I was taught. It's the best way to play basketball, the most fun way and most conducive to the kind of talent that comes off college campuses now. They are very agile, versatile, quick athletes whose instincts are to attack. I will always continue to be big on the wide-open running game.

"In this game you have to get easy baskets. You can't always grind it out, grind it out. There's more wear and tear on players in that kind of situation than there is in the free-lance running game. You've got to be able to get 20 percent of your offense on easy baskets—layups or opportunity jumpers off the break.

"The players don't like to have a leash around their neck all the time. You have to trust the players. You have to allow them to be able to create and to become spontaneous when the pattern breaks down. I think that's what players like about the breaking system so much, is that they're allowed to be instinctive."

Buss also felt that the theatrical touches and the blazing running game would make the Forum fans more enthusiastic and thereby strengthen the Lakers' home-court advantage.

"I really tried to create a Laker image, a distinct identity," Buss says. "I think we've been successful. I mean, the Lakers are pretty damn Hollywood."

And the resulting package is pretty damn sickening to some critics, most Celtic fans, and many basketball purists. The Lakers' exuberant and reckless style of play, coupled with the sideline circus, is not universally loved or admired. To some what Buss and the Lakers have done is as praiseworthy as hiring LeRoy Neiman to repaint the Sistine Chapel.

Nevertheless, the Lakers' Showtime philosophy has been successful in terms of winning games and influencing fans and advertisers coast to coast.

"I think the Lakers tugged basketball into the modern era, particularly when the Forum was built," says former 76ers general manager Pat Williams.

The Lakers certainly haven't hurt the league's overall clout with the networks. "The Lakers have generated a tremendous following, with their exciting offense and with Kareem and Magic," says Neil Pilson of CBS TV. "Their coach is an attractive, articulate guy with a distinctive style, and the Forum is a glamorous place to play. The Lakers are a very powerful part of our TV package.

"In the last four or five years, the ratings, in numbers and in quality demographics, have improved year by year, and that's very significant. Most other sports have been static or have declined. That's why the NBA's new TV contract is almost 100 percent bigger than the last one, at a time when other sports are not getting any contracts at all.

"The NBA is definitely swimming against the tide. They're going upstream while the others are going downstream. There is a fundamental public perception that the league is a well-managed, well-run, economically sound sports league not troubled by the labor strife, antitrust problems, and uncertainties that have plagued professional football and baseball."

A major factor in the rise of the league has been an influx of marquee players—Magic, Bird, Ralph Sampson, Patrick Ewing, Michael Jordan, Dominique Wilkens. . . .

Another factor, surely, has been the more solvent and competent level of ownership. The policies laid down by Jerry Buss—

the ticket-pricing structure and the marketing—have set a general trend.

Buss declines to take the blame for escalating salaries, pointing out that every time he raises the ante by writing a bigger contract, the other owners quickly bypass him in free-spending. Still, there's little doubt that Buss's generosity in writing huge contracts for top stars has goosed the league's salary structure.

But the overall result has been prosperity, a league that has pulled itself out of the bushes and into the big time. This is a league that once (in the early 1940s) featured as halftime entertainment accordian minisolos by Celtic player Tony Lavelli, who played for $125 a game, and now hires superstars like Willie Nelson to serenade the folks at the All-Star Game. The league has come far.

It didn't take Jerry Buss long to make an impact on the league, to create and execute a Showtime concept that paid off in good times, rich times, and winning times, exactly what he had in mind when he went into the basketball business.

Five seasons into his ownership, Buss found himself presiding over a cultural phenomena. He was a leader and policy shaper in a boom league. He had more money than ever, considerably more personal fame, increased clout at the discos, and he owned the grandest toy in the world—the Lakers. What more could he possibly wish for?

Just this: a win over the hated Boston Celtics. Without that, the show would never be complete.

12.

Showdown Time

THE LAKERS had been in Los Angeles for 24 years. It had been 24 years filled with lots of victories and a couple of titles, bigger crowds and bigger bucks than the old Minneapolis regime could have ever dreamed of.

But it had also been 24 years of frustration. The Lakers still couldn't seem to shake that monkey off their backs, the big green monkey with the cigar in its mouth. For the Lakers had *never* beaten the Boston Celtics in a championship series. They had *never* beaten the symbol of the old guard, of the Eastern basketball establishment, the ruling class of the game for the better part of two decades.

Oh sure, the Lakers had won three NBA titles since coming West, but there are peaks and then there are *peaks*. Beating Boston, settling old scores, ending a quarter-century jinx, proving that the finesse of Showtime could prevail over the muscle of the Celtics, fast-breaking your way past the greatest dynasty the game has known—that would be the ultimate peak.

Seven times the Lakers had met the Celtics in the NBA finals, and seven times it was the Lakers who went tumbling down, often missing that peak by just inches.

There was Frank Selvy's shot that hit the rim and bounced away, Sam Jones's bank shot that hit the rim and rolled in, Don Nelson's ridiculous rim shot that came down just right, and all those balloons that never came down.

All seven Laker–Celtic meetings had ended with an NBA championship banner headed for the rafters of Boston Garden.

The most recent and most embarrassing encounter with the Celtics ended with balloons in the Forum rafters. That was 1969. Jack Kent Cooke was sure this was the year. After all, the Lakers had the home-court advantage for the first time against Boston. They also had Wilt Chamberlain, Elgin Baylor, and Jerry West.

So with the series tied at 3–3, Cooke arranged a little celebration for the seventh game at the Forum. When the Lakers won he would release balloons from the ceiling and the USC marching band would play "Happy Days Are Here Again."

All day long the phones in the Forum rang and rang, but many of the secretaries were too busy to answer them. They were blowing up balloons.

As Laker P.R. man Jim Brochu, now an ABC publicist, raced up an aisle on his way out of the arena several hours before the game, he bumped into Red Auerbach, then the Celtics' general manager.

As they exchanged nods Auerbach glanced up at the ceiling. Instantly, Red got a lot redder.

"Those things," he growled, pointing to the balloons with his cigar, "are going to stay up there a hell of a long time."

With just under 10 minutes to play in the game, the Celtics, fired up to pop Cooke's balloons, had opened up a 17-point lead.

But West, despite a badly pulled hamstring, led his club back within reach. West would wind up with 42 points, 13 rebounds, and 12 assists.

With a little over five minutes to play and the Lakers just seven back, Chamberlain, the team's 7-2 center, hurt his right knee coming down with a rebound. Off he limped and in came Mel Counts.

The Lakers continued to narrow the margin until Counts' 10-foot jumper cut the Boston lead to one. Chamberlain was ready to go back in. But coach Bill Van Breda Kolff wasn't ready to put him in. It was to be the climax to a long-running feud between the two. Van Breda Kolff told his superstar center, "We're doing well enough without you." A furious Chamberlain returned to his seat.

With little more than a minute to play and Boston still clinging to a one-point lead, 103–102, West made a great defensive play, slapping the ball away from a Celtic. But the loose ball bounced directly into the hands of Boston forward Don Nelson, who was standing near the free-throw line. He fired a 15-foot shot that hit the rim, bounced up four feet above the basket, and came down cleanly through the net.

"It was lucky," says Nelson, now coach of the Milwaukee Bucks. "Sometimes luck does play a part. There had been nothing we'd been able to do to stop them. We couldn't get them down. But that one shot brought them back to reality."

The Celtics hung on to win, 108–106.

It was the second miraculous shot of the series. In Game 4, the Lakers, leading 88–87 with seven seconds to play, committed a turnover. Boston's Sam Jones grabbed the ball and threw it up off balance with two seconds remaining. The ball rolled around the rim and fell through for the game winner.

In the Celtic locker room Jones told sportswriters he had deliberately shot the ball higher than normal so that if he missed, center Bill Russell would have a chance to tip it in.

Russell wasn't in the game.

Three months after the series ended Russell announced that the 1968–69 NBA title, his eleventh in 13 seasons, would be his last. He was retiring.

West was named Most Valuable Player of that championship series, the only time the award has gone to a member of the losing side. Van Breda Kolff wound up losing his job to Joe Mullaney.

And the balloons?

"I sent them all to a children's hospital," Cooke says, "where the kids had a great time with them, certainly a better time than I did."

The Lakers began their championship rivalry with the Celtics the season before they crash-landed in that Iowa cornfield. In the 1959 NBA finals, Boston, behind Frank Ramsey (29 points in Game 1), Bill Sharman (28 points in Game 2), and Bob Cousy (23 points and 15 assists in Game 3), swept the Minneapolis Lakers in four games.

The teams met again in 1962 when the Lakers were calling the L.A. Sports Arena home. With the series at 1–1, Game 3 was played before a then-record Laker crowd of 15,180.

The night was vintage Jerry West. On a jumper and then two free throws, he tied the score at 115 with four seconds remaining. After a timeout Sam Jones tried to in-bound the ball to Cousy, but West intercepted the pass about 35 feet from the Laker basket. Three seconds left. Rather than fire up a jumper, West decided to go for the layup. The ball went in just as the buzzer went off.

"We were all yelling for him to shoot it at the free-throw line," Frank Selvy says. "But he knew exactly how much time was left. You wouldn't find anyone that smart now. They would all pull up and shoot from 40 feet."

Says Chick Hearn, "Auerbach said it was impossible to dribble nearly half the court and make the basket in three seconds. So he got the film of the game, ran that play 1,000 times, and it always came out the same—2.9 seconds."

The Lakers' 117–115 win had a whole city talking the next day. Pro basketball had arrived in Los Angeles.

There was a lot more to talk about before that series ended. In Game 5 Baylor scored 61 points (and grabbed 22 rebounds) in Boston Garden, a playoff record that stood until the Chicago Bulls' Michael Jordan scored 63 in a 1986 double-overtime loss to the Celtics.

Tom (Satch) Sanders guarded Baylor in his record game. Or tried to.

"It didn't matter who guarded him," Sanders says. "Elgin was just a machine that night."

Sanders remembers Baylor as "such an exceptional passer that we couldn't really double-team him. Before the game they'd tell me, 'Satch, you're on your own.' Which, to tell you the truth, did not exactly inspire me.

"People talk about his [Baylor's] fabulous right hand, but in one playoff game, two times in a row, he went to his left. The party was over after that. You didn't know where to play him."

The series came down to a seventh game. It came down to the final three seconds with the score tied at 100.

It came down to Frank Selvy, a Laker guard who once scored 100 points in a game for Furman University.

"He was senile at 28," Hundley says. "He led the nation in scoring in college [in 1954] with 41.7 per game. I asked him once what he averaged that year and he said, 'I don't remember. Somewhere around 41.7.'"

Two points would be enough now in these final seconds at

the Garden, enough to give the Lakers the title and perhaps end the Celtic dynasty. Boston had already won three straight championships and four of the last five.

"Hot Rod [Hundley] told me he had had a dream that he made the winning shot," says Fred Schaus, then the Laker coach. "Damn, he should have taken it."

"I turned to face the basket," Hundley says. "K. C. [Jones] got through [Rudy] LaRusso's screen, so West wasn't open. Cousy was on Selvy. Cousy was a *terrible* defensive player. We used to fight over who would be guarded by him. He would steal the ball a lot because he just ran around, but he never guarded his man.

Hundley bounced the ball to Selvy on the baseline. He was wide open when he got it. Three seconds remained.

"The screen delayed him [Cousy] just a second," Selvy remembers. "I had to get it off fast. I sort of hurried, but I thought it was going in."

"There was very little breathing in the Garden," Sanders says, "when the ball went to Selvy on the baseline. I thought, 'Anybody but him.'"

Selvy shot a 15-foot jumper. No miracles required. Just a routine shot, one he'd made a thousand times before.

Thought Auerbach, "It's all over."

Not quite. The ball missed by an inch, hitting the rim and bouncing away, into the large hands of Bill Russell. To K. C. Jones, then a Celtic guard, it seemed Russell "went about 12,000 feet above the rim" to get the ball.

"I was so relieved," Cousy remembers. "I don't think Frank had missed that shot since 1928."

"I was in good position to get the rebound," Baylor says, "and Sam Jones just shoved me out of bounds. He didn't get called for it. He kids me about it today."

Auerbach remembers that "my timekeeper froze on the clock. Our guys thought time had run out [the film shows otherwise]. There were only one or two seconds left when the ball was thrown to midcourt, then Hundley took one or two dribbles, threw to Selvy and he shot, and they *still* had time to get a tap on the thing. All within two seconds.

"Our timekeeper was an old guy from Harvard. He was 100

percent ethical and scrupulous, but he was an old gent. He had run the clock for 20-odd years and his reflexes weren't that good."

No argument about what happened when the clock did run out. The Lakers ran out of chances in overtime and Boston won, 110–107.

"I get the blame for missing that shot," Selvy says, "but I don't think that was the ballgame. We could have done better in overtime. I think a lot of people don't realize I made the last two baskets to tie the game up."

It was a key win in the Celtics' string of championships.

"We were an aging club," Auerbach says, "and if we hadn't won that one, it would have made it rougher psychologically for the guys in the future."

"Especially in Boston, they developed that invincible aura," Tommy Hawkins says of the Celtics. "Teams going in were psyched totally. It was nervous time. It wasn't, 'I hope we can win.' It was, 'I hope we can get out alive without getting embarrassed.' Even athletes have fear when they enter competition. They are in awe of certain things and Boston had developed that in other teams. If we had won that one game, it might have changed that significantly."

In the Laker locker room a lot of heads were hanging, especially Selvy's. Hundley came up to him, kneeled, a soothing look on his face, and said, "It could happen to anybody. Don't worry, baby. You only cost us about $30,000."

In another corner of the locker room Ray Felix stood up and told his teammates, "Don't worry, we'll get 'em tomorrow."

Tomorrow would be a long time in coming.

The two teams met again in the finals a year later and again Boston prevailed, this time in six games.

A Tommy Heinsohn steal and layup followed by two Heinsohn free throws were the keys to a 112–109 title-clinching win for the Celtics. When it was over a retiring Cousy hurled the ball toward the ceiling of the Sports Arena.

The Lakers and Celtics were back at it in 1965. This time Baylor was out with a knee injury and West responded by averaging 40.6 points over the 11 Laker postseason games.

K. C. Jones was given the task of guarding him in the finals. Jones, doing his best imitation of West's West Virginia twang, recalls the Laker guard telling him, " 'Kase, I just can't get things going.' I'd stand there, listening and saying, 'Yeah, yeah, yeah.' Here he was averaging 25 points and there I was, hoping to get four."

In one playoff game Jones held West to 16 points.

"In the dressing room after the game, I'd never seen that many reporters around me in my life," Jones says. "I must have talked a dictionary full. I'd forgotten that Jerry would also be reading the papers, and we had a game the next night. That night he got 43 points and they had to take me to the hospital the next day to take my foot out of my mouth."

Russell, although suffering from an eye injury, pulled down 30 rebounds in the fifth and final game of the 1965 finals, a game the Celtics won, 129–96. They clinched it at the start of the final quarter when they ran off 20 straight points, holding the Lakers scoreless for five minutes.

A year later it was Auerbach who was retiring. Up by 10 with 40 seconds to play in Game 7, Boston hung on for a 95–93 win with John Havlicek finally dribbling out the clock.

"I would have loved to have stuffed that damn cigar down his throat," says Schaus of Auerbach's traditional victory smoke. "We came awfully close to putting that damn thing out."

Close, but no cigar.

In 1968 the Celtics beat the Lakers in six, Havlicek scoring 40 points in the 124–109 clincher.

This was Russell's first championship as a player-coach. He did his part as a player, making a key block of a Baylor shot in a Boston overtime win in Game 5.

One season the Lakers were so confident of victory, they had their champagne on ice early in the series.

"We carried that champagne from coast to coast," Baylor says. "By the time we lost, the labels had come off the bottles. Schaus wanted to know if we could get our money back. I think we wound up selling the champagne to the Celtics."

The Lakers never got to taste it. With such journeymen as Felix, Jim Krebs, Gene Wiley, Leroy Ellis, and Darrall Imhoff on the front line, the team was never a match for Russell, who averaged 24.9 rebounds, 16.2 points, and who knows how many blocked shots (they didn't keep that statistic in those days) in 13 years of postseason play.

"I've always felt a little fortunate," Cousy says. "Jerry and Elgin should have had a championship ring long before they got one. But the Lakers didn't have a viable center."

"If Russell had been on the Lakers," Hearn says, "we'd have won all six [championship series]."

The 6-11 Felix was no match for the 6-10 Russell. In one Celtic–Laker battle Felix put up four shots and Russell blocked them all. The fifth time Felix faked Russell one way and then threw the ball—over his head, over the backboard, into the stands. He pointed at Russell, grinned, and said, "You didn't get that one, baby."

Most of his teammates had a Ray Felix story.

"We'd play high-low [poker]," Tommy Hawkins says, "where you have to declare high or low by showing one finger or two. He'd get confused. He'd have a lock on low and he'd display the high sign and lose the pot. He had the ability to forget. He'd make the all-eccentric, all-absentminded team. Invariably he'd forget to bring an overcoat to New York. He wasn't a guy who remembered every offensive play the Lakers had. We called him Count, or Baby Ray, which infuriated him."

A reporter in Cincinnati wrote that Ray was "gangling." The next time he saw the sportswriter Ray ordered him out of the locker room, then turned to a teammate and asked, "What does gangling mean?"

Looking back, Cousy feels only sympathy for his old rivals. "Active players are notoriously selfish," he says. "It's only when you get into middle age that you develop the quiet compassion."

At age 68, Auerbach is well past middle age. But *his* compassion still seems nonexistent.

"Why would I feel sorry for them?" he asks. "They were the enemy. They were continually building a better team. We didn't have any money, any draft choices, and we still beat them. [It] was more satisfying because of the Hollywood syndrome. Every year the writers out there raved how tremendous the Lakers were. We whipped them with Chamberlain, without Chamberlain, with Baylor, with West.

"We outpsyched them many times. One time [1966], they

came into Boston for the first game and whipped us [133–129]. That was the day I released the news that I was making Russell coach for the next season. That killed them. They beat the hell out of us and everybody was writing about Russell being the next coach. They hardly even mentioned the game.

"We used to psyche Schaus pretty good. He became a little confused. It got to the point he started Baylor in the backcourt."

Responds Schaus, "He always had a gimmick all right. It was called Bill Russell. It was amazing how great a coach he became after he got Bill Russell. Russell made a hell of a coach out of him. Before that, with Cousy and Sharman, he couldn't even win his division."

Says Cooke, "I echo in high 'C.' Of all the ridiculous nonsense. If he didn't have Russell, I don't think he'd be lighting up cigars."

The cast and crew were all new when the favorite series of the networks—Lakers against the Celtics—was brought back in 1984 after a 15-year hiatus. But the bitterness remained.

Auerbach was still around. But instead of Chamberlain and Russell, or West and Cousy, or Baylor and Sanders, it would be Magic and Larry Bird, arguably the game's two finest players. They had clashed their final year in college when Johnson led Michigan State past Bird's Indiana State club in the NCAA championship game.

When Magic had that memorable night against Philadelphia in the 1980 Championship Series, people were calling him the best in the game. A year later Bird was leading the Celtics to the NBA championship and the sentiment had shifted in his favor. Back and forth it went, depending on the fortunes of their respective teams, but never had they had the opportunity to settle this argument face-to-face with a title on the line. Until now.

There was so much at stake:

Lakers vs. Celtics.

Magic vs. Bird.

West vs. East.

Finesse vs. Muscle.

Glamour vs. Tradition.

Hollywood vs. Beantown.

New vs. Old.

Running vs. Rebounding.

Gold Chains vs. Blue Collars.

Perhaps the Next Dynasty vs. the Last Dynasty.

Jerry Buss felt it all.

"I still like finesse basketball more than I like intimidating basketball," he says. "I still like the West much more than I do the East. I had that battle running in everything I've done for 25 or 30 years, not just basketball. I worked back East for a year and my reaction is, they don't know what they're doing. I'm the one that keeps trying to get all the NBA offices to head-quarter in Los Angeles, because this is where it's at, not in the East. I'm very pro-West and anti-East. Intimidating vs. finesse, and old vs. new, and Laker vs. Celtic, all the traditions—yes, I do feel them all."

The images don't blur easily. Even after the Lakers beat the Celtics in the 1985 NBA finals there were many in the East who still considered this to be Team Hollywood, a collection of fleet-footed wimps playing in a circus tent.

"L.A. is a good team, but they're too nice," said Pat Williams, former 76er general manager. He said that *after* the Lakers had won it all three times in this decade. "The Lakers are fancy passes and limousines. Us against Boston is a black-eye series. Them against L.A. is a black-tie series."

And Williams is an *admirer* of the Laker franchise. The *detractors* see the Lakers as a cute team that breezes through a cream-puff conference every season and lacks muscle and substance and character.

"I think it's no more than a crock of shit," says Pat Riley of the Eastern view of the Western teams, the Lakers in particular. "That's just the perception of the public, born out of the comments of the Pat Williamses in the Eastern Conference, and of the media that cover the teams back there. They consider the Eastern Conference hard-hat and blue-collar. We have to deal with that all the time, and it takes a shot at your dignity. Anything that you do isn't good enough, because it's soft.

"This has an impact on the officiating. I don't think there's any doubt that the officials think, 'Well, this team plays this way and they're allowed to play that way, and that team isn't supposed to play that way.' They allow the Eastern teams to get away with more.

"We've won three championships in seven years and went to the finals four straight years. We win, and that's the only thing any team should be measured on. I think the enthusiasm of Earvin Johnson has created an emotional team that sometimes enjoys winning too much. People might think you're rubbing it in. I don't agree with that. Something that's spontaneous and joyful shouldn't be misconstrued as showing a lack of respect for the opponent.

"I don't think there's any doubt that Southern California and Hollywood and L.A. are considered to be filled with people who are soft and have no values and couldn't work a day in their lives, that everything out here is a free ride. Our road to success has always been a struggle, hasn't been easy, but they [critics] won't agree with that. They don't want to hear it. They think you're on a magic carpet or something, being lifted up by the bright lights of Los Angeles."

Who would say a thing like that? Boston play-by-play announcer Johnny Most, perhaps. Most's unabashed, unchecked love of the Celtics and hate for the Lakers, expressed on the air, reflects the nature of the L.A.-Boston rivalry.

During the '84–85 Finals, Most opined during one broadcast that Rambis had crawled up out of a sewer. In one game, Magic Johnson complained to the referee about a foul call. For the rest of the broadcast, Most referred to Johnson as "Crybaby," as in "Crybaby brings the ball upcourt. Crybaby passes over to Worthy . . ."

The feelings were pretty strong on the court too.

"I don't think we liked them particularly as players," says Cedric [Cornbread] Maxwell, then a Boston forward, of that '84 Laker squad. "We didn't like what they represented. And that was the Hollywood bourgeoisie, West Coast, laid-back-type style, Showtime.

"That Showtime attitude didn't fit well on the East Coast. If you win, you're going to win with hard-nosed play and some good baskets and stuff like that. But Showtime, the behind-the-back passes—that's a little like showing off. We took it to heart that we were going to try to put an end to some of that. The Lakers have that air about them that they're a very flashy team. The Celtics were a very workmanlike team. They worked for everything they got, like guys going to work every day. It was the steelworkers against the Hollywood movie stars."

Was the Celtic jinx still alive and lurking in the shadows, having waited 15 years for the next group of Lakers to come along?

On the eve of the 1984 finals, while the rest of the Lakers were tucked into their Boston hotel-room beds, catching their final hours of rest for the struggle ahead, Kareem Abdul-Jabbar was engaged in a struggle of a different sort, trying to shake off a migraine headache.

Migraines, caused by diet or nerves or a combination of both, had plagued Abdul-Jabbar throughout his career, and now he had one at the worst possible time. He missed the team meeting that morning, he missed breakfast, and he missed the bus to Boston Garden for Game 1, but he didn't miss much else.

The Laker center arrived at the Garden about an hour before tipoff, his head still throbbing, only to have trainer Jack Curran snap him back into shape—literally. Curran adjusted the vertebrae in Abdul-Jabbar's neck, sending a pain-free Kareem out onto the court.

For the next couple of hours the Laker center gave the Celtics headaches by scoring a game-high 32 points (12 of 17 from the floor and 8 of 9 from the free-throw line), along with eight rebounds, five assists, two blocked shots, and a steal as the Lakers won, 115–109.

Maybe it *was* a new era.

It sure seemed so when the Lakers found themselves just 18 seconds away from victory in Game 2. A sweep of the first two in Boston? That was more than they dared dream.

But then the Lakers fell asleep.

Kevin McHale had just missed a free throw, leaving the Celtics two points behind. Pat Riley had told Magic Johnson to call a timeout after the free throws only if Boston tied the game up. Johnson, however, misunderstood and called time anyway.

The break in the action gave the Celtics an opportunity to

set up their defense. Johnson flipped an in-bounds pass to James Worthy in the backcourt. Rather than toss it back to Magic, Worthy looped a cross-court pass in the direction of Byron Scott.

Boston guard Gerald Henderson, waiting and hoping for such a break, cut in front of Scott, stole the ball, and scored on a soft layup to tie the game.

Buss calls the play "a nightmare. If I shut my eyes, I can *still* see it. It's indelible in my mind. I can tell you who I was sitting next to at the time, what they were wearing, everything."

Johnson failed to get a shot off in the closing seconds of regulation time and the Celtics won in the overtime, 124–121.

It was ironic that Worthy had made the bad pass. This had been his coming-out night in the NBA. He had been in the national spotlight in his junior year at North Carolina when he led the Tar Heels to the 1982 NCAA championship. He was the tournament MVP after scoring 28 points in the title game against Georgetown.

During Laker negotiations with Cleveland for Jim Chones in the fall of 1979, Buss detected real anxiousness on the part of the Cavaliers to make a trade. So he instructed Bill Sharman to lean on the Cavs, get them to sweeten the deal by agreeing to swap first-round draft picks for, oh, say, three years down the road. The Cavs agreed. What the hell; both teams were drafting in the middle of the pack then, and the switch of picks didn't seem so significant.

But when 1982 rolled around, Cleveland was dead last, and that '79 side deal gave the Lakers the league's No. 1 pick. The Cavaliers used their No. 1 from the Lakers to pick John Bagley of Boston College, while the Lakers, who had a choice of Worthy, Terry Cummings, or Dominique Wilkins, went for the North Carolina forward. Jerry West, by then the Laker general manager, knew what he wanted.

"I pointed out at the time," he says, "that in Worthy we'd get the player who would combine the best elements of both of those other players, and also someone who, from the winning standpoint, would simply do more for our team."

But it took even a James Worthy time to find the spotlight on a stage featuring performers like Magic and Kareem.

"You sometimes wonder," West says, "what he [Worthy] might average [scoring]. James is a very team-oriented player, and a player who is sometimes asked to sacrifice personally for the good of the team. He just does that very easily."

Modest, soft-spoken, and self-effacing, Worthy was in no hurry to be a star. He has all the outward flash of an insurance salesman. Worthy described himself, upon his arrival in Los Angeles, as "just a plain old simple, down-home guy."

When his son first returned home to Gastonia, North Carolina (population 50,000), to visit, his father, Ervin, said, "He doesn't care about the spotlight. He's still down to earth."

But not on the court. Worthy was slowed by the fractured leg he suffered in the spring of 1983, but by the spring of '84 he was all the way back, using the tremendous acceleration that makes him about as easy to stop as a runaway train the last ten feet to the basket.

The night of Game 2 he was showing the nation his entire arsenal of moves as he scored 29 points, hitting 11 of 12 from the floor. He went up for a slam, found Dennis Johnson in his path, switched hands after leaving the ground, and jammed the ball through with his left hand.

Earlier that year he went up for a hook against the Golden State Warriors, found he couldn't make it with Larry Smith all over him, made a 360-degree midair turn, and softly put the ball in.

Magic named that shot "The Dipsy-Doo-360-Clutch-Skin-And-In."

It wasn't all good times and glory. The Lakers have been disappointed in Worthy's rebounding. In his five-year career in Los Angeles he has averaged just 5.8 rebounds per game. He has been known to disappear on defense. And he has been slow to develop a medium-range jumper to prevent defenders from waiting down low for his explosive charge, although he seemed to have finally perfected it in 1986.

"He's a very selfish player and I hope you understand what I mean by that," Riley says. "If he's got a 17-footer, he wants a 10-footer. If he's got a 10-footer, he wants a five-footer. He always wants better shots."

Worthy always knew what he wanted. His father remembers

when his "little son—James was 6–5 in junior high—found Ervin shaking his head sadly while shuffling through a large stack of unpaid household bills spread out on the dinner table.

James told his father there was one expense he wouldn't have to worry about. The younger Worthy announced that he planned to go to college, but would do so on a scholarship.

He kept his promise.

Worthy's bad pass was just a bad memory after Game 3 when the Lakers regained the momentum with a 137–104 romp in the Forum. Magic had 14 points, 21 assists, and 11 rebounds.

When it was over the *Herald-Examiner* announced that Worthy deserved to be the series MVP.

"You guys have already written us off," an angry Dennis Johnson told the L.A. media. "Why even bother going on with the series?"

Worthy's vote total, however, went down after he missed a crucial free throw in the closing seconds of overtime of Game 4 and the Celtics went on to win. Boston's M. L. Carr—reserve player, No. 1 cheerleader, and designated woofer extraordinaire—had told Worthy in advance that he would miss and Cedric Maxwell added the coup de grace by making the choke sign afterward.

The Celtics were trying a new tactic—intimidation—and to their own surprise, it was working.

"We just used whatever we could to try to distract them," Maxwell says, "or to try to take their minds off the game. And they did the same thing to us. So it wasn't that we went in with the idea of using it [intimidation], but eventually it kind of worked out like that.

"As players, you'll do anything to win. It's psychological warfare. Anything you can do, you'll do it. We were trying to abuse them psychologically and trying to beat them physically."

Wasn't he surprised that such tactics could rattle a team of professionals?

"Yeah, I was, because you play in front of 200,000–300,000 people and millions of people watching you on TV. So to be upset about what 12 other guys were saying about you really didn't make a lot of sense."

Magic calls the Celtics "a special breed."

Says Michael Cooper, "They don't talk so much anymore, but they did in 1984. And I'll tell you, they backed it up. They were the Muhammed Alis of basketball. That was something new to me that I kind of enjoyed about them, because that's what you do on the playgrounds—you do a little talking to see where the opponent's heart is, try to intimidate 'em."

Any other team talk like that?

"No, not like they did. You might get a couple of players here and there, but not like the Celtics, constantly, the whole game, the whole team almost. They'll tell you something each quarter, keep something on your mind.

"Larry Bird tells me one time, 'I'm gonna wear you out on this play, Mike.' So I'm getting keyed up for this play coming up. He comes off a pick, a cross pick underneath by [Danny] Ainge, and I'm trailing Bird like I'm supposed to, around Robert Parish. Bird takes one dribble, Kareem just raises his hand up a little bit, Parish rolls to the hoop, Bird makes a great pass and Parish dunks.

"And all Bird does is laugh at me, 'Ha, ha, ha.' That kills you when they do that kind of shit.

"There are times I might get into a defensive groove, Larry'll get the ball out on a wing, and I'll tell him, 'Well, okay, let's go now, come on, take me.' He'll go into his move, try to break me down and he can't, so he'll end up passing the ball and I might laugh at him, or grin, or catch his eye, and he *knows.* That's our little individual battle."

There were a lot of individual battles in the '84 finals, but none more memorable than the McHale–Rambis Incident in Game 4. With Rambis headed for a sure breakaway basket in the second quarter, McHale tackled him around the upper body and sent him crashing to the floor with the most celebrated hit this town had seen since Kermit Washington teed off on Rudy Tomjanovich.

Pat Riley labeled McHale's foul "thuggery."

"It was a freak play," Maxwell says. "Kevin, among all of us that were there at that time, was, by far, the most timid so far as tackling. So when he tackled Rambis, nobody could believe it. We were all in shock."

From then on it was the Lakers who seemed in shock. They blew a five-point lead with less than a minute to play in regulation time. Magic threw a pass away to Robert Parish in the closing seconds and then missed two key free throws at the end of the game as Boston won in overtime, 129–125, to tie the series.

Game 5 was played in a sauna bath. The Garden was a pit, a throwback to the grimy, squalid arenas of the early years of the NBA. With Boston experiencing a heat wave, the temperature in unventilated Boston Garden soared to 97 degrees and the Lakers melted into the parquet floor, going home 121–103 losers and facing possible elimination in Game 6.

The oppressive heat had hit Kareem especially hard. The 37-year-old captain, oldest player in the league, had sucked wind from the pregame layups on. He missed 12 of his first 14 shots from the floor, wound up seven for 25, and ran the court like a man carrying a refrigerator on his shoulders.

What did it feel like? a reporter asked.

"I suggest," Kareem said, "that you go to a local steam bath, do 100 pushups with all your clothes on, and then try to run back and forth for 48 minutes.

"The game was in slow motion. It was like we were running in mud."

Not Larry Bird. He was as hot as the temperature, hitting 15 of 20 from the field and winding up with 34 points along with 17 rebounds.

Kareem and his teammates cooled Boston down in Game 6. Abdul-Jabbar had 30 points and the Lakers won, 119–108.

It had come down to another Game 7, another Garden showdown.

Tempers were now warmer than the Garden floor. After Worthy shoved Maxwell out of bounds into the post supporting one of the baskets in the first quarter of Game 6, M. L. Carr labeled the series "all-out war."

Said Carr, "We are not going to come out and be soft anymore. I know what James did he did in the sense of battle. That just shows they are going for the gold too. But we are not going to be soft. I'd like to meet them at the airport tomorrow."

When a fan threw a beer in Carr's face as the Celtics were leaving the Forum floor after that game, Bird exploded.

"I'm not predicting anything will happen in the Garden [in Game 7]," he said. "But after what happened to M. L., the Lakers better wear hard hats on the bench instead of oxygen masks. Our fans can do anything. You never want to do that [the beer throwing] and then go back to the other fellow's home. You don't want to turn the Boston fans loose. If the guy had walked up to M. L. and done it face-to-face, it would have been different. But to do it from 20 rows up . . . if our fans got wind of it or saw it on TV, they will do something. I hope they don't, but I think they will be ready to explode."

The explosion came early. Early on the morning of Game 7 the fans seemed to start chanting "Beat L.A.! Beat L.A.!" on the streets of Boston. Not since the days of King George had this city been so fiercely united against a common foe.

The Lakers needed a police escort to get them out of their hotel and onto a bus after fans barricaded the front of the building.

The crowd inside the Garden was even uglier, many of them pausing between swigs of beer to shout threats and spit at anyone they could identify as being from the greater Los Angeles area.

In the Celtic locker room the emotion was buoyed by confidence rather than alcohol.

"I think we felt we were the best team going in," Maxwell says. "We felt they had more talent than we did, but I felt if we stuck together, we were going to win the series. I think we were a better team all around, in areas like rebounding, defense, team-type things. If you had to get us in a Superstars competition with the Lakers, I think they would have had 100 points and we would have had about 20 because they were faster than we were and they could jump higher. Natural talent, they had the advantage. We did the things fundamentally like boxing out, rebounding, battling for loose balls. We had the grips on those things because we were more the dirty players and they were more like the tuxedo players."

For Pat Riley it had come down to the white tuxedo.

He had had the dream more than once. It had haunted him for two years. And it was always the same.

He's on the sidelines at Boston Garden, wearing a white tuxedo and staring across the court at a girl in a front-row seat wearing an avocado-green dress.

The game is down to the last few seconds. A faceless Laker puts up a shot at the final buzzer with the game on the line. One time it's Laker trainer Jack Curran taking the crucial shot.

Does it go in?

Do the Lakers win?

Does the girl in the green dress live happily ever after?

Riley never knew. He always woke up as the shot was hanging in midair. But he became convinced that if there was ever a seventh game at the Garden, he was going to have to wear that tuxedo to find out what happened.

Riley believes in such signs and he really thought about wearing the white tuxedo and perhaps seeing his faceless Laker put up a winning shot.

But at what cost?

If he was to march out onto that parquet floor in a white tuxedo, he knew it wouldn't stay white for long. He might as well have worn a red shirt and walked into a ring containing 14,890 mad bulls.

And what about the reaction across the country? Wouldn't he be accused of trying to steal the spotlight from his players, upsetting their concentration with a crazy coaching stunt?

But still, there was that dream. . . .

Riley even found the avocado dress. His wife, Chris, had an old green dress in her closet she had saved from her first date.

She refused to wear it into the Garden, but a white jacket was brought in for the coach.

Riley decided against wearing it. And his dream turned into a nightmare.

The Celtics had their own traditional magic working in Game 7 in the Garden, where they had never lost an NBA final.

Maxwell, who had been doing his best shooting with his mouth earlier in the series, came alive with 24 points, eight rebounds, and eight assists. Bird had 20 points and 12 rebounds, Parish, 14 points and 16 rebounds, Dennis Johnson, 22 points.

And yet the Lakers, down by 14, had cut the margin to just three, 105–102, with a little over a minute to play in the season.

Magic brought the ball downcourt only to have Dennis Johnson strip him of it.

Cooper got the ball back and fed Magic. One more shot at Winnin' Time. Again Magic headed downcourt. His eyes widened. James Worthy was wide open under the basket.

That sight is a frozen frame Magic will carry with him the rest of his life. But it will never be followed by a picture of the ball reaching Worthy's waiting arms. Maxwell, waiting in ambush, batted the ball out of Magic's hands. Dennis Johnson picked it up, was fouled, and converted the free throws that sealed a 111–102 Celtic triumph.

When it was over the dam burst and a sea of humanity rushed onto the court to claim their fifteenth NBA title.

This was not, however, a gathering of joy. It was ugly. Chris Riley, Pat's wife, and her parents were jostled. The mob went after Kareem, trying to grab his goggles. The fans chased anything they could find in purple and gold. Outside, a car on the street was dismantled. A window in the press bus was smashed.

In the Celtic locker room Larry Bird was informed he had been named Most Valuable Player of the series.

In the Laker locker room Magic and Cooper found their only solace in the showers. They sat in a corner and let the warm water run over their bodies. But nothing could wash away the hurt.

Another Boston series. Another Game 7.

And after a quarter century, still no balloons.

13.

Redemption

DAWN was breaking over the city of Boston. The streets running past Boston Garden, which rides piggyback on old North Station, were still littered with debris from the rioting the night before, wild celebrating touched off by the Celtics' victory over the Lakers in the seventh game of the 1984 NBA Championship Series.

A few of the cars that had been dented and walked on and pounded, batteries ripped out, tires ripped off, hadn't yet been hauled away. The drunken revelers who had rampaged down Causeway Street after the game had been long since ushered off, some to jail.

Inside the Garden, the square brick building that for years has served as a trash compactor of Laker dreams, only the rats were stirring, breakfasting on spilled popcorn and beer.

The Celtic party was over, temporarily; the Laker wake was still very much rolling along. Winners sleep; losers weep.

At the Copley Plaza Hotel, Magic Johnson sat in his room, still trying to sort it all out. He'd been up all night, hadn't even tried to sleep. He'd been talking and playing music with his two best pals, Isiah Thomas and Mark Aguirre. The two had come to town to cheer Magic on and had stayed around to help cheer him up.

It was no small challenge. Magic had failed in the clutch, lost his touch in Winnin' Time. Magic and his friends played music and talked about everything except basketball. The old days. Girls. Anything but hoops. What could they possibly say to make Magic feel better? That he played a great series, except for his lapses in Games 2, 4, and 7? That maybe even those lapses weren't entirely his fault?

Forget it. There was a dark cloud that wouldn't be sweet-talked away or rationalized or philosophized away. Not tonight.

Not ever. Sometimes there's nothing you can do but suffer, ride it out, let it hurt. They put another cassette in the stereo and turned up the volume.

Michael Cooper preferred to suffer without musical accompaniment. No music, no TV. He and his wife, Wanda, had been up all night analyzing. Cooper went over each game, each key play, over and over, as if he might find something that would change the outcome of the series.

"If only . . ." he would say to Wanda, and rehash another play. They had ordered from room service, but Michael wouldn't eat a bite. Some of Wanda's relatives had knocked at the door, but Michael didn't want visitors, couldn't face company. Wanda had talked to them in the hallway, sent them away. One was a college professor who couldn't comprehend all this deep mourning over a basketball game.

The sun was peeking into Jerry Buss's hotel room, cutting through the heavy smoke. Buss was well into his third pack of cigarettes since last night. He and a friend had gone over every play in last night's game a dozen times, it seemed, and now all Buss could do was sit quietly, stare at the walls, tap out another cigarette, and curse the daylight.

Pat Riley was also doing some serious brooding. He and his wife, Chris, had had some company in their room after the game—a few other couples, including assistant coach Bill Bertka and his wife, Solveig. They had ordered up a case of beer and hors d'oeuvres. After the company left Pat tried to catch some sleep but couldn't. For the first time in months there was no videotape to study, no reason to get out the yellow legal pad and doodle "X's" and "O's." This was one game Riley would never watch on videotape, not ever.

"It was the longest night of my life," Riley says. "I couldn't wait for the pain to go away. It was the total essence of misery."

For the Lakers the day was already shot to hell. The plane ride home would be worse, what with all the sufferers thrown together in one closed space. Since 1959 Laker teams had now lost eight NBA championships to the Celtics in eight meetings. And this one was the worst, the most humiliating.

This time there were no excuses, not like in the old days when you could blame it on Bill Russell. This time the Lakers had come into the series with the talent and teamwork to match the Celtics. The Lakers had come into the series sharp and confident and proud.

But, in the end, they had been chased off the Garden's creaky old floor and into their cramped, sweatbox locker room by a stampeding mob of whooping, wild-eyed Celtic fans.

The Lakers had seen enough of this city. Given the choice, most of the players probably would have preferred to leave town after the game, even if it meant taking a Greyhound. Anything to avoid having to face Boston again by the light of day. The city had not been kind.

For the Lakers the only consolation when it was all over was being spared having to witness the spectacle of the postgame trophy presentation in the Celtic locker room. With the CBS cameras rolling, club president Red Auerbach brandished that same type of fat cigar with which he had taunted and tormented three generations of Lakers and their fans and accepted the trophy from commissioner David Stern.

"What ever happened to that Laker *dynasty* I've been hearing so much about?" Auerbach growled sarcastically, snatching the trophy, stamping this shining Celtic moment with all the class and compassion of a cartoon villain foreclosing on the fair damsel's mortgage.

But Red had a good point. There *had* been some discussion in the media about the birth of a Laker dynasty. That talk *did* seem a little premature now.

The would-be dynasty had been nipped in the bud by the cocky, opportunistic, gritty, and talented Celtics. They had talked big and carried big sticks. The Celtics had woofed and boasted and bullied and hustled and played well and won.

This was one wound time wouldn't heal. The Lakers knew the only way they could wipe out the pain and embarrassment and frustration would be to beat the Celtics in the finals someday.

This would be the summer of the big brood.

"It was a devastating loss for us," says Riley, "because of the *way* we lost. We really felt that we were the better team that year. . . . But that's life and we have nobody to blame but ourselves. It all goes back to this—there's one winner and there's one miserable son of a bitch, and we were the miserable ones that summer. We felt we gifted Boston, and that was tough to deal with.

"The second thing was the total lack of respect they showed for us as a team, not just that year, but every year. You would think that somewhere along the line, we could have walked away with some dignity, but they wouldn't let us. They called us chokers and all those things. You should let the defeated just lie there and wallow in his wounds by himself.

"They're a proud team, but pride can be defined in different ways. One way is humility, and being proud of your accomplishments, but not puffing yourself up and thinking you're better than everybody else. I think they're a proud team to the point of being arrogant and cocky, letting everybody know about it, and I think that's something that rubs every team in this league wrong. I think every team in this league gets more pleasure out of beating them than any other team.

"I don't think we're that kind of team. I think we're a very humble team. We celebrate, and our players have fun playing, but we're not cocky or arrogant. We're taking joy in playing the game.

"To me, they have no class at all. Psychological warfare—if that's what their ploy was—so be it. That's their personality. But it is classless. I think there [should be] a certain professional conduct, born out of respect for each athlete. . . . Their whole philosophy is to take a step first, create situations that are going to put the opposition in a reacting mode. They play a very physical, very aggressive game, and I think they cross the boundary. They'll do whatever it takes to win, to turn the game around. I think the Kevin McHale shot on Rambis was testimony to that philosophy. . . . That play turned the whole game around, got our players very angry, and they [Celtics] succeeded in doing what they had to do. That doesn't make it right. That's just the way they are.

"It took us a long time to get over that loss," Riley continues. "It took us a month into the next regular season to get over it. We realize you should keep your perspective and tell yourself that getting to the finals means you've had a very, very successful year, and whether you win or lose you should find some joy in the experience. But that isn't the way it is.

"The fan in L.A. and Boston will not allow their teams to get that far and not come away with the gold. They will just not *allow* it. That's just the nature of both cities and the demands they put on the teams to win. You do get caught up in that and feel it, sense it.

"It was a very difficult summer for all of us."

Buss suffered unrelentingly. He moped around Pickfair and when he did venture out, to the Forum or to football games or to his favorite discos, he dreaded the questions people would ask: *What the hell happened to the Lakers, Jerry? You guys shoulda won it in four. What happened? How could you guys let Boston win again?*

"Being from Los Angeles," Buss says, "all those years that the Celtics kept pinning our ears back, well, I was part of all that tradition. Here's a team that's been beating you, and we finally had a chance to take them. To lose was a terrible, terrible disappointment. It was very hard."

When Magic got back to L.A. he locked himself in his apartment for three days, couldn't even talk to his mom when she phoned. Magic had just bought his mansion in Bel-Air, but the furniture wasn't in yet, so he would pace slowly through the house, his footsteps echoing down long corridors, the gloomy memories of the series dogging him like a long shadow.

Kareem, better than any other Laker, shrugged off the Boston loss. It had been unpleasant and embarrassing, but life goes on. Kareem spent some time in Hawaii, and worked hard on his conditioning and his flexibility. He wasn't going to give the Boston Celtics the pleasure of ruining his off-season; he had another season to begin preparing for.

When the Lakers gathered in Palm Springs for training camp, they were a team with a mission. In the NBA—in any pro sport— you don't build your preseason dreams around meeting one certain team in the championship series. There are far too many variables, too many unforeseen twists in the road. You worry about your *own* team. The Dodgers don't open spring training praying for a World Series shot at the Yankees.

But this time the Lakers wanted the Celtics. It wasn't something they talked about, certainly not to the press, and not even much among themselves. But they were quietly obsessed. On long bus rides, on plane flights, even during team scrimmages and regular-season games, the Lakers were seeing Celtic green.

They even secretly rooted for the Celtics, tracking their progress in the sports pages. At least make the finals, you bastards. *We'll* be there. Give us one more shot. You owe us that.

For the Lakers to reach the NBA finals and face any team but the Celtics would be like being granted an audience with the Pope's second cousin. As the song goes, ain't nothin' like the real thing, baby.

The Lakers seemed a solid bet to make the finals again. The finale in Boston in '84 would have broken the spirit and confidence of many teams, but the Lakers had come a long way from the first two seasons of the Buss–Magic Era, when they won a championship, then fell apart.

"At that particular time," Riley says, "the team was just in the process of maturing, forming an identity. They were winning on talent. They hadn't really become a team yet. I think that was indicated the next season when the team ultimately broke down and fragmented and fractured after the initial success. They didn't know how to win championships year in and year out. They fell prey to all those things you fall prey to after a championship year. If you don't know how to grow, those things will destroy you. And they ultimately did.

"We won a championship in '80, we totally fragmented in '80–81, and my first year ['81–82], we were beginning to fracture again. It was all that immaturity. The players had not grown together and learned enough about each other to totally accept and tolerate each other. There were times my first two years that this team could crack immediately, and it's not that way anymore.

"We've established some policies and some rules and concepts about what comes out of the locker room and what stays in. I think we're one of the most uncontroversial teams in the league, as far as quotes and as far as pointing fingers and blaming. Every now and then we get a new player on the team who pops off. We get him in line quick, let him know that's not the way it works here."

Even after the shocking loss to Houston in the 1986 finals,

there was no talk of dissension on the Lakers, no finger-pointing. Those days were over. After the earlier loss to Houston, in the '80–81 playoffs, there was a feeling the team had cracked from within. By '86, however, the feeling was that the team had been cracked from without by a superior force. It was no longer a question of morale or character or heart. The question now was talent.

None of that, however, was evident in the early months of the 1984–85 season.

The Lakers were solid, they were motivated, and, after a rocky first month, they were digging steadily toward their single-minded goal of revenge against the Celtics. But suddenly, just after midseason, the organization was rocked with reports of impending collapse of the Buss sports empire.

One February evening Jim Mitchell, a respected, veteran investigative reporter for L.A. TV station KCBS, went on the air with a report that Buss had missed payments to a bank on loans of more than $100 million, putting his vast holdings in danger. He had used the Lakers, Kings, and the Forum as collateral, Mitchell reported. He said that Buss had fallen behind on his payments on Security Pacific Bank loans six months previous, and the institution was considering forcing Buss into bankruptcy.

Mitchell also said bank officials weren't eager to foreclose on Buss, but, just in case, they had contacted Sam Gilbert, a wealthy UCLA booster, about running the Lakers and Kings if Buss were forced out.

There were denials all around.

"I am solvent and I am not in default on any loan whatsoever," Buss said.

A bank spokesperson said no Buss loans were in default, and no collective action had been taken.

Gilbert denied having talked to bank officials about Buss.

The rumors and reports of Buss's financial difficulties didn't seem to adversely affect the Lakers' performance or morale. As Magic Johnson said, "The checks keep coming in."

CBS management and Mitchell stuck by the story. But no new developments were reported in succeeding weeks, and the story gradually faded away. Mitchell has since left the station, saying he was dissatisfied with management.

Another rumor soon took its place. One month after the bankruptcy rumor *The Los Angeles Times* broke a story that the county attorney's office in Phoenix was threatening to file felony charges against Buss and Frank Mariani. A deputy county attorney, Joe Abodeely, said Buss and his associates underpaid property tax on 206 Arizona properties over a five-year period. According to Abodeely, an informant said the underpayment was deliberate.

Three months later Buss and Mariani settled up by paying $1 million to Arizona's Maricopa County for the back taxes and penalties.

"He got his hand caught in the cookie jar," said Abodeely. ". . . We asked him to put the cookies back and asked him to put some more in."

Abodeely later resigned after charges of "unprofessional conduct" were leveled at him by the county attorney's office, then dropped as part of a settlement.

Buss, however, didn't get his money back.

Buss claimed ignorance of the underpayment, said that his involvement with the Lakers and Kings had caused him to delegate authority to others to run his real estate empire. Buss said he was devastated at having been publicly portrayed as a tax-dodging felon.

"As a sports owner, I have children looking up to me," he said, "and I encourage them to work hard, to study hard, to be good people and to stay away from drugs. I want to help the disadvantaged and give children a role model. Have I lost my ability to help people with this kind of publicity? I don't know."

If Buss's empire truly was in trouble, he seemed to have bailed himself out nicely. By the '85–86 season the national Forum Entertainment Network and his L.A. Prime Ticket Network cable TV stations were in operation. Prime Ticket was 10 years in the planning and features Lakers, Kings, local sports, and various Forum events.

"I have a toy [Prime Ticket Network] and it's got a tremendous number of gadgets on it," Buss says. "It's only limited by your creativity. This is a real fantasyland for me. It's one thing to come to the Forum and say, 'Wow, that's my team down there.' That's really a great feeling. But there are about 120 people in the United States who can say that. When I go home and go around the channels, and hit 12, and see Prime Ticket and know that's my channel, that's a total fantasy. To own your own channel in a city the size of L.A. is unbelievable. It's just absolutely like a Disneyland. I'm really proud of myself. It's my fantasy."

He has other sports fantasies too. He has resolved to pump more money and energy into his woebegone hockey and indoor soccer teams, and has gotten involved in an indoor volleyball league. Buss also offered $1 million to buy the Hawaii Islanders minor-league baseball franchise, but was turned down.

One night he was at a charity banquet also attended by Angels owner Gene Autry. During the program Buss sent Autry a note: "How about selling me 25 percent of the Angels?"

Wrote back Autry: "No."

Buss would love to get a shot at buying the Rams or Angels, but doesn't think the Raiders or Dodgers will be for sale in his lifetime.

And Buss says he and Jerry West have fantasized about starting over from scratch with an expansion NBA team, possibly one based in Honolulu, a city Buss loves.

He once told an aide, "I'm going to go until I get down to my last million. Then I'm going to take that and live on a desert island somewhere."

A more immediate fantasy is finding a replacement for the soon-to-retire Kareem Abdul-Jabbar. Buss has always coveted Ralph Sampson, and would have had Ralph back in 1982 but for Donald Sterling.

Sterling owns the Clippers, which were then based in San Diego. Going into the '82 college draft, the Clippers and Lakers had the league's first two picks, and an official coin flip would determine which team would draft No. 1 and which No. 2.

Sampson, the sensational 7–4 center from Virginia, had just finished his junior year, and there was speculation that he might forgo his senior season and declare himself eligible for the NBA draft. However, there were strong indications that he wouldn't leave school early unless he could be guaranteed he'd be drafted by the Lakers. He liked the Lakers and Kareem. He wasn't willing to miss his senior year if it meant risking being drafted by a second-rate team like the Clippers.

One night at Pickfair, Sterling stopped by to drop off his friend and business associate Frank Mariani for a poker game, and Buss made Sterling an offer he thought the Clipper owner shouldn't refuse.

"Let's flip a coin *now*," Buss said. "If I win, I can guarantee Sampson a spot with the Lakers, and so he will skip his final college season. If that happens, you'll get to draft James Worthy.

"If we don't flip now, Sampson will have no guarantee of playing in L.A. and, therefore, he will stay in school.

"If we flip now, you can't lose. You get Worthy, no matter what. If we don't flip now, you only have a 50 percent chance of getting Worthy."

Sterling said no.

Buss persisted. As an inducement he offered to set up an organization to help Sterling sell Clipper season tickets. Buss would guarantee Sterling $1 million worth of tickets a year for five years.

"Let's flip right now," Buss said, reaching into his pocket for a coin.

Sterling either didn't buy Buss's logic or didn't believe Sampson had his heart set on playing for the Lakers. Maybe Sampson wouldn't mind playing in San Diego.

Sterling held firm. There would be no early flip.

Sure enough, Sampson, not willing to take a 50 percent chance of winding up in San Diego, stayed in school. The Lakers won the flip and drafted Worthy. The Clippers took Terry Cummings, whom Sterling says they would have taken even if they'd drafted first. But the Clippers subsequently traded Cummings.

And Buss has never given up on the fantasy of landing Sampson.

In the spring of 1985, Jerry Buss's No. 1 sports fantasy was for his Lakers to beat the Boston Celtics in the NBA finals.

He was going to get his chance.

In the '85 playoffs the Celtics mowed down Cleveland (3–1), Detroit (4–2), and Philadelphia (4–1), while the Lakers were slapping aside Phoenix (3–0), Portland (4–1), and Denver (4–1).

There was no doubt these were easily the league's two best teams, maybe two of the best ever. There was no question that CBS was elated to have a Laker–Celtic showdown. This was one matchup the public would buy.

Then, one game into the series, the dream matchup turned into a mismatch.

On Memorial Day the Celtics humiliated the Lakers, 148–114, in the dreaded Garden. Kareem, who was 38 years old, played like he wasn't a day over 60. The Big Fella finished with 12 points, 3 rebounds, and only a vague idea of what Celtic center Robert Parish looked like. Parish had promised to outrun Kareem, but even Parish hadn't imagined it would be *this* easy.

Considering the circumstances, it was easily the worst basketball game Kareem had ever played.

"The play was always, like, going *away* from me," Abdul-Jabbar says. "It's like I was always between the tops of the keys, and everyone else kept passing me going the other way."

At a team meeting the next morning, at the film study session, Kareem sat directly in front of the TV screen rather than taking his customary seat to the rear of the team gathering. He had some serious music to face. Riley, grim-faced, jammed the cassette of the game into the VCR. Every time Parrish zoomed past the floundering Abdul-Jabbar, Riley reversed the tape and played it again. And again. Kareem never lowered his head.

"I wasn't embarrassed, but I thought I'd really let my team down," Kareem says.

He spoke to each teammate, promised each one he would kick himself in the butt from here on out, and urged his teammates to do the same. Play hard and proud, and let the Celtics fall where they may.

At the Lakers' hotel the evening of Game 2, Kareem asked Riley's permission to have his father ride to the game on the team bus. Watching Kareem and Big Al Alcindor together, Riley thought about his own father.

Lee Riley's last words to his son, not long before he died of a heart attack in 1970, were, "Just remember—somewhere, someplace, sometime, you're going to have to plant your feet, make a stand, and kick some ass."

Shades of Knute Rockne and the Gipper. Riley, in his pre-game locker-room talk, told the Lakers what his father had said. They liked it. It seemed to fire them up.

Yeah. Take a stand and kick some *ass*. It became the Laker theme for the rest of the playoffs.

"The Celtics had pushed us around and beat us the year before," Cooper says. "These guys, they hung Kurt, they beat us up, they pushed us around, they taunted us, they talked about us. After a while you get tired of it. Then we come out the first game of the playoffs and they kick our ass real royally. After the first game it was time to make a stand, man."

Remembering back to the disastrous seventh game at the Garden the season before, Cooper says, "For some reason their fans sensed they had a victory even before the game began. It was like leading the people [Lakers] into the lion's den. You know they're gonna run, and run, and run, but sooner or later, the lions are gonna catch 'em and eat 'em up, and that's what the fans come to see.

"I wouldn't say we were intimidated, but we were in a tough situation. . . .

"The Celtic players would talk to us. 'Magic Tragic,' things like that. They'd sing to us—'Off to see the Fakers . . .' [to the tune of 'Off to see the Wizard']—that kind of shit, and you don't want to hear that. But I guess we *were* fakers, because they beat us."

Now, down 1–0, the Lakers took a stand.

They beat the Celtics by seven in the Garden. Kareem had 30 points, 17 rebounds, eight assists, and three blocks.

The second-leading scorer was Michael Cooper with 22 points, including eight of nine from the floor, several coming at key moments when the Celtics were making a charge. That in itself was a story.

There was a time when Michael Cooper didn't know if he could be a big scorer on a playground team, much less in an NBA Championship Series. For a long time nobody on the Lakers had more natural talent and less confidence in himself than Cooper.

No confidence for Michael Cooper, high-wire performer su-preme, creator of the gravity-defying Coop-a-Loop, master of versatility, feared nemesis of almost every offensive whiz kid thrown his way?

No matter how many Coop-a-Loops he sunk, no matter how many times he'd shut down an opposing player to retain his reputation as one of the league's best defenders, no matter how often he'd switch from small forward to off guard to point guard without losing a bit of effectiveness, no matter how many three-point shots he'd hit, Cooper was never really sure he belonged in the NBA.

Maybe his insecurity began in childhood when two-year-old Michael Cooper slashed his knee so badly on a coffee can that it required 100 stitches. Doctors didn't even know if he'd ever walk without a brace, much less play basketball, and indeed he wore a brace for nearly eight years.

Maybe it was caused by the fact that he played for the University of New Mexico rather than a larger school. Or that he wasn't picked in the 1978 NBA draft until the third round. Or that he played only seven minutes his rookie season after tearing a knee ligament. Or that he was almost cut the next year.

But for a long time Cooper kept waiting for the ax to fall.

In 1982 the Lakers were suffering through a miserably cold Midwestern trip. Cooper was particularly miserable after spraining an ankle. When the Lakers reached Detroit, Riley pulled Cooper aside prior to the game.

"Michael, why don't you go home?" the coach said. "You're not doing yourself any good staying with us. Go home, rest the ankle, and by the time we get back, you should be ready to play."

Cooper nodded, but didn't reply.

At halftime he sat down next to a couple of Laker beat writers at the press table.

"This is it," he said, staring off into space.

"This is what?" asked one of the sportswriters, barely looking up.

"This could be the end," Cooper said. "Why do you think the Lakers are sending me back? If I go home, I just might wind up off the team. They might use this opportunity to cut me."

"What are you talking about, Coop?" the sportswriter asked. "You're one of the most valuable guys on this team."

"Do you re-e-e-ally think the Lakers are just sending me home to rest the ankle?" Cooper insisted. "I'm not falling for that. They'll probably put me on waivers."

The sportswriter just shook his head.

When he saw Cooper in the locker room later, he asked the Laker swingman if he still feared he was going to be cut.

"N-a-a-a," Cooper said, "I'm just—what's that word you used, Jack?"

Trainer Jack Curran looked up from an equipment trunk he was leaning over and said, "Paranoid."

"Yeah," said Cooper, nodding, "I'm just paranoid."

Still, Cooper *didn't* go home. No sense taking any chances.

"If you leave," he explained, "you may not come back. They don't have time to wait on stragglers."

Says Riley of his favorite straggler: "He has cleaned the skeletons from his closet, and he found some self-esteem. He's older, he's grown as a player, and he has some perspective. He has become a man, finally. He is not as fearful. I've told him, you can't worry about tomorrow. If you do, you can't play today.

"We have had many long talks. I have told him I never had any doubts about him. He had the doubts. I've told him as long as I'm here, he'll be here. We'll never get rid of him unless it's for some incredible offer. He's too valuable, too versatile. Now that he's learned to handle the ball, he may be more versatile than Magic, although it probably sounds like a sin for me to say that."

For a long time Riley had to watch what he said and did in regard to Cooper. It was always Cooper first off the bench before the arrival of Worthy. But one night Riley put both Worthy and Bob McAdoo in first.

Riley looked over and saw Cooper, dejected, on the bench, a towel over his head.

"I knew I had to get him in fast," Riley said, "or I would lose him."

When Mike McGee came along, when Byron Scott came along, it was the same thing. Would they start ahead of me? Cooper wondered.

"Soon he was thinking they would be bringing in Jack Curran ahead of him," says Wanda, Michael's wife. "It was something he had to overcome."

"He's fine until he thinks of something else to worry about. I think he's always going to have some of that because it makes him play harder. Sometimes he'll shut a guy down totally on defense, but he'll come home and say, 'Damn, I scored only four points.' Sometimes I feel like slapping him. Even after a superb game, he'll come home and get upset about a pass he could have had or should have made.

"One reporter told him about a trade rumor one year, and the more he thought about it, the more he thought himself into a funk and a slump. I told him he ought to ask the coach or Jerry West if he had his doubts about himself, but he said you don't do that. Instead, he just plays through it and plays harder to make himself more indispensable. It's a way of getting up. He'll say, 'Damn, I'll show them they can't do without me' or 'I'll show those other teams what they are getting.' "

When he's down Cooper always has his New Mexico film to soothe him. He kept film from his collegiate days to remind himself what he was like before his game fell apart—fell apart, that is, in his mind.

"He gets a real boost from that," Wanda says of the film, "watching himself play well."

Nothing seemed to help Cooper's doubts when he first played for the Lakers.

"It was kind of hard to play with those second thoughts on my mind," he says, "and they were always there. I needed someone I could take the frustration out on. I couldn't scream at practice. So I'd come home and there was my wife to take it out on."

Recalls Wanda, "We were just married and I couldn't figure out why he was so grumpy. Once I knew what the cause was, I just kept telling him how good he was. I'm confident enough for both of us."

He's certainly not lacking for boosters at the Forum. The crowd will begin to chant "Coop! Coop! Coop!" as soon as he takes off his warm-up pants.

In Cooper's initial seasons with the Lakers, crowds could expect a Coop-a-Loop nearly every game. Cooper would slip behind the defense and take off down his personal runway, Norm Nixon would throw a lob pass and, ideally, ball and man would arrive at the basket at the same instant for a thunderous slam dunk.

True aficionados of the Coop-a-Loop hoped for an errant pass, because that's when their man was at his best. Cooper, when he arrived at the rim and found the ball or himself out of position, was occasionally able to stretch his airborne body, pull the ball in—from behind, below, or above him—and still dunk it, providing an aerial show not seen since in the skies above the Forum baskets.

These days the Coop-a-Loops have become almost extinct because opposing players have gotten wise. Instead, Cooper has found a new crowd-pleaser—the long-range bomb. In 1986 he set club records for most three-pointers in a game (five) and a season (63) as well as most attempts (163). He continued firing away from three-point range in the playoffs, producing one game breaker after another.

It's hard to believe this guy, at one time, had no confidence in his ability to shoot.

"He always had the feeling," Riley says, "if he missed two or three shots, I would take him out. I have never done that to a player."

If Cooper missed his first shot of the game in those days, he might not shoot again. The misses stay with him.

Others had doubts Cooper could be effective at handling the ball, but when Magic has been hurt Cooper has produced assists at a double-figure level.

When he fails to produce, however, he goes back into a funk.

A few years ago he missed a crucial free throw in Dallas and the Lakers lost. Two sportswriters, knowing Cooper's habit of avoiding them after a bad game, decided to wait him out in the locker room.

Nearly an hour passed, everyone else was gone, and still no sign of Cooper, who had disappeared into the shower.

Finally one of the sportswriters walked over to the shower area and peeked in. There was Cooper, waiting for them to leave, spending his time playing hopscotch with the soap.

Cooper is very sensitive about what the media writes about him. Most players *claim* they never read the paper. Not Cooper. He reads it. Every word.

Once when Rich Levin of the *Herald-Examiner* quoted Cooper in the paper on something Cooper thought was off the record, the Laker star became angry. Extremely angry. In the world of Michael Cooper, there's no telling what form that anger might take.

At first he called up the *Herald* the morning after the story appeared and threatened to sue. Then he told another reporter he was going to slap Levin around.

Finally, that night, Levin approached Cooper at his locker stall, their first face-to-face meeting since the story appeared.

Cooper glared at the sportswriter as a crowd of media people gathered around for the anticipated confrontation.

"I'll tell you what I'm going to do," Cooper said to Levin. "I'm going to put you on probation. That's what I'm going to do. Three games probation. If I like what you write, I'll go back to talking to you. If not, I'll never speak to you again."

Cooper liked what he read.

Levin found a screw in a locker room one time and asked Cooper if it had fallen out of his head, if that's what made him so crazy.

"Yeah," Cooper told him, "but you'd better hang on to it, 'cause I'm going to get a lot crazier."

Levin carried the screw for several years, then, when he left the beat, passed the screw on to Steve Springer of the *Register.* Cooper would periodically check to make sure the screw was still around in case he needed it.

Dealing with Cooper, one often feels like the straight man in a comedy routine.

Example No. 1: It is 2:30 on the morning after Game 1 of the 1985 NBA finals. Laker P.R. man Josh Rosenfeld is asleep in his Boston hotel room. The phone rings. It's Cooper.

"Josh, what are you doin'?"

"I'm trying to sleep," says a groggy and annoyed Rosenfeld.

"*I* can't sleep," Cooper says. "I'm still up from the game."

"Coop, it was a day game. It's been over for almost 12 hours."

"Yeah, well, I'm hungry. Maybe I'll get something to eat."

"You do that."

Click.

A minute later Rosenfeld's phone rings again.

"Josh."

"Yeah, Coop."

"I thought I'd call room service. You know the number?"

"It's on your *phone*, Coop. How many years you been traveling? Haven't you ever called room service before?"

"Oh yeah."

The next day Rosenfeld sees Cooper in the lobby.

"You ever get to sleep last night, Coop?" he asks.

"What do you mean?"

"Well, you called me at 2:30 in the morning because you couldn't sleep, remember?"

"What are you talking about? I was asleep by 11."

Example No. 2: Cooper approaches Steve Springer in Phoenix to tell him how much he enjoyed a story Springer did on Cooper that had run that day in *The L.A. Times*.

"Oh, you saw it?" Springer says.

"Nope."

"Then how do you know it was good?"

"Because Wanda called and told me." Cooper pauses, then asks, "Do you have a copy of it with you?"

"I have one back at the hotel," Springer says. "Do you want to see it?"

Again Cooper pauses. "N-a-a-a," he finally says, "it'll just piss me off."

"Well, anyway," Springer says, "I'm glad you enjoyed it."

Beneath all the craziness, though, is a caring person. Whenever he scores at the basket near where Wanda always sits, he points to her in tribute. He is, according to Rosenfeld, the most charitable of the Lakers, whether it's funding a hotline for troubled kids in New Mexico or offering to buy Laker tickets for the classroom in a nearby school that can boast of the best attendance level. When the Lakers came out with a cookbook Cooper came up with the idea of buying some and reselling them, with the money going to the homeless. In 1986, Cooper was a co-winner of the league's J. Walter Kennedy Citizenship Award, given for outstanding community service.

Cooper's unique. Just ask Pat Riley. At Riley's fortieth birthday party at an exclusive Beverly Hills club last year, in the middle of a dance, Cooper suddenly fell to the floor, clutching his right knee and moaning in pain. Team trainer Gary Vitti rushed to Cooper's side, as did Riley.

The music stopped. Vitti examined Cooper for a moment, then uttered the dreaded words "Torn ligament." Riley was dumbstruck. Speechless. The other guests had gathered around and talked in whispers.

Then Cooper suddenly leapt to his feet, grinned at Riley, and moonwalked back across the dance floor.

The Lakers won Game 3 of the '85 finals by 24 points (Worthy 29 points; Kareem 26 and 14 rebounds). The Celtics won Game 4 by two points (Dennis Johnson's 21-foot jumper at the buzzer) to tie the series, but the Lakers came back to win Game 5 by nine (Kareem had 36 points).

That sent the series back to Boston, back to the Garden, where all the banners of past championships and all the retired uniform numbers of Celtic legends hang from the rafters like a giant leprechaun's laundry.

Banging and bruising had been an ongoing theme of the series, but this game wouldn't be decided on muscle. The Lakers would break out a strategy that had worked nicely five years earlier, in another Game 6.

They would run.

They would run until one team dropped, or threw in the towel, or threw up their breakfast.

Win or lose, they would play their game—Laker basketball, Showtime. The Celtics knew what to expect. It was like Nolan Ryan facing Reggie Jackson and giving Reggie the nod—fastball coming your way, big man. Down the pipe. Take your best cut.

In Los Angeles sportscaster Tommy Hawkins was seated in front of his television set in a Laker uniform. Former Laker coach Fred Schaus, now athletic director at West Virginia University, was pulling weeds in his yard, too nervous to watch. His wife fed him bulletins. Frank Selvy, now a salesman in South Carolina, caught the game on TV while vacationing in Hilton Head. Jerry West, too superstitious to return to the haunted grounds of the Garden, stayed home in L.A. to watch.

Magic ran to exhaustion, then sucked it up and ran some more. Kareem, the oldest basketball player on the planet, kept up with the pace. Worthy quietly soared above the rim. Rambis and Magic pounded the boards. Johnson would wind up with 14 points, 14 assists, 10 rebounds; Abdul-Jabbar with 29 points; Worthy with 28 points on 11-for-15 field-goal shooting.

The final score was 111–100.

As time ran out on the Celtics, the Boston crowd became almost silent. In the shoe-box arena where the fans had nearly blown the roof off a year earlier, sounds that had been drowned out were now clearly audible—the echo of each dribble, the squeak of shoes, the sound of the players panting and grunting and shouting at one another under the basket. You could almost hear the Celtic egos crumbling.

At the final buzzer, near the Laker bench, Kareem and Magic embraced. Each man now knew how much he needed the other.

Future generations of basketball fans would see that these two had played on the same team and wonder how they ever lost. It was like the union of Ruth and Gehrig in another time and another sport.

Buss pulled a scrap of paper from his pocket and wrote the sentence "The Lakers have never beaten the Celtics." Then he crossed out the "never" and made a mental note to have this scribbled message transposed exactly as he wrote it onto a billboard near the Forum.

The Celtic fans, instead of storming the court as they had the year before, filed out into the cool afternoon as quietly and humbly as a church congregation. The only action on the court was Buss and a friend having their pictures taken at midcourt to commemorate the occasion.

In the Laker locker room Magic slumped on a bench.

"We had to go to another level," he said. "We had to play on a higher level, past what we played the rest of the season and in the playoffs. In your guts you can feel it."

Yet even now Magic couldn't forget the pain of a year ago.

"Nothing is gonna make up for that," he said. "That's one championship I don't have, and I want every one I have a chance to get. I can't go back now. You don't get another chance. You always get other chances to win again, but you never can get that one. I want that one."

In the losers' dressing room Auerbach snapped an answer

to the reporters, "No, I don't think the better team won. We had a bad game is all. We didn't shoot." Then he turned and left.

The White House had issued an invitation to the winning team to fly to Washington to meet President Reagan. But in the locker room Michael Cooper obviously had forgotten about the side trip to D.C. He said he was planning to rush home the next day to celebrate with his children.

"What about the Prez?" a reporter asked Cooper.

"I'm *through* with you guys," Cooper said with grin.

"No, Coop, not the *press*—the *Prez*. Reagan."

"Him too," Cooper said.

But the next morning, 24 years after the franchise had flown to L.A., 25 years after another group of Lakers almost died in a DC-3 floundering in a Midwest snowstorm, the Lakers caught a flight from Boston to the White House.

Nice place, they thought. Real pretty. But, in all honesty, kind of a comedown after you've seen the beautiful Boston Garden.

EPILOGUE

EPILOGUE

Losin' Time

Let's start at the end.

The Forum scoreboard showed a 112–112 tie, with one second remaining in the Lakers' season. The Rockets had the ball out of bounds. The Lakers chose not to pressure Houston's Rodney McCray, the man entrusted with making the crucial inbounds pass. McCray hurled the ball to 7–4 center Ralph Sampson, 12 feet from the basket. With his back to both defender Kareem Abdul-Jabbar and the basket, Sampson jumped to meet the ball, then twisted his body toward the basket and tossed up an off-balance, no-look, no-form shot.

He had done the only thing he could do: He received the ball and got rid of it in the single second allowed him before time expired.

The ball bounced on the front rim, then on the back rim as the buzzer sounded. The fate of the Lakers was now out of human hands. It would be decided by the bounce of the ball.

Sampson, falling sideways in the confusion, never saw the final bounce, nor the ball settling softly into the net.

Not that he needed to see the shot. A quarterback knocked flat on his back as he throws a pass knows immediately from the crowd reaction whether or not his throw is complete, and perhaps whether it's a touchdown.

As Sampson's shot dropped through the net, the 17,505 fans in the Forum seemed to suck in their breath as one, and a deathly silence fell over the house. It was a spontaneous moment of silence for the death of a dynasty.

Michael Cooper, under the basket looking up when Sampson's shot finally dropped to earth, felt his knees buckle. Cooper dropped to the floor on his back and shut his eyes against the glare of the lights and the pain of the loss. He felt the shock waves of the Forum floor as Rocket players leapt and whooped in joyous celebration.

In Philadelphia, Bob McAdoo, watching on TV, fought back the tears. Those were his guys out there, his friends, his teammates. If only he had been there, maybe a few of his jumpers would have made a difference in the series and it would be the Lakers leaping and shouting and celebrating.

What *happened?*

Five months before, off to a roaring start, the Lakers had the league buzzing. The team had replaced the aging, oft-hurt McAdoo with power forward Maurice Lucas and rookie forward A. C. Green, a first-round draft choice, to plug the team's big weakness—front-line rebounding. The champions were back, seemingly stronger.

The Lakers had a chance to get Clipper center Bill Walton, a free agent, but were scared off after reviewing the results of an extensive physical given him by the Laker medical staff. It was felt that Walton, with a history of foot problems, wouldn't be able to last through a long, tough season.

Also, the Lakers were wary of what the Clippers would demand from their crosstown rivals in exchange for their not matching an offer to Walton.

So the Lakers passed on the former UCLA star, a move they would regret in hindsight when he would go on to have a healthy, productive season and help the Celtics win the NBA championship.

But for the moment it looked like the Lakers had all the weapons they would need. The team got off to its best start ever, its record soaring to 4–0, 11–1, 19–2, and then 24–3. Some basketball insiders were wondering whether the 1985–86 Los Angeles Lakers were the best team in basketball history.

Five trips to the finals in the previous six seasons, two championships, the most recent one a win over the dreaded Celtics, and now the Lakers seemed to be even better than the season before. Would winnin' time last forever?

The glow of victory had burned brightly for Jerry Buss since that magic moment in the Garden the previous spring.

"I was just waiting," he says, "for people to come by and ask, 'What happened?' Then I could say, 'We won. We're just the best team, that's all.'"

Jerry Buss wasn't the only one waiting for former critics to come by and gaze in wonder. NBA commissioner David Stern was presiding over a league that had soared into some winnin' times of its own. Had it really been only four years earlier that clubs were facing the abyss of bankruptcy, that league meetings were highlighted by talks of the possible mergers of failing clubs? In the 1980–81 season 16 of the league's 23 teams were losing money and four were on the block with no buyers in sight.

In the ensuing seasons the NBA had become this nation's bona fide third big-time professional sports organization, joining major-league baseball and the National Football League. At the start of the 1985–86 season the league's financial comeback was a cover story in *Business Week.* League revenues for the 1980–81 season were $108 million. That grew to $123 million the following season, then $141 million in 1982–83, $165 million in 1983–84, $192 million in 1984–85, and an estimated $250 million for 1985–86. All clubs were expected to make money by the 1986–87 season.

Attendance continues to rise. For the 1985–86 regular season a record 11,214,888 fans paid their way into NBA arenas, an increase of 6.7 percent over the season before and the third straight time a new attendance mark had been set.

Television, which had long relegated many NBA playoff games to a late-night slot where they battled Johnny Carson and old Sherlock Holmes movies, now proudly displays pro basketball, a rising force in an age where the ratings of other sports are often dropping. Regular-season ratings on CBS in 1985–86 were up 11 percent, after posting a 2 percent increase the season before. Cable ratings were up 14 percent. The NBA just concluded a four-year, $88 million contract with CBS and signed a new one for an additional four years at $175 million. That's still a long way from the billions given to football and baseball, but it's also a long way from the days of cold, empty NBA arenas and $7-per-day meal money.

What's behind this surge in the league's fortunes? Many things, from the bright new stars like Akeem Olajuwon, Ralph Sampson, Patrick Ewing, and Michael Jordan to better marketing techniques and better management. The league has avoided strikes, has taken the lead over rival sports in handling drug problems, and has invoked a salary cap that has helped spread the wealth.

But don't forget Showtime, either. The rise of the NBA has coincided with the rise of the Lakers. The team drew 689,905 fans at home during the 1985–86 regular season, an average of 16,827 per game. Both are records. Twenty-six of the 41 regular-season games were sellouts—this despite continually rising ticket prices. The Lakers now outrate the Dodgers in some head-to-head telecasts, something unheard of several years ago.

These numbers are as sweet for Buss as the final numbers posted on the Garden scoreboard in the 1984–85 season finale. He was once ridiculed by some league owners for jacking up league salaries with his huge contracts for Magic Johnson and Mitch Kupchak. But with his unique mix of big names, both on his roster and in the crowd, with his unique blend of entertaining yet winning basketball, he proved that Showtime could work.

"Jerry Buss recognized that this is the entertainment capital of the world," Stern says. "Jerry Buss gave the people an exciting product. The team matches the community. He made the Forum the place to be. He gauged it right for Los Angeles. You can't charge $100 or $150 for a front-row seat in Indiana or Atlanta. Buss had a unique sense of the culture of the community he was appealing to and he exploited it."

But the glow from past seasons can only shine so far into the next. The 1985–86 season brought new problems for the Lakers.

At first it appeared the main roadblock on the team's march to another title would be boredom. They were so much better than most of their competition, the Lakers were in danger of shutting down their engines and coasting into the playoffs, which could leave them vulnerable to revenge-hungry Boston.

Indeed, the Lakers were less than awesome coming into the playoffs. In mid-March they won nine in a row, but then lost to the lowly Los Angeles Clippers by one point as Kareem was outplayed by an erratic but enthusiastic young center, Benoit Benjamin.

Little things: The Lakers then beat San Antonio handily, as Maurice Lucas had his best game of the season—16 points and 11 rebounds in 27 minutes—but Riley said afterward, "Luke's played real hard, but he has got to be more consistent, night in and night out."

When informed of Riley's words Lucas replied, "Maybe playing time would take care of that."

The Lakers won four in a row, then lost to Seattle, 88–87, squandering their last shot attempt as Lucas charged the hoop like a bull and was called for an offensive foul.

The Lakers beat Portland for win No. 60, but Trail Blazer guard Clyde (the Glide) Drexler said, "They looked like they were bored stiff."

Still, the Lakers finished the regular season at 62–20, 11 games better than the next best team in the Western Conference, the Houston Rockets. The Lakers also had the league's highest scoring average (117.3 points) and field goal percentage (.522).

Their regular-season won-lost mark was the same as the year before when they'd won everything. Were they ready to do the impossible, to become the first team since the 1968–69 Boston Celtics to win back-to-back NBA titles?

If so, they would make their mark on the NBA, silence the Eastern critics once again, and earn the label of "dynasty." Their greatness would be a matter of fact, of hoop history. But in order to get to Boston and the finals, the Lakers had to march through Texas.

They opened the playoffs against the San Antonio Spurs, who were short-handed due to injuries and badly overmatched. It was little more than a glorified scrimmage as the Lakers swept the miniseries in three games, winning by a total of 95 points. That broke an all-time playoff record for largest total victory margin, a record set in a four-game series.

Then the fun began. The Lakers opened their series against the Dallas Mavericks by winning the first two. They lost the next two by two points each. Suddenly the Lakers seemed mortal. They were unable to contain hot-shooting Mark Aguirre, Rolando Blackman, and Derek Harper, and were unable or unwilling to ignore the verbal snipes and jabs of Dallas coach Dick Motta, who was seeking to upset his opponents with psychological gamesmanship.

Still, the Lakers were able to rally and win the next two games, by three points and then by 13 points, to win the series. Aguirre went down shooting—literally. He was forced to the bench late in the third quarter of the sixth and final game of the series due to a sprained ankle. Aguirre had scored 14 of his 28 points that night in the third period and was leading one last charge when he went out.

Two Texas clubs down, one to go. In order to win the Western Conference, the Lakers had to get past Houston.

The Rockets had dropped their regular-season series to the Lakers, four games to one, and had proved spectacularly inefficient at controlling Kareem Abdul-Jabbar. In one game Houston coach Bill Fitch let center Akeem Olajuwon guard Kareem one-on-one, and Kareem responded with 38 points.

The next time Fitch tried a double team, and Kareem got 43.

But the Rockets' lone win over the Lakers came in the last meeting of the regular season, a win that might have given the young Houston team the psychological lift it needed going into a series against the NBA's perennial kings of the West.

The Lakers beat Houston in the series opener by 12. But the Rockets won the next three games, by margins of 10, 8, and 10. Now the Lakers would have to do the same, win three in a row, to reach the finals for the fifth straight time.

They had been completely unable to contain the man-child Akeem, who was frolicking like a young buck, scoring at will, dominating both backboards, and firing up his teammates with his hustle and enthusiasm. This was a player to whom the game was still new, and fun. A native of Lagos, Nigeria, and a former soccer player, the 6–11 (or 6–10, depending on whose yardstick you believe) Olajuwon has been playing basketball for only six years.

"You throw the ball to me," he told one of his guards during a game earlier in the season.

"But, Akeem," the guard said, "they've got you covered with three guys."

"It does not matter," Akeem said, "I dunk the ball anyway."

Akeem the Dream was causing a Laker nightmare. Concentrating on him, the Lakers were creating breathing room for forward Ralph Sampson and for Rocket guards Lewis Lloyd and Robert Reid.

The Rockets were outplaying, outrebounding, outpoising their elders. Were the Lakers through?

Wilt Chamberlain, from his house high atop Mulholland

Drive, said he figured the Lakers could come back from this desperate 3–1 situation, a feat accomplished only four previous times in league history.

"If you asked people before this series," Chamberlain said, "I guarantee you about 95 percent of them would have said the Lakers would win in four games, maybe five. Now, if all us Laker fans believe they can run over the Rockets in the first place, there's no reason we can't believe it now."

It was going to take more than just strong belief. The Lakers had been getting beaten badly on the backboards. Wilt, naturally, blamed Kareem.

"Can he get more rebounds?" Chamberlain said. "Sure he can. I find it hard to believe he can be so animated on offense, but only get three, four rebounds. I tell you, he's not *trying* to get rebounds. He's even ducking away sometimes. He's like an old batter up at the plate, bailing out, afraid of the inside fast-balls."

But Kareem wasn't the only Laker on the spot. By now all the Lakers knew they were in trouble. Michael Cooper had spent hour upon hour the previous two days studying films. Magic Johnson was so intense and single-minded that when his mother came to L.A. to be with her son before Game 5, Magic, despite his five-bedroom mansion in Bel-Air, put her up in a nearby hotel. He would brook no distractions before this game.

A year earlier, after being blown out in Game 1 of the finals by the Celtics, the Lakers had rallied around Riley's stirring pregame talk.

This time the message was simpler. The team got together the day before Game 5 against Houston and adopted a new slogan: "Let's get it done!"

"I wish you were out there tonight," a fan told a nervous Jerry West prior to the start of Game 5.

"I wish I was too," West replied. "I used to love games like this."

He would love watching this one, until the very end.

The Lakers dominated the backboards in Game 5, playing hard and hungry. They would finish the night with an incredible 51–31 rebound advantage. Kareem, answering Wilt one more time, had 13 rebounds, one more than the combined total collected by Sampson and Olajuwon, the Twin Towers. The Lakers did not trail the Rockets once in the first 47 minutes and 59 seconds.

With 5:14 left in the game and the Rockets trailing, 103–99, Mitch Kupchak, not known for his politeness or finesse, and Akeem, not known for his patience with bullies, began to mix it up. Elbows were exchanged. Then Akeem threw a punch at Kupchak and referee Jess Kersey quickly tackled Akeem around the waist and drove him back toward the Laker bench, where Maurice Lucas applied a headlock. Both benches cleared. Kupchak and Olajuwon were ejected.

"I think that was the turning point," Cooper would say later. "Sometimes a fight like that will get a team fired up. It got us fired up, but it got them fired up more."

There were so many lost opportunities at the end—a seemingly easy stuff that Lucas blew, an even easier layup that Magic couldn't convert.

Still, the Lakers had a chance to win it after Robert Reid's three-pointer from the corner tied the game with 15 seconds to play.

The ball went in to Kareem, who saw nothing but Rocket red blocking his view of the basket. So the ball went back out to Magic, over to Cooper, and then to the open man, Byron Scott, standing 17 feet from victory. The same Byron Scott who had joined the Lakers as The Man Who Replaced Norm Nixon; who had found his shots repeatedly blocked during those early days with the Lakers—by his own teammates in practice because of their lasting bitterness over the Nixon trade; who had raised doubts about his ability in the clutch with his performance in the '84–85 finals, when he shot just 39.5 percent from the floor; who was shooting just 44 percent from the floor in this series.

As he stood with the ball in his hands, the clock running down to the final seconds of Game 5 against the Rockets, Scott was only 4-for-10 on the night from the floor. No matter: A game-winning shot with the season on the line was just what he needed to change his image, restore his confidence. Free of defenders, he paused, a city paused, and then he fired a straight-arrow shot.

It was long. Just long. Just long enough to hit the back of the rim.

The ball bounded into the anxious hands of Houston guard Allen Leavell, who furiously signaled for a timeout, which he got one tick before overtime.

That gave the Rockets one last chance. One last desperation shot, by Ralph Sampson . . . and the Lakers were dead.

The Celtics had been cheated out of their chance at revenge. The league's fans had been cheated out of a battle of the titans—although by now the word for the Lakers was less titan than *Titanic,* as the team that was thought to be unsinkable had run into twin icebergs.

Johnson and Cooper were devastated. They left the court, went into the Rockets' dressing room to congratulate the new Western Division champs, then immediately found themselves a quiet room, a back room the Kings hockey team uses for weight training. Magic and Cooper sat there for nearly an hour, alone, mourning, rehashing, shaking their heads in despair at the utter frustration and finality of it all.

Wait till next year? That didn't sound like such a resounding battle cry right then. The Lakers, the wonder team of the '80s, a team that five months earlier was the essence of precision and power, a team that had shattered the Celtic aura of invincibility and formed one of its own, was now a team riddled with exposed weaknesses, their hopes of a dynasty suddenly peppered with holes, as if from a shotgun blast.

Nobody ever lives happily ever after in sports, but this was a hell of a fall. A year earlier, after winning their third title in six years, the Lakers were paraded through downtown Los Angeles while their fans showered them with confetti. Now they were being showered with criticism. A year earlier they had been greeted at the White House like visiting heads of state. Now they were being treated like deposed dictators.

Suddenly only Magic's future with the team was certain, only his value was unquestioned.

Kareem would play one more season, but he would be 40 years old when next the playoffs came around. . . . Cooper was a free agent. . . . James Worthy had again shown himself to be one of the league's premier offensive weapons, but basically a one-dimensional player. . . . Riley was saying the Lakers could no longer afford the luxury of a nonscorer, Kurt Rambis, at starting forward. . . . Byron Scott, three seasons a Laker, had yet to emerge from the shadow of Norm Nixon. . . . The Laker brass was hinting broadly that if Mitch Kupchak would retire, they could use his salary to sign a big star. . . . And Mike McGee, Larry Spriggs, and A. C. Green had become forgotten men in the playoffs, relegated mysteriously to the doghouse, unused and unwanted. Several weeks later McGee was traded to Atlanta.

Four finals in four years. Three world titles in six years. The long-time goal of victory over the Celtics realized. Ancient history. What about now?

It could all change again just as quickly but until it does, old wounds are open.

The Nixon trade is rehashed. So are the lost opportunities to get Larry Nance, Bill Walton, and perhaps even Terry Cummings or Dominique Wilkins instead of James Worthy.

Even Riley, the kid phenom of coaches, is under the gun. Why had he abandoned his bench in the '86 playoffs, forsaken the muscle and hustle of Kupchak, and the defense and perimeter shooting of McGee?

Why had the last shot gone to Byron Scott? Why had there been no pressure on the final in-bounds pass? And why had Sampson, the logical choice to receive that pass, been left so lightly guarded so close to the hoop?

The questions would fade in time. The accomplishments would not. This team had traveled a long way since that snowy night in the Iowa cornfield. So had Jerry Buss since those snowy mornings of ditchdigging back in Wyoming.

All concerned had found fame and fortune in Los Angeles and had helped to lead a league into a bright new world. Four championship banners graced the walls of the Forum, mute evidence of the glory days.

But while Showtime continues to play on, Winnin' Time has run out—at least temporarily. The spotlight has shifted to Boston, Houston, perhaps Philadelphia, or Dallas, or who knows where else?

Old memories and aging banners will be of little use in future battles. Perhaps it is time for new warriors.

Looming largest on the horizon is the imminent retirement of Kareem Abdul-Jabbar, the anchoring force through all of Winnin' Time. Soon the bulkhead seat on the left aisle of Los Angeles Laker flights will again be empty.

Will anybody ever again fill it so well?